Political Journalism in Comparative

CU00542637

Political journalism is often under fire. Conve
arly research suggest that journalists are me
Political news is void of substance and overly focused on strategy and persons.
Citizens do not learn from the news, are politically cynical, and are dissatisfied
with the media.

Political Journalism in Comparative Perspective challenges these assumptions, which are often based on single-country studies, with limited empirical
observations about the relationship between news production, content, and
journalism's effects. Based on interviews with journalists, a systematic content analysis of political news, and panel survey data in different countries, the
book tests the way different systems and media-politics relationships condition
the content of political news. It shows how different content creates different
effects and demonstrates that under the right circumstances citizens learn from
political news, do not become cynical, and are generally satisfied with political
journalism.

Erik Albæk is Professor of Journalism and Political Science and Research Director at the Center for Journalism, Department of Political Science and Public
Management, at the University of Southern Denmark. His work has appeared
in numerous journals, including *Journalism, Journalism and Mass Communication Quarterly, Political Communication, Journal of Communication, European Journal of Communication*, and *Party Politics*. He is the former chairman
of the Danish Social Science Research Council and the Nordic Political Science
Association.

Arjen van Dalen is Associate Professor at the Center for Journalism, Department of Political Science and Public Management, at the University of Southern
Denmark. His work has been published in *The Global Journalists in the 21st
Century* (edited by David Weaver and Lars Willnat, 2012) and journals such
as the *European Journal of Communication, Political Communication, International Journal of Press/Politics, Journalism*, and *Journalism Studies*. He has
lived, studied, and worked in the Netherlands, the United Kingdom, Austria,
Germany, Spain, Belgium, and Denmark.

Nael Jebril is a Career Development Fellow at the Reuters Institute for the
Study of Journalism, Department of Politics and International Relations, at
the University of Oxford. He holds a PhD in journalism (2011) from the Cen-
ter for Journalism, Department of Political Science and Public Management,
University of Southern Denmark, and an MA in global journalism (2006) from
Örebro University, Sweden. His research has received support from the Danish
Social Science Research Council.

Claes H. de Vreese is Professor and Chair of Political Communication and
former Director of the Amsterdam School of Communication Research at
the University of Amsterdam. He is the founding Director of the Center for
Politics and Communication (www.polcomm.org) and Adjunct Professor of
Political Science and Journalism at the University of Southern Denmark. His
research interests include comparative journalism research; the effects of news,
public opinion, and European integration; and the effects of information and
campaigning on elections, referendums, and direct democracy.

Communication, Society and Politics

Editors

W. Lance Bennett, *University of Washington*
Robert M. Entman, *The George Washington University*

Politics and relationships among individuals in societies across the world are being transformed by new technologies for targeting individuals and sophisticated methods for shaping personalized messages. The new technologies challenge boundaries of many kinds – between news, information, entertainment, and advertising; between media, with the arrival of the World Wide Web; and even between nations. *Communication, Society and Politics* probes the political and social impacts of these new communication systems in national, comparative, and global perspective.

Other Books in the Series

(continued after the index)

Political Journalism in Comparative Perspective

ERIK ALBÆK
University of Southern Denmark

ARJEN VAN DALEN
University of Southern Denmark

NAEL JEBRIL
University of Oxford

CLAES H. DE VREESE
University of Amsterdam

CAMBRIDGE
UNIVERSITY PRESS

CAMBRIDGE
UNIVERSITY PRESS

32 Avenue of the Americas, New York, NY 10013-2473, USA

Cambridge University Press is part of the University of Cambridge.

It furthers the University's mission by disseminating knowledge in the pursuit of education, learning, and research at the highest international levels of excellence.

www.cambridge.org
Information on this title: www.cambridge.org/9781107674608

© Erik Albæk, Arjen van Dalen, Nael Jebril, and Claes H. de Vreese 2014

First published 2014

Printed in the United States of America

A catalog record for this publication is available from the British Library.

Library of Congress Cataloging in Publication Data
Albæk, Erik.
Political journalism in comparative perspective / Erik Albæk, Arjen Van Dalen, Nael Jebril, Claes H. de Vreese.
  pages cm. – (Communication, society and politics)
Includes bibliographical references and index.
ISBN 978-1-107-03628-4 (hardback)
1. Press and politics. 2. Journalism – Political aspects. I. Van Dalen, Arjen, 1980– II. Jebril, Nael, 1980– III. Title.
PN4751.A57 2013
070.4'4932–dc23   2013027556

ISBN 978-1-107-03628-4 Hardback
ISBN 978-1-107-67460-8 Paperback

Contents

List of Tables and Figures

TABLES

FIGURES

Preface

During our first years at the University of Southern Denmark, two of us, Erik Albæk and Claes H. de Vreese, fantasized about creating a large-scale comparative study of political journalism that would show how different conditions can produce different types of news, which in effect will have different implications for citizens' functioning in democracies. With a grant from the Danish Social Science Research Council (grant number 275–06–0038) and the arrival of Arjen van Dalen and Nael Jebril as PhD students in this project, the fantasy became a reality. From 2008 to 2012 we worked on the project, which led first and foremost to interesting conversations about journalism, media effects, analyses, and writing styles, and also to journal publications, two PhD dissertations, and this book with Cambridge University Press. We believe that the book tells an interesting and important story, and we hope that colleagues, politicians, and journalists will strenuously debate what we have written so that the field of political journalism research is advanced.

We are indebted to several people and institutions. In a non-systematic and non-exhaustive list, these include: The Danish Social Science Research Council and The Educational Fund of the Danish Press (Pressens Uddannelsesfond) supported the project financially with grants of 4.4 million Danish kroner and

900,000 Danish kroner, respectively. We are grateful to TNS Opinion for a very smooth collaboration on the panel surveys.

We thank Sage Publications for generously granting us permission to draw on material from articles of ours that had previously been published in several of Sage's journals: "The people behind the political headlines: A comparison of political journalists in Denmark, Germany, the United Kingdom, and Spain," *International Communication Gazette*, 2012: 74(5); "Suspicious minds: Explaining political cynicism among political journalists in Europe," *European Journal of Communication*, 2011: 26(2); "Infotainment, cynicism, and democracy: Privatization vs. personalization," *European Journal of Communication*, 2013: 28(2); and "Different roles, different content? A four-country comparison of the role conceptions and reporting style of political journalists," *Journalism, Theory, Practice and Criticism*, 2012: 13(7).

Without the help of the following student assistants and coders, this project would not have been possible: Alessandra Bertino, Anders Christian Frederiksen, Anne Mørk, Carles Samper, Claire Segijn Davide Giacalone, Dietmar Benndorf, Fernando Morente, Inga Materna, Imma Alberch Chamorro, Kari Anne Janisse, Katrin Radtke, Luz Gutierrez, Malte Fischer, Maria Barcenilla, Morten Bang Jørgensen, Niels Asger Wille-Jørgensen, Nina Rømer Gylling, Rebecca Natalie Bjergegaard Fretté, Rosalba Osorio, Yasir Waled Hashim Al-Gailany, Zenia Nørregaard, and Zita Burkeviciute.

We wish to thank colleagues from SDU and the Amsterdam School of Communication Research *ASCoR* as well as reviewers, respondents, and audiences at various conferences. At SDU, we want to thank in particular Morten Skovsgaard, David Hopmann, Christian Elmelund-Præstekær, and Anders Bo Rasmussen for comments on earlier drafts of the manuscript. Asbjørn Sonne Nørgaard, Thomas Pallesen, Jesper Strömbäck, Frank Esser, and Sara Binzer Hobolt all gave valuable input in the design phase of the studies. Rens Vliegenthart provided insightful comments and support in the analysis of the data. When designing the journalist survey, Christine Pihlkjær Jensen, Sophie

Lecheler, Christian Baden, and Noemi Mena Montes generously helped with the translation and adjustment of the questions. Collecting the data would have been impossible without the help of Maria Rosa Berganza and Marian Chaparro Domínguez of the Universidad Rey Juan Carlos in Madrid, Michael Agner of the University of Southern Denmark, and the help of the Institute of Communication Studies at the University of Leeds. We are grateful to Alicja Kozlowska for copyediting the first draft of the manuscript.

On a personal note, Erik Albæk would like to thank Ann Skovly, Anette Schmidt, and Tina Guldbrandt Jakobsen from the University of Southern Denmark for administrative support. In addition, Erik is grateful to the Amsterdam School of Communication Research for hosting him as Visiting Professor in the spring of 2009. Arjen van Dalen expresses his gratitude to Peter van Aelst (Antwerp University) and Claudia Mellado Ruiz (University of Santiago de Chile) for fruitful discussions and collaborations, which helped shape the arguments in Chapters 3, 4, and 5. Arjen furthermore thanks Peter Bro (University of Southern Denmark), Klaus Schönbach (University of Vienna), and Jesper Strömbäck (Mid-Sweden University, Sundsvall) for challenging and thoughtful opposition during his PhD defense. Finally, Arjen would like to thank Joke, Jan, Thijs Charlotte, and most of all Ania for their support over the course of this project.

Nael Jebril thanks the Department of Political Science and the Center for Journalism at SDU, and the Amsterdam School of Communication Research at the University of Amsterdam for providing an ideal and dynamic research environment during the completion of this project. In addition, Nael extends his thanks to all academic colleagues during his PhD studies, in particular Asbjørn Sonne Nørgaard, Rens Vliegenhart, Klaus Levinsen, Peter van Aelst, and David Hopmann for their valuable feedback on Chapters 6, 7, and 8.

Claes H. de Vreese thanks the Hans Christian Andersen Foundation and the Department of Political Science and the Center for Journalism for providing him with the opportunity to work on this manuscript, and the Netherlands Institute for Advanced

Studies (NIAS) for providing the peaceful setting where the last revisions were made.

Finally, we all are indebted to Lance Bennett and Bob Entman, the editors of the series; the anonymous reviewers of the manuscript; and Lew Bateman at Cambridge University Press. Without their help, the book would not have become a reality. All errors are, of course, solely our responsibility.

Erik Albæk, Odense, Denmark
Arjen van Dalen, Odense, Denmark
Nael Jebril, Oxford, UK
Claes H. de Vreese, Amsterdam, the Netherlands

I

Introduction

Political journalists play a crucial role in a democracy. Democracy and journalism develop side by side, and a healthy democracy is characterized by free media and well-functioning journalists. Norris (2000, xv) writes that "journalism is often venerated as a beacon of light that helps to sustain democracy, a force for freedom lying between venal government and the citizens, a protector of the innocent." The crucial word here is "often." The role of journalism is not carved in stone, neither in terms of location nor time. The relationship between politics and journalism is evolving, and the news that journalists produce is under constant public and scientific scrutiny. Changes in society, journalism, and politics over the past decades have affected the nature of political communication systems. As argued by Blumler and Kavanagh (1999) more than a decade ago, power relationships among key message providers are shifting, the culture of political journalism is undergoing transformation, and conventional meanings of "democracy" and "citizenship" are being questioned and rethought. These changes raise questions about the nature of political journalism: Are political journalists and journalism similar across countries, or are they different? Does political journalism inform citizens? Does it help or hinder their engagement in politics? And what are the conditions under which political journalism functions optimally?

In the scholarly literature and public debate, some point to a positive impact of the news media on citizens' knowledge and engagement in politics (e.g., Norris, 2000, Aarts & Semetko 2003). However, mostly negative views of news content dominate. Many believe in a current demise of news journalism, and most studies highlight the detrimental effects of that demise on citizens and democracy. Concerns are voiced about dominance in ownership structures, poor content, lack of good journalism, reliance on and misinterpretation of opinion polls, and ill-informed citizens who are losing interest in politics (e.g., Barnett & Gaber, 2001; Bennett, Lawrence, and Livingston, 2007; Blumler and Kavanagh, 1999; Cappella & Jamieson, 1997; McChesney, 1999; McNair, 2000a; Patterson, 1993, 2005).

Is this pervasive pessimism justified? We doubt it. We believe the conclusions reported here to be too sweeping and too general. Moreover, many arguments are based on single-country studies with limited empirical observations about both news content and journalism's effects. Our book offers the first systematic, internationally comparative assessment of political journalism – its production, content, and the effects that it produces. Our fundamental claim is that when conditions are right, political journalism makes an important and positive contribution to democratic processes. We show that different conditions create different kinds of political journalism that affect citizens in a variety of ways. The book analyses and compares political journalism cross-nationally, and it tests, re-assesses, and further develops a set of key propositions on the influences of news media on the general public.

What are the right conditions? Central to this book is the thesis that when political actors and journalists view each other with a minimum of suspicion, when journalists perceive that they have autonomy, and when political journalism serves both an informing *and* entertaining role, citizens are more knowledgeable, more satisfied with the media, and less cynical. Specifically, we identify a high degree of professionalization in journalism, a low degree of political parallelism, a strong public broadcasting system, and moderate degrees of commercialization and competition as the *right mix*. This specification of the conditions is important because it straightforwardly defines what is needed. But it is the *combination* of conditions that is required. The presence of one of the elements is in most cases not sufficient. For example, American journalists may feel that they have a high degree of freedom (i.e., score high on the professionalization dimension and low on the political parallelism dimension), but this by itself does not lead to higher news quality. It is the combination, the mix, that is required. As will become clear in the book, the one-million dollar question is: what is the right mix of conditions? Ultimately, the book strikes an optimistic note about the nature of political journalism and its societal role.

CHANGES IN POLITICAL JOURNALISM

An ever-growing body of research in political communication shows how political coverage can have an impact on democratic processes through its effects at the individual, societal, and institutional levels. Developments in political journalism go hand in hand with larger societal and democratic developments. The relationship between the media, politics, and the public is complex and dynamic, and the literature suggests that the current phase of political communication is marked by several major developments.

First, politics is changing. Campaigning has gone from short and decentralized political campaigns to a state of permanent campaigning in which campaign professionals such as pollsters, marketing consultants, and spin doctors play key roles (de Vreese, 2009). These recruits are familiar with the different news outlets and their audiences, and they are able to plan campaigns in elaborate detail and organize prompt responses to daily events and opinion trends (Blumler & Kavanagh, 1999). The professionalization of politics has meant increased use of communication technologies, more sophisticated targeting of key voters, and increased expenditure on publicity (see also Norris, 2000). These developments have affected the mutual perceptions of journalists and of politicians and their staffs, with journalists allegedly increasingly making the strategies and behavior of political actors the object of their reporting.

Second, the media landscape is changing, and has become a commercial industry. Commercialization here refers to the decline of party press and the emergence of a catch-all media that is committed to an informational and commercial model of journalism (Hallin & Mancini, 2004b). The process features increased liberalization and competition, which have led to the multiplication of news outlets and to an upsurge of specialist journalism forms (Blumler & Kavanagh, 1999). Scholars argue that commercialization has undercut the public broadcasting system with its cultural, pedagogic remit of giving the public what it needs (Brants & van Praag, 2006). They perceive the process to be threatening since the news content tends to be produced and marketed as a commodity (McQuail, 2005). This development potentially affects the role conceptions of political journalists and the content they produce.

Third, politics and media have become more intensely intertwined, a process often referred to as "mediatization" of politics. This process refers to the shift from political logic to media logic. In the former case, the needs of the political system and of political institutions take center stage and shape the way political communication is played out, covered, and understood. In the latter case, the requirements of the media take center stage, and they ultimately determine how political actors, the media, and citizens use and understand political communication (Strömback, 2008. p. 7). Thus the content of news reporting must fit the frame of reference that the media uses to socially construct reality and to frame issues and people. Political actors adapt their performance to the media's needs regarding time, place, and format (Brants & van Praag, 2006, p. 30). The mediatization of politics, it is argued, undergoes four successive stages. The first stage is whenever the mass media in a particular setting constitute the most important source of information and communication between the citizenry and political actors. In the second and third stages, the media gain greater independence from the government and political bodies, which forces political and social actors to adapt to the media. The final stage is reached when these actors allow media logic and standards of newsworthiness to become a built-in part of the governing processes (Strömback, 2008, 9–13). These developments raise questions about both the content of political journalism and its effects on citizens' perceptions of politics, satisfaction with the media, and gains in knowledge.

Lastly, wide-reaching changes within society include personalized consumer behavior, a focus on individual ambitions, and decreasing conformity to traditional societal pillars, such as religion, group-based working conditions, and standard family compositions (see also Blumler & Kavanagh, 1999). Citizens are increasingly viewed as individual consumers of political products rather than as an electorate or a mass. This view affects politicians' behavior (together with the media, they focus more on their own personae) and is also reflected in news reporting, where typically an individual's fate takes center stage (for example, a story about a policy's impact on a particular person). Finally, individualization is also seen in media use patterns: citizens in the post-Second World War period were captive audiences who had a hard time escaping the evening news (Prior, 2007; Schönbach & Lauf, 2002). Today, it is much easier to create a personal media diet that may consist of either plenty of or virtually no political information.

As an antidote to such general accounts, we note that, as with all typologies and overviews of developments, great injustice is done to differences in the speed and scope of changes. It is indeed noteworthy that although most research speaks of developments as universally applicable, they are not necessarily uniform, and may well create different conditions for the functioning of political journalism in different countries.

The characteristics of current political communication have significant consequences for the relationship between journalists and politicians and the nature of political news reporting. While campaigns and elections in the past were considered newsworthy per se (Blumler & Gurevitch, 1995), politics must now fight for its place in reporting and scheduling on the basis of its news value or likely audience appeal (Blumler & Kavanagh, 1999, 218).

In other words, the "sacerdotal" approach toward politics has been replaced by a pragmatic one (Blumler & Kavanagh, 2001; de Vreese, 2009). It appears that political journalism has shifted from descriptive to interpretative styles of reporting, which manifest themselves in less substantive and more negatively focused news (Brants & van Praag, 2006). Journalists tend to increasingly cover elections with a focus on candidates' strategies – somewhat in the spirit of horse racing (Patterson, 1993; Cappella & Jamieson, 1997) – and they uncover politicians' publicity efforts, emphasizing the role of the media in the campaign (Esser & d'Angelo, 2003; Kerbel et al., 2000). Further, the presentation of politics has become more dramatized (Bennett, 2001) and people-oriented, often resorting to "infotainment" styles (Adam & Maier, 2010). This is reflected in the breakdown of the public/private divide when covering politicians, the greater receptivity of quality media to stories initiated by tabloids, and the significant growth in scandals coverage (Blumler & Kavanagh, 1999).

Coverage and framing of national politics can, for instance, influence an individual's knowledge (e.g., Delli Carpini & Keeter, 1996; Schönbach & Lauf, 2002; Iyengar et al., 2010), political cynicism, participation, and interest (Cappella & Jamieson, 1997; Norris, 2000; De Vreese, 2005; Strömbäck & Shehata, 2010), or the turnout in elections (Banducci & de Vreese, 2011; Kahn & Kenney, 1999; Jackson & Carsey, 2007). At the level of institutional politics, media attention to different issues and politicians can have an effect on the political agenda (Robinson, 1999; Walgrave & van Aelst, 2006, Blach-Ørsten & Bro, 2009), the careers of politicians (van Aelst et al., 2010; Sheafer, 2008), or the tone in political debates (Kepplinger, 2000). At the societal level, the range of voices and viewpoints expressed in the media has, for example, been related to political polarization (Prior, 2007; Iyengar & Hahn, 2009) and the composition of public agenda (McCombs & Reynolds, 2009).

The way political journalists work results in the political news coverage that causes these effects. Political news presents a mediated version of reality, "an account of the existing, real world as appropriated by the journalist and processed in accordance with the particular requirements of the journalistic medium" (McNair, 1999, p. 9). To better understand *why* political news looks the way it does, and why the media produces the effects it does, we need to go back a step to study how news is produced. In the words of Shoemaker and Reese (1996, p. 258), "We cannot fully understand the effects of that version of social reality if we do not understand the forces that shape it."

Media sociology and journalism studies have developed theories and models to help us understand the antecedents of news. Examples include the hierarchy-of-influences model (Shoemaker & Reese, 1996), the concept of news values (Galtung & Ruge, 1965), and theories of socialization and social interaction in the newsroom (Breed, 1955; Tuchman, 1978; Gans, 1979). However, media sociology (studying news production) and political communication (studying news content and its effects) still largely stand apart from each other. Benson (2004, p. 275) summarizes this divide by noting that while journalism research has often been too "media-centric" (Schlesinger, 1990), political communication research seems to suffer from "media phobism."

Our book bridges this divide by taking a look at the mediating role of political journalists in the production of political news. We study their role conceptions and their relationships with sources, and the influence of these two features on political coverage. We also study the effects of different kinds of political journalism. Studying the antecedents, characteristics, and consequences of political news in countries with different media systems has three concrete goals: (1) to investigate journalists' backgrounds and their attitudes toward reporting on politics, (2) to identify, analyze, and define different types of political news reporting, and (3) to investigate the effects of different types of political reporting on the public's political perceptions. Each component is part of the central ambition to specify the mix of conditions that ensure that political journalism can make a positive contribution.

EXPLAINING CROSS-NATIONAL DIFFERENCES IN POLITICAL JOURNALISM

In our quest to specify the right mix of conditions, we take a cross-nationally comparative perspective. We first look at the variation in political journalism across countries. Media-sociological theories and models of forces that shape (political) news distinguish between influences on different levels, including the micro-level of individual journalists, the meso-level of news organization, and the macro-level of the system in which journalists work (Shoemaker & Reese, 1996; McQuail, 2005; Dimmick & Coit, 1982). Based on the observation that political news content varies from country to country, several scholars have called for more attention to be paid to the macro-level influences (for example, Blumler & Gurevitch, 1995; Esser & Pfetsch, 2004). Ignoring macro-level characteristics in the study of news production can lead to the assumption that findings in one context automatically apply to other contexts, putting research at risk of "naïve universalism" (Blumler & Gurevitch, 1995, 75). Heeding macro-level characteristics in the study of news production will expand our understanding of the antecedents of political news.

By comparing the way journalists in different systems work, we can determine the generalizability of theories that are developed in particular contexts, and even adapt these theories to become more widely applicable. Studying journalists working in other systems makes researchers view familiar systems afresh and "renders the invisible visible" (Blumler and Gurvitch, 1995, p. 76). Comparative research can shed light on the question of how macro-level forces – such as the structural arrangements of the media and political systems, or journalistic and political communication cultures – affect the way political journalists work (see also Chapter 2).

Although the notion that *context* affects political journalism is widely acknowledged (see, for example, Benson, 2004), our knowledge of the influence of macro-structures on political journalists is still limited (Norris, 2009; Benson & Hallin, 2007). Benson and Hallin (2007) identify two main reasons for this paucity of knowledge. First, the production of political news is generally studied in single-country studies, making it impossible to test the way system-level variation influences news production. Second, when political news is studied cross-nationally, this mostly entails descriptive accounts rather than systematic tests of predefined hypotheses. We can add yet a third explanation for our limited understanding of the influence of macro-structures on political journalism. While both production processes and news content have been studied cross-nationally (by means of surveys and observations and by content analysis, respectively), the two branches of research have so far been largely separate and distinct (Esser, 2008, 425).

In this book, *nations* are chosen as the unit of analysis. Although media markets have become transnationally connected (Hallin & Mancini, 2004b), media systems in Western Europe are still largely nationally organized (Livingstone, 2003, p. 480). Press laws and media subsidies are developed on a national level. International media, such as the *International Herald Tribune*, *Financial Times*, or *Euronews*, reach a fraction of the population compared with national newspapers or television channels. Public service broadcasters and commercial television stations aimed at national audiences reach a large proportion of the population. Finally, journalistic practice is heavily influenced by the historical development of the press, which is often nationally determined (Curran & Park, 2000, pp. 11–12).

DIFFERENT JOURNALISM, DIFFERENT EFFECTS?

Since national traditions and systems condition the functioning of political journalism, one would not expect the content of political journalism to be universal. This concept again is important to take as a starting point when identifying the right mix of conditions. Indeed, comparative studies have confirmed observations that the availability of political information in different European countries varies over time and by country (Aalberg et al., 2010; Esser et al., 2011). These variations in supply result in a variety of conditions and parameters, which help fashion citizens' political awareness and knowledge (Curran et al., 2009; Iyengar et al., 2010). Overview books, such as Kaid and Strömback's (2008) *Election News Coverage across the World*, certainly show that some content features are shared cross-nationally, but their effects vary in intensity. For example, the shift toward more episodic, sensational, and critical reporting styles has spawned important questions in relation to the media's function in a democracy, but these questions are not universally pertinent. Scholars fear that infotainment and cynical and negative approaches toward politics may have negative effects on the public. But the evidence for such effects is both fragmented and mixed (see e.g., Baum, 2003 versus Prior, 2003b). Indeed, it is not uncommon for the effects of news media on the public to be assumed rather than tested empirically.

If we scan the field of media-effects research historically, we can observe that it has passed through several more or less successive phases. The first phase began at the turn of the twentieth century and lasted until the 1930s, when the media was perceived as having considerable power to shape opinion and belief (McQuail, 2005, p. 458). In the second phase, the theory of powerful media effects was put to empirical analysis. Scholars did not find a one-to-one link between media stimulus and audience response (McQuail, 2005, 459), and a limited-effects model for mass communication emerged from these empirical studies (McCombs and Reynolds, 2002). The third phase took hold in the 1960s with the arrival of television, and witnessed a shift away from the minimal consequences of media (Chaffee, 2001): scholars found much evidence that the media plays a key role in constructing our picture of reality (McCombs & Shaw, 1972) and that the media could indeed have important social effects and be an instrument for exercising social and political power (McQuail 2005, p. 460).

Today, research on the effects of political communication has come to include an increased array of effects models, augmented conceptions of media messages, and greater emphasis on diverse types of effects and their conditional nature. The complexity of voting decisions and political behavior has led political communication researchers to realize the significance of additional types of effects (for example, cognitive, affective, and perceptual) not merely as pathways to ultimate behavioral political choices (see McLeod et al. 2002, 225–226) but as important outcome in and by themselves.

This book focuses on the relationship between the characteristics of news content and individual-level effects. The micro-level approach assumes that a person's exposure to a specific message, or a series of messages, may affect his or her response (Schulz, 2008). Several studies in the past have dealt with the media's ability to (1) influence the public salience of issues (agenda-setting), (2) affect understanding of and attitudes toward issues (framing), and (3) affect the standards by which the public evaluates political leaders (priming) (see de Vreese [2009] for a review). Our studies touch on these effects, but they center on a number of key dimensions of political journalism that specify the conditions that are instrumental for its optimal functioning. In the effects studies, our central dependent variables are changes in knowledge, cynicism, and satisfaction with the media. These effects are studied as a function of differences in media content (which is conditioned by context and journalistic roles). Collectively these dependent variables constitute key ingredients for assessing the role of political journalism for citizens in a democracy.

THE KEY CONCEPTS

We put three key concepts center stage in our investigation of the production, contents, and effects of political journalism. These concepts stem from international research conducted both in media sociology and journalism studies and in media effects and political communication research. We focus on these three concepts as the unifying factors throughout the book. We will return to them as the guiding light when assessing the implications of our empirical findings about the production, contents, and effects of political journalism.

Sacerdotal-Pragmatic

We investigate how political journalists view and approach politics. The distinction between sacerdotal and pragmatic is used to understand how important journalists deem politics to be and how politics is treated in the news (Blumler & Gurevitch, 1991). This perception of politics on the side of journalists may translate into the amount of attention devoted to politics in the news, and it may affect the way in which the news is framed. The more pragmatic the approach to politics, for example, the greater the likelihood of applying news frames such as conflict and human-interest (see, e.g., Chapter 5). These frames may in turn have implications for determining how much citizens learn from the news (see Chapter 6).

Impartial-Partisan

We investigate the relationship between politics and journalism and the extent to which political journalists perceive autonomy from, in particular, political pressure and political spin in their work. These are crucial conditioning factors (Hallin & Mancini, 2004b). We relate these factors to the notions of impartiality and objectivity to assess the degree to which political news might be favoring one or more sides in politics (see, e.g., Chapter 5). The perception of objectivity and factuality of political news may affect how citizens view and rate political journalism and the news media (see Chapter 8).

Information-Entertainment

We investigate the degree to which political journalists see themselves as having an informative or entertaining function (e.g., Chapter 5). Entertainment features in the news are often assumed to have negative consequences (e.g., Nair, 1999). Such features may on the one hand entice and excite audiences, but they may on the other also spark political cynicism (see Chapter 7). We assess the presence of infotainment in the news and test the effects of different infotainment features.

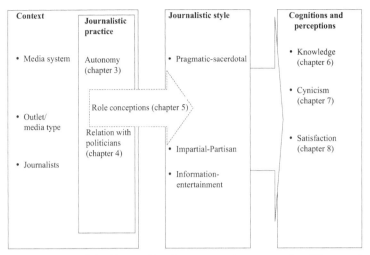

FIGURE 1.1. Political journalism in comparative perspective: Illustrated plan of book.

THE KEY QUESTIONS

Our central research questions connect political journalists and political news stories with the macro-level characteristics of the countries in which the journalists work: How do political journalists and the news they produce vary across countries? How can this variation be explained, and what kinds of effects does it produce?

The central argument is that in a healthy democracy, political journalists enjoy sufficient autonomy from political and commercial pressures to produce news that has the potential to both inform and entertain citizens without increasing public political cynicism or dissatisfaction with the media.

The structure of the book is as follows (see Figure 1.1). Chapter 2 asks how to study political journalists, their news, and the effects from a *comparative* perspective. The chapter briefly presents the key data that we rely on in this book. It outlines the studies conducted, which comprise comparative political journalist surveys, media-content analyses, and two-wave panel citizen surveys, all identical and conducted in Denmark, Germany (journalist survey only), the United Kingdom, and Spain. (All surveys are large-sample surveys; for more technical and detailed information, see the Appendix.) Chapter 3 is an analytical, descriptive chapter on the composition of the political journalist corps in the four countries. We focus especially on the differences in the perceived autonomy. Chapter 4 deals with the relationship and mutual suspicion between journalists and politicians and how this varies according to the political and media systems. Chapter 5 shows how political journalists see and define themselves and how this self-definition translates into the news content they produce.

Both Chapters 6 and 7 draw on media-content analyses and two-wave panel studies. In Chapter 6 we turn to effects. This chapter compares the countries' reporting on politics, and investigates under what circumstances political reporting leads to citizens' gain in knowledge. Chapter 7 assesses the degree of infotainment features in political journalism and shows how infotainment affects political cynicism. Chapter 8 looks at the relationship between the different journalistic approaches in political reporting and the degree to which citizens are satisfied with the media and political journalism in their country. In the conclusion (Chapter 9) we ask if political journalism is ultimately similar or different in different media and political systems. We answer the following questions: Do journalists perceive themselves differently in different systems and how does that affect their coverage? What effects does political journalism have in different countries? And are citizens satisfied with their political news? As we stated earlier, the book's central claim is that different conditions create different kinds of political journalism and that quality journalism has the potential to both inform and entertain citizens, which leads to higher levels of satisfaction with both democracy and political journalism itself. However, as we will show, this only happens when the *mix of conditions* is right and citizens choose to consume political journalism.

2

Comparing Political Journalism

In Chapter 1 we presented the book's focus and rationale. We study the influence of the conditions under which politicians, journalists, and audiences interact on the contribution which political journalism makes to democratic processes. To study this we (1) investigate journalists' backgrounds and attitudes toward covering politics, (2) define, identify, and analyze different types of political news reporting, and (3) investigate the effects of different types of political reporting on political perception and cognition. We address this question using a cross-national, multi-methods comparative design combining the following methods:

- Surveys among political journalists in Denmark, Germany, the United Kingdom, and Spain
- A content analysis of political news in Denmark, Germany, the United Kingdom, and Spain
- A panel study, combined with a content analysis, of political news and news about the U.S. presidential elections in Denmark, the United Kingdom, and Spain.

Before briefly presenting the studies, we first lay out two key requirements for the study of the link between the structural conditions in which journalists work and the content and effects of the news they produce. Comparative research can clarify the way characteristics of the media system (Hallin & Mancini, 2004b) affect the way political journalists work and the news they produce. But in order to do so, the first requirement is a *careful case selection*. Like many comparative studies, our case selection takes its starting point in Hallin and Mancini's media system framework. We present the Hallin and Mancini model, discuss potential pitfalls when applying it in comparative research, and present the way our countries fit within this framework. A second requirement in order to link structural conditions to production, content, and effects is a *multi-method design*. We explain why this is required and lay out the connection between our three types of studies. But first we take a step back to introduce the comparative nature of our endeavor.

COMPARATIVELY SPEAKING

Throughout the book, we take an explicit comparative perspective. Comparative political communication science has resulted in empirical knowledge, instruments, typologies, theories, and standards, all of which inform the design of the studies. However, the cross-national comparative study of the production of political news is a young discipline compared with other social sciences, such as political science (de Vreese, 2012; Munck, 2007). While the comparative approach was already being debated in the political and social sciences in the 1970s (Prezworksi & Teune, 1971; Sartori, 1970), Blumler and Gurevitch described comparative political communication research in 1975 as "a field in its infancy" (despite some isolated pioneer comparative studies: for example, Lasswell et al., 1952).

Between 1975 and the early 1990s, cross-national comparative communication research expanded considerably to include not only media structures but also the journalists working in these structures and the content they produced (see Donsbach, 2010). Based on the observation that "comparative studies address themselves to the different conditions that prevail rather than to those who practice their profession under these conditions" Köcher (1986, 44) was one of the first to study the differences and the similarities between journalists in different countries

(Germany and the United Kingdom) in a truly comparative design. At the same time, American studies of journalistic professionalization (Weaver & Wilhoit, 1986) were replicated worldwide (Weaver, 1998). Television news became the object of comparative content analysis (Hallin and Mancini, 1984; Heinderyckx, 1993). The creation of a forum for exchange between European communication scholars with the launch of the *European Journal of Communication* in 1986 and the 1989 conference of the International Communication Association entitled "Comparatively speaking . . . " were further signs of the growing interest in the comparative perspective (Holtz-Bacha, 2004). Assessing the development of the field, Gurevitch and Blumler (2004, p. 326) describe comparative political communication research in 1990 as "progressing from infancy to – if not full adulthood – at least late adolescence."

Between 1990 and 2004, comparative research expanded still further, resulting in the publication of books synthesizing the findings of studies on similar themes in different countries (Weaver, 1998 for journalists; Gunther & Mughan, 2000 for the relationship between democracy and the media; Kelly et al., 2004 for structures of European media markets). At the same time, rather than merely replicating research conducted in other countries, more cross-national comparative studies used instruments that were specifically designed for comparative research. Donsbach and Patterson (2006) applied this strategy in surveys of news journalists in Germany, Italy, Sweden, the United Kingdom, and the United States. De Vreese et al. (2001) used a similar approach in their study of television coverage on the introduction of the euro. These studies have provided insight into the differences and similarities in political journalism and have been beneficial in the development of instruments and procedures for comparative communication research (see, for example, Peter & Lauf [2002] on assessing intercoder reliability in cross-national content analysis).

On a more theoretical level, researchers and scholars have wrestled with various concepts. The German communication research community debated the appropriate analytical level for inter-country comparisons. Building on the work of Niklas Luhmann, the systems-theory perspective was introduced into journalism research. The idea took hold that the system of journalism fulfills a societal function (Görke & Scholl, 2006) and should therefore be analyzed at a macro-level. This approach has been extensively debated (Görke & Scholl, 2006; Löffelholz, 2008) because of the abstract nature of the theory and the neglect of the role of individuals. On the one hand, such debates have led to an increased interest in the link between individuals and systems (see Donsbach, 2004). On the other hand, they have resulted in a shift away from systems to middle-range theories, which apply to limited sets of phenomena and data (Esser, 2000, 133). Reese (2001) suggests that the "'hierarchy of influences' levels-of-analysis model" (Shoemaker & Reese, 1996) is particularly useful in comparative research because it reminds researchers that factors at different levels (the individual journalists, news routines, and organizational, extra-media, and ideological factors) simultaneously shape the work of journalists and news content.

In 2004, Hallin and Mancini published their book *Comparing Media Systems; Three Models of Media and Politics*. On the basis of historical developments and structural relationships between the worlds of media and politics, they classify the media systems in Western democracies into democratic corporatist, liberal, and polarized pluralist media systems. Although the classification of particular countries in the models, as well as Hallin and Mancini's selection of underlying dimensions, were criticized (see, for example, Norris, 2009), the book soon replaced *Four Theories of the Press*. It initiated a series of studies testing the way media structures influence the content produced by journalists working in these structures (for example, Strömbäck & Dimitrova, 2006; Strömbäck & Luengo, 2008). Hallin and Mancini's approach also sparked discussions that centered on the applicability of their model to other parts of the world and on possible additional dimensions that would distinguish other media systems from their models (Dobek-Ostrowska et al., 2010).

In their subsequent review of the state of the discipline in 2004, Gurevitch and Blumler described comparative political communication research as a field poised for maturity. Their description is supported by reflections on the state of the discipline in review articles (Livingstone, 2003; Norris, 2009), books (Esser & Pfetch, 2004; Esser & Hanitzsch, 2012), and conferences (see Proceedings in Löffelholz & Weaver, 2008; Dobek-Ostrowska et al., 2010), as well as in the growing interest in comparative designs and techniques developed in political science and sociology (see Hanitzsch, 2009; Wirth & Kolb, 2008). Empirical progress has been steady, with comparative studies testing directional hypotheses and proceeding beyond mere descriptive accounts (Esser, 2008; Benson & Hallin, 2007). More large-scale comparative projects are being conducted relying on uniform instruments, such as the project *Political Communication Cultures in Europe – A Comparative Study* by Barbara Pfetsch (European Science Foundation, 2009), the *World of Journalism* project by Thomas Hanitzsch (2009), the *Media System and Informed Citizenship* project by Toril Aalberg and colleagues, the *Foreign News Project* by Akiba Cohen, and the *Communication and Europe* project by Claes de Vreese (see de Vreese et al., 2010).

Despite this tremendous headway, Gurevitch and Blumler (2004) as well as Norris (2009) still do not see comparative political communication as a mature field. Gurevitch and Blumler (2004) argue, first, that the focus on the Americanization of election campaigning and election coverage has left other political communication topics unexplored and, second, that there is a lack of theoretical exchange and an accompanying underdevelopment of conceptual frameworks. This criticism is echoed by Norris (2009, p. 322), who argues that "the subfield of comparative political communications has not yet developed an extensive body of literature that establishes a range of theoretically sophisticated analytical frameworks, buttressed by rigorously tested scientific generalizations, common concepts, standardized instruments and shared archival datasets, with the capacity to identify common regularities that prove robust across widely varied contexts. "

In our book we build on previous research in several ways. Expectations are developed on the basis of theoretical frameworks and earlier empirical findings. Designs and instruments that have been developed and suggested for comparative journalism surveys and content analysis are adapted for the studies in this book. The media systems models by Hallin and Mancini (2004b) inform the case selection and the hypotheses about influences of system-level characteristics on journalistic practice. Recent reflections on comparative political communication (Esser & Pfetsch, 2004; Löffelholz & Weaver, 2008; Norris, 2009) are taken into account in the design of these studies.

Furthermore, our book aims to contribute to the emerging research tradition that we have just described. We have developed new measures to study journalistic role conceptions and content characteristics cross-nationally. We attempt to expand the empirical database by studying variations in political journalism in Denmark, Germany, Spain, and the United Kingdom. But the insight gained is not limited to these four cases. Gurevitch and Blumler (2004) defined a set of maturity criteria for comparative political communication research. We have been mindful of these criteria, and in each study the purpose of comparison is explained in detail, relevant macro-level dimensions are identified, and hypotheses are developed about how these dimensions influence political journalism.

LINKING CONDITIONS AND POLITICAL COMMUNICATION

In Chapter 1 we posed the question: how do macro-level forces – such as the structural arrangements of the media system or the political system, as well as journalistic and political communication cultures – affect the way that political journalists work? To study this, a comparative perspective is required. Most prior studies have focused on single countries, making it impossible to make inferences about the impact of the macro-level. Also, most cross-national studies have offered largely descriptive accounts;

TABLE 2.1. *Ideal Typical Description of Three Western Media Systems*

	Polarized Pluralist	Democratic Corporatist	Liberal
Development of mass press	Low	High	High
Political parallelism	High	High	Low
Professionalization	Low	High	High
State intervention	High	High	Low

Source: Hallin and Mancini 2004b, 299.

our aim is to provide a systematic test of a priori outlined expectations. This requires a careful case selection and a framework that lays out relevant dimensions along which a country's media systems may vary.

We use the typology developed by Hallin and Mancini (2004b) in their seminal work *Comparing Media Systems: Three Models of Media and Politics* as a starting point for our analysis. They identify three models for media systems. First, the *polarized pluralist model* is closely tied to the world of politics, with a high degree of political parallelism and a weak commercial press. Media instrumentalization by government, political parties, and industrialists with political ties is common, and the professionalization of the media is not as strong as in the other models. The *democratic corporatist model* has three major coexisting features: a strong mass-circulation commercial press and media that are tied to political and civil groups, the presence of both political parallelism and professionalization, and the traditions of both press freedom and active state intervention. In the *liberal model*, press freedom and mass circulation developed quite early in the media's history, commercial newspapers dominate, political parallelism is low, and internal pluralism dominates (with the exception of the British press). The professionalization of journalism is strong, and journalistic autonomy is more likely to be limited by commercial pressures than through political instrumentalization. The characteristics of the three media systems are summarized in Table 2.1.

A wide range of comparative political communication studies builds upon Hallin and Mancini's media systems framework. At the same time, the applicability of this framework to cross-national comparative research has been debated (see Norris, 2009 and Hallin & Mancini, 2012 for a discussion). A first point of debate deals with the applicability of the systems typology after a period of rapid cultural and structural changes (see Chapter 1). While the typology and models have been criticized for simplicity and lack of important parameters (e.g., Norris 2009, Hallin and Mancini, 2004a themselves acknowledge that media systems are not static. Over time, the media systems of the countries in this study have all undergone similar structural developments (Hallin & Mancini, 2004a). Media organizations became more profit oriented, and due to growing competition, audience reach became more important. Journalists became more highly educated, often completing university degrees or training in professional journalism. The politicians' world has also been changing, as political communication has become professionalized. News management techniques and spin have become increasingly common, and the employment of press officers has expanded from the United States via the United Kingdom to other countries in Europe (Esser et al., 2001). Though skeptical that convergence toward the liberal model is the result of a separation of media from systems of power (Hallin & Mancini 2004b, 83), the authors confirm that strong forces of convergence are present. A variety of theories can explain these forces, including Americanization, modernization, secularization, globalization, and commercialization (see also Chapter 1).

The fact that media systems and political journalism go through similar developments have lead to fears that it will no longer be possible to draw conclusions about the impact of country-specific variables (Esser & Pfetsch, 2004, p. 401) as we "enter into a world in which N=1" (Goldthorpe, 2000, 54). At the same time, these processes are subject to significant countertendencies, however, and are shaped by the characteristics of individual countries (that is, differences in national political systems, media market structures, or journalistic cultures), which

limits the spread of the liberal model to other countries (Hallin
& Mancini 2004a). Blumler and Gurevitch (2001) adopt a critical view toward the notion of Americanization: the concept, on
the one hand, implies a false impression of an unchanging U.S.
system, to which the rest of the democratic world is inexorably
adapting, and, on the other hand, points to the influence of the
United States as the only source of change in political communication arrangements.

Although it does not address developments taking place over
time, our book does shed light on whether cross-national differences in political journalism have indeed disappeared, or whether
traditional differences remain influential. We compare our findings with previous studies that have used similar approaches (for
example, surveys among journalists by Donsbach and Patterson
(2004) or Algarra and Gaitano (1998) and in the final chapter we discuss our findings in the light of four trends that are
expected to drive convergence: professionalization, commercialization, mediatization and individualization.

A second point of debate about the applicability of Hallin and
Mancini's media concerns the usefulness of this framework for
the understanding of cross-national variation in political journalism, its news and effects. The media-system models are based on
structural characteristics and historical developments of the relationship between the worlds of politics. In their book, Hallin and
Mancini (2004b, 297) stress that the models are ideal-types, that
individual countries do not fit perfectly in either of the models,
and that many countries (such as the United Kingdom) combine
features of different models. Although Hallin and Mancini propose numerous hypotheses about the meaning of system differences for news content, the models are not based on differences
or similarities in news content.

Therefore, testing the Hallin and Mancini model is not a goal
of this book, and it would be wrong to conclude on the basis
of our studies that the media-systems theory does or does not
work. Nevertheless, this book follows numerous other empirical
studies that, as well as in many other empirical studies, refer
to these media-system characteristics to understand variations in

journalistic practice and news content (Esser, 2008; Benson & Hallin, 2007; Strömbäck & Luengo, 2008 among others).

In a discussion of the reception of their book, Hallin and Mancini warn that researchers should not use the models as a "shortcut to comparative research" (Hallin & Mancini, 2010, xiii). Expecting to find similarities or differences in journalistic practice only because journalists work in different media systems would be a wrong application of the media-systems models. The four dimensions that underlie the country groupings (development of the mass press, political parallelism, professionalization, and state intervention) are more useful to explain cross-national differences in political communication than the country groupings. Which dimensions are most relevant to explain cross-national variation depends on the feature of news production the researcher is interested in. The four dimensions that Hallin and Mancini distinguish are not by definition the most relevant ones. When describing differences between countries along these structural dimensions, we are careful to avoid treating them as dichotomies (present or absent; high or low) since that might lead to an underestimation of differences between countries in the same media system, or an overestimation of differences across systems. Apart from the four dimensions underlying Hallin and Mancini's media models, this book includes several other structural dimensions that were relevant for variations in roles and news content. In particular, competitiveness of the media market (Chapter 3) and professionalization of communication by politicians (Chapter 4) play a role in addition to these four dimensions, and in some cases, a more important role. In addition, the size of the country is taken into account (Chapter 4).

CASE SELECTION

Based on these considerations, we include Denmark, Germany, the United Kingdom, and Spain in our design to study the influence of the context in which journalists work on news content and media effects. The selection of countries is suitable for addressing the various research questions raised in this book.

On the one hand, the contexts in which political journalists in these countries are, to a great extent, comparable. Each of the four parliamentary democracies has high levels of press freedom, a dual television market with strongly positioned public service broadcasters, and a pluralistic media landscape (Kelly et al. 2004; Colomer, 2008).[1] On the other hand, the structural differences between the three media and political systems are expected to affect journalists' attitudes and professional autonomy as well as the nature of political reporting. The countries represent different media systems, and show variation on a number of other central dimensions.

The media systems of Denmark and Germany belong to the democratic corporatist model, which is characterized by an early development of the mass press, institutionalized self-regulation, a tradition of state intervention in the media market, and political parallelism. The political system in these countries follows a consensus model with a tradition of coalition governments in which parliament has more formal and de facto power than does the executive branch. An important difference between Denmark and Germany is the size of the country, which is reflected in the size of the political press corps and the level of competition on the media market. In the panel study, only Denmark was chosen to represent the democratic corporatist model.

The media system of the United Kingdom combines elements from the liberal model (low levels of state intervention in the shape of press subsidies and non-institutionalized self-regulation) with characteristics of the democratic corporatist media system (a strong, independent position of public broadcasting and a tradition of political parallelism in the written press). The British media landscape is generally considered competitive and commercialized (Strömbäck & Shehata, 2007). The political system of the United Kingdom is a prime example of a majoritarian system, with dominance of the executive branch over parliament and

---

[1] See European Journalism Centre. Media landscape. http://www.ejc.net/media_landscape/; Freedomhouse. Freedom of the press 2008 survey release. http://freedomhouse.org/template.cfm?page=362 (both accessed November 2011).

a tradition of single-party governments. In the late 1990s, during the Tony Blair Labour government, the United Kingdom was the second democratic country, after the United States, in which political communication was professionalized, and spin doctors gained a strong position in politics. The United Kingdom has the strongest separation between quality and sensationalist press.

Spain belongs to the polarized pluralist media system. This is the most distinct model of the three, with a late development of the mass press and a weakly developed professional culture, a tradition of state intervention in the media market, political parallelism, and control of the media by outside actors. The political system of Spain follows the majoritarian model. By comparison with the practice in other countries, the democratic tradition in Spain is less developed, and the political culture is characterized by polarization and clientalism. While the Spanish newspaper market is characterized by low circulations reaching mostly an elite audience, the television and radio markets are highly competitive, and audiovisual media reach large parts of the population. Spain offers relatively weak public-service regulation compared with the other sampled countries.

This case selection allows the study of the way the context in which journalists work affects news production and news content. For the study of *media effects*, the cross-national perspective is specifically employed to increase variations both in the dependent and the independent variables. In the effects section we focus on Britain, Denmark, and Spain. While we are well aware of the moderating function that political, social, and cultural contexts can have on media effects (e.g. Peter, 2004; de Vreese, 2005; Schuck et al., 2011), we limit ourselves to studying micro-level effects and do not specify formal expectations regarding cross-national differences. In other words, we set out to investigate the effects of exposure to different types of political reporting; for example, we are interested in how citizens learn from the news, depending on the amount and content of the news they receive, regardless of the country they live in. Of course, if the news varies between countries, then this is exactly the type of dynamic that is of interest to us. What the cross-national design provides us with is maximized variation, increased analytical leverage and power, a higher degree of generalizability, and the opportunity to understand differences at the aggregate level.

MULTI-METHOD DESIGN

A second requirement to successfully address of research question is a multi-method design. As stressed in Chapter 1, the fields of media sociology (studying news production) and political communication (studying news content and its effects) have remained independent. We explicitly aim to bridge this gap in our book. The research investigates political communication from the moment news is produced until the moment news is consumed by its audience. This book combines a survey among political journalists with a content analysis of political news in four countries and a panel study in three countries. Such a combination of methods offers important advantages for the study of the connection between context, production, and effects, since it allows us to follow the whole political communication process, and the methods are often complementary. However, these research methods are seldom combined in comparative research (for exceptions, see Iyengar et al., 2010; Aalberg & Curran, 2012). Comparative (political) communication research knows different emerging methodological traditions, and the advantages, disadvantages, and best practices of each method are discussed in several publications (see Löffelholz & Weaver, 2008; Esser & Hanitzsch, 2012 for general discussions on comparative communication research and methods; Weaver, 2008 for a discussion of survey research; Rössler, 2012; Peter & Lauf, 2002, on comparative content analysis or Harkness, 2012 on comparative surveys). Studies using different methods often find comparable cross-national patterns. In his study of political news cultures. Esser (2008, p. 425) therefore calls for a combination of different methods in comparative political communication research:

The cultures identified here bear similarity to Patterson's (2008) mapping of Western journalists' role positions and Hallin and Mancini's (2004) typology of Western news systems. Patterson's study is based on survey responses, Hallin and Mancini's on institutional features, and our own – much more modest undertaking – on actual news content. All three data sources have to be seen together, and ideally combined in one project, to investigate the fundamental assumption behind comparative political communication research. This assumption states that specific constellations of media and political structure (as manifested on the organizational, national, and transnational level) characteristically shape the facets of culture (as manifested in news journalists' ideas, practices, and products, among other things).

By combining journalism surveys, content analysis, and panel surveys, we follow the whole political communication process. This is necessary in order to make inferences about the influence of context on news production and, ultimately, media effects. The three central dimensions laid out in Chapter 1 form the red threat through the design. These concepts (pragmatic-sacerdotal; impartial-partisan and information-entertainment) have been operationalized so that they can be studied in role conceptions (with journalism surveys) in television news and newspapers (with content analyses) and their effects on knowledge, political attitudes, and satisfaction (in the panel study). In cross-national comparative research, instruments must be valid and reliable across cultures to assure that the results are not biased (Wirth & Kolb, 2004). In our study, several attempts were made to assure equivalence in the design of the journalism surveys, panel surveys, and content analyses. Later we briefly describe the different methods and how they contribute to the understanding of the influence of the context in which journalists work on political journalism, and its effects. The technical details of the methods, translation procedure, and data can be found in the Appendixes of this book.

LINKING CONTEXT AND PRACTICE: JOURNALISM SURVEYS

Surveys among political journalists serve to investigate the way the attitudes and working practice of journalists vary across different contexts. Comparative journalism surveys are a fast-growing research technique. Until the turn of the twenty-first century, most comparative media studies focused on institutions and macro structures rather than the people working within these structures (Köcher, 1986). Despite remarkable exceptions (for example, Kocher, 1986; Patterson & Donsbach, 1996; Weaver, 1998; Reese, 2001, p. 177), they concluded in 2001 that not many studies had looked into the link between media systems and journalistic role conceptions. Almost ten years later, in the 2009 *Handbook of Journalism Studies* (Hanitzsch, 2009, p. 413) signals an increased interest in these kind of studies. "The attempt to probe deeper into the similarities and differences in journalistic cultures around the world has become one of the most fascinating sub-domains in the field of journalism studies."

This interest in cross-national differences in journalistic perceptions and attitudes comes from the idea that these are, on the one hand, influenced by the contexts in which journalists work and, on the other, influence the way they work. Donsbach (2008), for example, argues that role conceptions "can have a strong influence on journalists' professional behavior and thus can explain differences between news cultures." Pfetsch (2004) sees the mutual attitudes of political journalists and political actors as the defining characteristics of political communication cultures, and argues that these are influenced by the structures in which they operate. Building on the work of these and other scholars (Weaver & Willnat, 2012; Hanitzsch, 2011; Van Aelst et al., 2008), we conducted comparative surveys among parliamentary journalists in Denmark, Germany, Spain, and the United Kingdom. The survey included questions on the personal backgrounds, perceived autonomy, role conceptions, and attitudes toward politicians, and forms the backbone of Chapters 3, 4, and 5. The technical details of the survey data, such as the definition of the research population, method of data collection, and the response rate can be found in the Appendix to Chapter 2.

LINKING PRACTICE AND STYLE: CONTENT ANALYSIS

A crucial point in our argument that the conditions under which journalists work matters for news content is the link between their role conceptions and journalistic style. Behind many surveys among journalists is the assumption that their role conceptions matter for the content they produce. Previous studies have looked at this relationship at the individual level (Starck & Soloski, 1977; Weaver et al., 2007, 233) or comparatively by aggregating news decisions in survey experiments to the national level (Patterson & Donsbach, 1996; Scholl & Weischenberg, 1998). We combine the findings from our political journalist survey with a content analysis of political news to address this link. Several scholars have called for a study of political journalism using this combination (Weaver, 2008; Vos, 2002), in particular in cross-national comparative research (Esser, 2008). Studies based on surveys among journalists and studies based on content analysis often refer to each other, but these two methods have so far not often been used in combination (for an example, see Vos, 2002). The two methods are complementary. Each method is appropriate for the study of some aspects of news production, but has its limitations in the study of others. Surveys can provide insight into the background and occupational characteristics of journalists – for instance, their political leanings, attitudes, and role conceptions – but are of limited use in studying the outcome of the production process. Content analysis can describe the characteristics of news, such as the attention paid to different political actors or the way political coverage is framed, but is limited in its ability to study the decisions that lie behind news coverage. By combining the two methods, we are better able to justify our claims about the relationship between the views of political journalists, who report the news, the news production process, and the news content that is the outcome of this process.

Chapter 5 describes the reporting styles of political news in the different countries and compares these with cross-national differences in role conceptions. For this purpose, we conducted a content analysis of two constructed news weeks during a routine period in Denmark, Germany, the United Kingdom, and Spain. In each country, news broadcasts of a public service and a commercial channel were included in the analysis, as well as right- and left-leaning broadsheets and a tabloid newspaper.[2] To compare journalistic roles and styles, we operationalized the three key dimensions (*sacerdotal-pragmatic; impartial-partisan; information-entertainment*) so that they can be measured both with content analyses and with surveys. The content dimensions in the study were operationalized with indicators which have been used in previous studies (De Vreese et al., 2001; Benson & Hallin, 2007; Strömback & Luengo, 2008; Esser, 2008).The technical details of the sample and the content analysis are described in the Appendix to Chapter 2.

LINKING CONTENT AND EFFECTS: PANEL SURVEY

To study the effect of news content on receivers, we conducted two-wave online panel surveys with a representative sample of the Danish, British, and Spanish populations. *Panel data* refers to a group of individuals surveyed repeatedly over time (Frees, 2004). Data gathered in this way provide a clearer picture of causal influence than do cross-sectional analyses, because one can control the time ordering of effects and the influence of prior scores on the outcome measures (Slater, 2004, 173).

Panel surveys have advantages over experimentation as they do not involve forced exposure; when investigating the effects of news media on the public, panel surveys ensure a natural viewing and readership environment (see also Kinder, 2007). Furthermore, surveys, unlike laboratory experiments, have the inherent advantage of drawing on a more heterogeneous sample than, for example, students. This heterogeneity allows for more advanced analyses of the way individual-level characteristics and predispositions may moderate some of the effects.

We opted for a panel survey in combination with content analysis, rather than self-reported media use alone. The use of self-report measures alone to investigate the effects of news media on the public leaves researchers uncertain about the exact nature

---

[2] Spain does not have the equivalent of a tabloid newspaper.

of the media content to which respondents report exposure (see Slater, 2004, 169). Such methods are also likely to suffer from the "methodological problems inherent in a failure to distinguish between reliance on a medium and exposure to a message, or between exposure in general and exposure to particular message content" (Miller et al., 1979, 68). Thus, with surveys alone, the effects of news content on the public can only be assumed but not empirically verified. Content analysis is therefore important for exploring more directly how individual-level processes and effects relate to message characteristics (Riffe et al., 2005). This form of analysis is often used to identify the characteristics of news messages as well as to make "replicable and valid inferences to unobserved elements of the communication process" (Schulz, 2008, p. 349). The demonstration of causal media effects presupposes a connection between content analysis and panel data.

When panel studies and content analysis are used in combination, media content must be analyzed in the period between the panel waves. Combining panel and content data makes it possible to track responses and opinions at the aggregate level as well as at the individual level. We can see how media content affects changes in survey responses. To analyze news media effects (see Peter, 2003 for a review), several studies have used similar multi-method designs in the past, but most studies have utilized only media exposure and media attention measures (i.e., Newton, 1999; Norris, 2000). In this book, we incorporated the content analysis data into our news exposure measures so as to construct a more precise measure of the news content to which each respondent was actually exposed (see de Vreese & Semetko, 2004; Schuck & De Vreese, 2008 for a similar approach). Each respondent was given a weighted exposure score determined by his or her frequency of exposure to the different news outlets in his or her country as well as by the average presence of certain content features in each news outlet during the period between the panel waves.

The panel study was conducted during the U.S. elections in 2008. The panel surveys measure change in political knowledge, political cynicism, and satisfaction with political news. The Appendix to Chapter 2 describes the data collection for the survey panel data, as well as the content analysis during the panel period. The data form the backbone of Chapters 6, 7, and 8.

CONCLUSION

To summarize, this book utilizes a cross-national, multi-method design to assess the production, content, and effects of political news. We build upon a growing tradition of studies that employ multiple methods *and* a comparative perspective in order to determine the right mix of conditions for political journalism. Our country selection takes its starting point in the Hallin and Mancini (2004b) framework, but also allows us to study the influence of other system-level characteristics. Surveys are used to investigate journalists' backgrounds and attitudes toward covering politics, content analysis is used to identify and analyze different types of political news reporting, and panel surveys are used to examine the causal effects of content characteristics on the general public. The items in the journalist surveys and the general population panel surveys, as well as some of the measures in the content analyses, have been used, tested, and validated in prior research. Other items have been developed by us in an attempt to link the production of political journalism with its contents and effects. Our design is a unique feature, involving three types of newly collected data, in an integrated, cross-nationally comparative project.

3

Journalists

The People Behind the Headlines

In our study of political journalism, political news, and its effects, we focus first on political journalists. Understanding who political journalists are and what their relationship is to politics and politicians is important for specifying the conditions under which journalism operates. Political journalism has been described as "'the most sacred part' of journalism" (Neveu, 2002, 23) because of its intermediary position between the political elite and the people. This central role in the democratic process makes political journalism one of journalism's most prestigious beats (Tunstall, 1970, 41, 71): political journalists are close to the center of power and in an exclusive position to report on matters of great national importance, such as national elections or cabinet decisions. Political news is highly visible, often covered on the front pages of newspapers or at the beginning of the evening news (McNair 2000). But given this proximity to the center of power, political journalism is also one of the most criticized beats. With a prestigious position come high expectations, and politicians, media scholars, the general public, and other journalists criticize political journalists for not living up to their role as the "fourth estate." Critiques of political journalists are common and often center around journalists' autonomy, roles, and demographic profiles. This position in the 'front line' in terms of critique will be investigated in the light of our three key concepts.

We address the validity of this criticism across our four chosen national contexts and answer the questions: who are the political journalists and how do they view their role in the political process?

CRITIQUE FROM EVERYBODY

Journalistic Autonomy: Dealing with Pressures

As mentioned in Chapter 1, there is a largely negative discourse about journalists. A first critique centers around autonomy. Journalistic autonomy is the journalist's "latitude to carry out his or her occupational duties" (Weaver et al., 2007, 70). Deuze (2002, 5–6) describes autonomy as one of the defining features of a universal journalistic occupational ideology. Critics claim that journalists lack the necessary autonomy to fulfill their roles as democratic watchdogs.

Political pressure. Owners and other stakeholders who pursue political agendas may limit the autonomy of political journalists (Hallin & Papathanassopoulos, 2002). An owner of a media outlet could directly interfere, for example, by dismissing a journalist or an editor who refuses to toe the editorial line. Political pressure is often more subtle, however, and influences the editorial process in less visible ways (Breed, 1955). Political pressure bears direct relevance to the notions of impartiality and objectivity.

Commercial pressure. Increasing commercial pressure on journalism is seen as a threat to democracy (Roland, 2009, 267) and has led to discussions of a crisis in political communication (see McNair, 2009, 242–3). The need of media organizations to make profits may limit the freedom of journalists to do their work according to their professional norms and ethics. For example, budget cuts may mean allocating journalists less time and fewer resources to do their work (Neveu, 2002, 35). This pressure relates directly to our information-entertainment axiom (Chapter 1).

Spin doctors. When public relations techniques were introduced into politics, the number of spin doctors rapidly rose.

They tightened control over access to information and prepared politicians to avoid critical questions (McNair, 2004). This development has seriously frustrated political journalists by undercutting their capacity to engage in investigative reporting and pose challenging questions. When journalists ignore spin doctors' demands, they can expect aggressive complaints to their editors and may well be excluded from press conferences (Esser et al., 2000).

Journalistic Role: Approach to Politics

A second type of criticism is related to the way political journalists see their democratic role. Role conceptions have been described as a "type of self-image" (Cohen, 1963, 22) and refer to the way journalists believe they should do their work. Criticism has been aimed at three aspects, which relate to the three central concepts introduced in Chapter 1.

Pragmatism. Political journalism has been accused of taking an overtly pragmatic approach when covering politics (Blumler & Gurevitch 1995, 50). Political journalists no longer treat politics as newsworthy in itself (as the sacerdotal approach would imply; see Chapter 1). Instead, the focus lies on conflicts and contests (Neuman et al., 1992, 64–6; Patterson, 1993; Cappella & Jamieson, 1997) and on reporting events "laced with drama, conflict, novelty, movement and anomaly" (Blumler & Gurevitch 1991, 55). Politicians have also complained about this pragmatic approach in relation to political agendas (Brants et al., 2010; Van Aelst et al., 2008) since pragmatic journalists no longer respectfully follow the agendas put forward by politicians. Instead, these journalists seek a role in setting the political agendas and in actively determining the main issues of the day.

Partisanship. Political journalists have been criticized for not being impartial and balanced in their approach to politics. An impartial, objective, and factual style is characteristic of the journalistic watchdog model. But political journalists are criticized for giving preferential treatment to certain politicians and for expressing the political stands of the particular news media to which they belong (see Albæk et al., 2010).

Entertainment. Critics claim that political reporters no longer take their democratic task seriously; they entertain rather than inform (see McNair, 2009). Political news continues to "dumb down" as journalists place too much emphasis on scandals, remarkable incidents, and emotions. Rather than providing citizens with the information they need, political journalists give audiences the relaxation and sensation they desire.

Demographic Profile

A third and major criticism leveled at all journalists (Shoemaker & Reese, 1996), but most particularly at political reporters, is that their demographic backgrounds are not representative of their national populations (Henningham, 1995; Hess, 1992).

Academization. Previous studies have shown strong similarities between political reporters and politicians in terms of social background and level of education (Reese, 2001; Dahlgren, 1995). Increased levels of education – the "academization" of journalism – have been linked to a patriarchal stance toward the audience and the risk that journalists will become political insiders, copying the same frames and using the same language as the political elite while losing the perspective of the general population (see Schönbach et al., 1994, 141; Shoemaker & Reese, 1996).

Masculine beat. Political news is a prime example of a "masculine" news domain (Van Zoonen, 1998, 127), in which female journalists are traditionally a minority. A study of Westminster lobby correspondents published in 1970 found that only 2 out of 109 lobby correspondents were women (Tunstall, 1970). Male dominance in political journalism has been linked to gendering of journalistic content – for instance, a preference for objectivity over subjectivity, a dominance of male sources, and a focus on conflict and power (Klaus, 2009).

Left-leaning. Journalists have been criticized for their predominantly left-leaning political preferences, which are expected to lead to political bias in news content (see D'Alessio & Allen, 2000; Albæk et al., 2010). Political journalists have been called "left-wing missionaries" (see Albæk et al., 2010, 108), indicating

TABLE 3.1. *Characteristics of Political Journalists in Denmark, Germany, the United Kingdom, and Spain*

	Denmark (%)	Germany (%)	United Kingdom (%)	Spain (%)
At least a bachelor's degree	99	84	89	97
Degree in journalism	90	39	18	93
Female	28	29	23	41

that they intend their journalistic work to have a social mission. Henningham (1995) showed that political reporters in Australia were more left-wing than their colleagues on other beats.

In sum, political journalists are under scrutiny from politicians, audiences, researchers, and media pundits, and criticism is widespread. However, the empirical basis for such criticism is rather thin. The characterization of political journalism and the criticism of general trends are based on particular incidents (such as scandals) or particular periods (such as elections). In cases where political journalists are criticized on the basis of systematic research, such research is usually conducted in single national contexts. Our systematic, cross-national comparative design allows us to answer the following four questions: Who are the political journalists? How do they perceive their autonomy, and which pressures do they believe limit their freedom to work according to professional journalistic norms? How do political journalists see their journalistic role?

DEMOGRAPHIC BACKGROUNDS OF POLITICAL JOURNALISTS

We start with an account of the demographic composition of political journalists in Denmark, Germany, Spain, and the United Kingdom. Political journalists in these countries share certain characteristics: they are highly educated, predominantly male, and with a left political leaning (Table 3.1 and Figure 3.1). Across

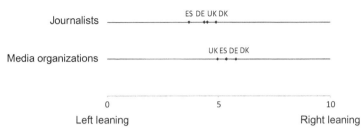

FIGURE 3.1. Political leaning of political journalists and their media in Denmark, Germany, the United Kingdom, and Spain. *Note:* Figure shows mean scores on a scale from 0 (completely left leaning) to 10 (completely right leaning). Based on a survey among 425 political journalists (see Appendix to Chapter 2). Mean scores and standard deviations can be found in the Appendix to Chapter 3.

countries, a large majority of political journalists are highly educated – about 90 percent have at least a bachelor's degree. For Denmark and Germany the level of education among political journalists is higher than on other journalistic beats.[1] The type of education differs markedly across countries. In Denmark and Spain, a majority of respondents have a degree in journalism, while this is the case for only a minority of journalists in the United Kingdom and Germany. These results confirm that political journalists are highly educated and that the educational level of political journalists is closer to that of the political class than that of the general population.

More than thirty years ago, studies in the United Kingdom (Tunstall, 1970) and in the United States (Hess, 1981) showed that political journalism was clearly a male profession. Although overall female participation in the journalistic profession may have risen since then (see Weaver et al., 2007 for the United States), the political beat still lags behind. More than two-thirds of British, Danish, and German political journalists are male. Spain is the only country in which more than 40 percent of the political beat is female. This percentage is mainly due to the

---

[1] Seventy percent of Danish journalists (Skovsgaard et al., 2012), 66 percent of German journalists (Weischenberg et al., 2006), and 49 percent of British journalists (Henningham and Delano, 1998) have completed a higher education.

unusually high number of women in the 30-40-year age group; female reporters actually outnumber males. Gender imbalances are less prevalent in the younger age groups than among older generations. Comparisons with the gender balance among whole populations of journalists in Denmark and Germany (Skovsgaard et al., 2012; Weischenberg et al., 2006) show that the gender balance is more skewed on the political beat.[2] For example, while 46 percent of all Danish journalists are female (Skovsgaard et al. 2012), in the case of political journalists, the corresponding figure is only 28 percent. This confirms that the journalistic profession is still horizontally segmented between men and women across different beats.

Political journalists positioned their own political leaning as well as the political leaning of the medium they work for on a scale from 0 (completely left leaning) to 10 (completely right leaning). The political leaning of journalists who report about politics can best be described as slightly left of center (for similar results for news journalists in general, see Patterson & Donsbach, 1996). In Denmark, Germany, and the United Kingdom, the majority of political journalists position themselves on or immediately next to the neutral middle position, with a mean score within one point left of the middle position. Only 7 percent of political journalists position themselves on one of the three outer-left positions of the 11-point scale. Spanish journalists have a more left political leaning than their colleagues in the northern European countries.

These results challenge critics who accuse the media of a left bias. First, political journalists are less left leaning than the general population of journalists (Henningham & Delano, 1998; Weischenberg et al., 2006; Skovsgaard et al., 2012). The mean political leaning of political journalists is closer to the neutral

---

[2] Although data from Germany are not directly comparable, only the 50-65-year age group (7 percent of the general journalistic population) has a lower share of women than those on the political beat (Weischenberg et al., 2006). In the United Kingdom, the share of women in the general journalistic population in 1998 was roughly the same as the share of women on the political beat in this survey (25 percent versus 23 percent) (Henningham & Delano, 1998).

middle position than the political leaning of general reporters in Germany (Weischenberg 2006) or in Denmark (Skovsgaard et al., 2012).[3] Second, political journalists are less left leaning than other people with similar educational backgrounds. In Denmark, political journalists voted less often for the two most left-wing parties than non-journalists with similar demographic profiles (Albæk et al., 2008). Third, in all countries, the journalists' own political leaning – slightly left of center – is balanced by the political leaning of the media outlets, which is slightly right of center (Figure 3.1).

AUTONOMY

Journalists have an autonomous position when "control of the work process in journalism is to a significant extent collegial, in the sense that authority over journalists is exercised primarily by fellow journalists" (Hallin & Mancini, 2004, 35). We have already mentioned that autonomy is one of the characteristics of a universal journalistic ideology (Deuze, 2002, 5–6) and of the journalist as democratic watchdog. In practice, levels of autonomy vary widely across countries (Hanitzsch et al., 2010; Benson, 2004). Journalists' autonomy has been less commonly studied in comparative research than have other topics (such as role conceptions). Several studies that have compared the influence of political and commercial pressures on journalism across countries have found significant differences. Weaver (1998, 462) showed that the percentage of journalists who perceive a great deal of autonomy varies from 6 percent in Taiwan to more than 80 percent in Finland and North America. Country differences seem to be mainly related to the competitiveness of the media markets (Kelly et al., 2004) and the strength of the journalistic profession (Hallin & Mancini, 2004b).

Political journalists were asked to describe the main limitation to their freedom in their work (Table 3.2). The most frequently

---

[3] Danish journalists have a mean political leaning of 3.99 on a scale from 0 (left) to 11 (right) (Skovsgaard et al., 2012). German journalists have a mean political leaning of 38 on a scale from 1 (left) to 100 (right).

TABLE 3.2. *Most Frequently Mentioned Limitations of Freedom to Do Journalistic Work (in Answer to an Open Question)*

Denmark (total N=71)	Germany (total N=201)	United Kingdom (total N=87)	Spain (total N=66)
Time/space (25)[a]	Time/space (72)	Time/space (21)	Political pressure from within organization (17)
Access to politicians and spin (5)	Commercial pressure (21)	Access to politicians and spin (20)	Time/space (11)
Commercial pressure (2)	Access to politicians and spin (18)	Libel and privacy laws (6)	Access to politicians and spin (8)
	Political pressure from within organization (7)	Political pressure from within organization (5)	Commercial pressure (1)

[a] Number of journalists mentioning limitation.

mentioned answers were coded into five categories. Across countries, limitations inherent in the routines within the news organization and the format of the news outlet (time and space) are seen as the most important limitations (for similar findings, see Hanitzsch et al., 2010). This is the most often mentioned category in Denmark, Germany, and the United Kingdom, and the second most often mentioned in Spain. Apart from this main limitation, "limited access to politicians and spin" is the only other category that is in the top four in each country.

Among the four countries, the Danish political press corps sees itself as the most autonomous. Danes hardly report any limitations other than time and space. None of the Danish journalists reported that they experience political pressure, while only two journalists report commercial pressure. In fact, nine Danish journalists explicitly mentioned that they do not experience any limitations at all. In Denmark, it appears, the traditionally strong professional status of journalists, combined with a well-established public service tradition and a robust newspaper market, remain influential and limit the effects of increased competition on the daily work of political journalists. Although Germany belongs to the same media system as Denmark, German political journalists experience more constraints on their autonomy than do their Danish colleagues. Compared with that of Denmark, the German media system is more competitive – with more competition in the television market and more newspapers competing for readers. In Germany, commercial pressures (*boulevardisering*) and access to politicians and spin ("attempts by official bodies to hide information") come in second and third place, followed by pressure from within the news organizations to adhere to the political lines of the papers.

Twenty British political journalists (23 percent) stated that "government secrecy" and "spin and counter spin" limit their freedom (for similar findings, see Esser & Spanjer, 2005). The United Kingdom was the only country in which journalists mentioned libel laws and privacy laws as the most important limitations on their work. Although the United Kingdom is generally classified as belonging to the liberal media system, with a preference for neutral, objective journalism, five British journalists reported that political pressure from within the newsroom – such as "editorial control (agenda set by the paper's editor/owner)" – limits their journalistic freedom. This shows that political parallelism in the British press (Seymoure-Ure, 1974) continues to influence the work of political journalists today. The press in Britain is highly competitive, with a strong tabloid segment and high reliance on loose sales rather than subscriptions. In recent years, several observers have expressed their concern about an increasing profit orientation and budget cuts in news media organizations (see McNair, 2009). Nevertheless, none of the British journalists in this study mentioned commercial pressure as the most important limitation to their freedom.

In Denmark, Germany, and the United Kingdom, the most often mentioned limitations are related to the routines in the news organization and the formats of the news outlets; in Spain, these take second place. In Spain, as in other countries belonging to the polarized pluralist media system, owners of print and commercial media may use their influence over media outlets to gain political favors (Hallin & Papathanassopoulos, 2002). At the same

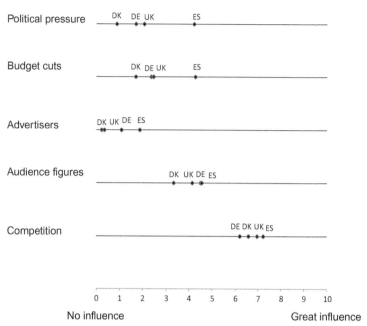

FIGURE 3.2. Influence of political and commercial pressure on the work of political journalists in Denmark, Germany, the United Kingdom, and Spain. *Note:* Figure shows mean scores on a scale from 0 (no influence) to 10 (large influence). Based on a survey among 425 political journalists (see Appendix to Chapter 2). Mean scores and standard deviations can be found in the Appendix to Chapter 3.

time, the Spanish government has a stronger influence in public service broadcasting than in other media systems where public service media are not directly financed by the state. According to Spanish political journalists, these structural characteristics remain important today: the most often mentioned constraint on the autonomy of Spanish political journalists is political pressure, trumping even constraints due to time and space.

On a scale from 0 (none) to 10 (great influence), the political journalists indicated the degree of political pressure and of four types of commercial pressure (Figure 3.2) that they experience. Across countries, journalists experienced little direct pressure from advertisers, while they experienced most pressure from competition with other media. Country differences are largely in line with those presented in Table 3.1.

Political pressure provides the most variation across the four countries. Criticism that political journalists cannot fulfill their roles as independent watchdogs due to political pressure finds most support in Spain and the least support in Denmark. In line with their answers to the open questions, Danish journalists score low on the political-pressure scale. Spanish newspaper journalists and those working for commercial media experience significantly more political pressure than journalists in Northern Europe. Spanish political reporters working for public service media, however, are no different from their colleagues working in other media systems.

Spanish journalists clearly experience the most political pressure. They also experience significantly more pressure from threats of budget cuts and from advertisers than do their colleagues in Denmark, Germany, and the United Kingdom. In the 1980s and 1990s, media policy in countries belonging to the polarized pluralist media system was characterized by "savage deregulation" (Traquina, 1995), leading to a growth of media conglomerates and greater focus on profits. Since Spanish journalists had not yet developed a strong institutionalized professional culture, these developments have had a negative influence on the autonomy of Spanish political journalists. But, as in the case of political pressure, there is one group of Spanish journalists that is less affected by commercial pressure: those journalists working for public service broadcast organizations do not experience significantly more commercial pressure than do their foreign colleagues. Contrary to what would be expected, based on discussions concerning the commercialization of journalism (Roland, 2009; McNair, 2009), political journalists in Denmark, Germany, and the United Kingdom do not overwhelmingly experience commercial pressure from advertisers or budget cuts. They do, however, experience somewhat more pressure from audience figures.

British newspaper journalists do not experience more pressure than journalists in the democratic corporatist media system. This is surprising, since the professional position of journalists is considered to be weaker in the liberal media system than in the democratic corporatist system: they have fewer and weaker unions, and self-regulatory mechanisms are not as strongly institutionalized (Tunstall, 2004). The low levels of commercial pressure experienced by British journalists are in line with Donsbach and Patterson's earlier findings (2004, 262) on American journalists, who likewise scored "medium" on the commercialization scale used in their study.[4]

ROLE CONCEPTIONS

Role conceptions are compared along the three dimensions introduced in Chapter 1: the status of political news (pragmatic versus sacerdotal), the degree of partisan commitment (impartial versus partisan), and audience goals (information versus entertainment). Each of these dimensions has been used in previous journalism surveys, observational studies, and content analyses (Donsbach & Patterson, 2004; Semetko & Canel, 1997; De Vreese, 2001).

Figure 3.3 shows the position of the political journalists on the pragmatic-sacerdotal scale.[5] Danish and Spanish journalists are significantly more sacerdotal than journalists in Germany and

---

[4] The commercial pressure experienced by journalists may differ from what could be expected based on a structural account of the liberal media system (Tunstall, 2004; McNair, 2009) or on an analysis of content characteristics in this system (Strömbäck & Shehata, 2007). Certainly, studies of journalists' perceptions of autonomy should not be seen as a substitute for, but rather as a useful addition to, studies in which news content produced in different countries or by different outlets is compared (Benson & Hallin, 2007; Esser, 2008). In addition, surveying journalists' perceptions can be valuable in understanding news production because it "renders observable social structures that are otherwise invisible to researchers" (Hanitzsch et al., 2010, 18).

[5] The pragmatic-sacerdotal scale is measured using the following question: To what extent do you agree or disagree with the following statement about the newsworthiness of national politics: "Mass media should report about national politics in full detail, even when the public is more interested in other topics"? Scale from 1 (totally disagree) to 5 (totally agree).

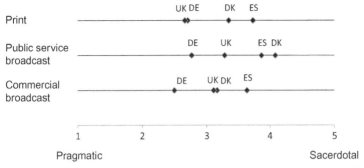

FIGURE 3.3. Pragmatic versus sacerdotal role conceptions of political journalists working in Denmark, Germany, the United Kingdom, and Spain. *Note:* Figure shows mean scores on a scale from 1 (pragmatic) to 5 (sacerdotal) for journalists working for print, public service broadcasters, and commercial broadcasters. Based on a survey among 425 political journalists (see the Appendix to Chapter 2). Mean scores and standard deviations can be found in the Appendix to Chapter 3.

the United Kingdom. The sacerdotal Spanish journalistic culture goes back to the democratic transition period, when Spanish journalists saw it as their task to help "resocialize Spain's adult population to acknowledge the legitimacy of the new regime and to internalize fundamental norms of democratic behavior" (Gunther, Montero, & Wert, 2000, 51). Danish political journalists also believe that national politics deserve special attention. This impression is consistent with the findings of a survey of the general Danish journalist population, which concluded that Danish journalists "have a strong sense of public obligation, and they strongly adhere to objectivity and relevance rather than dramatic appeal in the news selection" (Skovsgaard et al., 2012). The country differences are significant for print and public service journalists but not for journalists working for commercial broadcasters.

Figures 3.4 and 3.5 show the position of British, Danish, German, and Spanish journalists working for different outlets on the impartial-partisan and information-entertainment dimensions.[6]

---

[6] The impartial-partisan index summed the score for agreement with the statements that (1) the medium I work for has a specific political color that guides

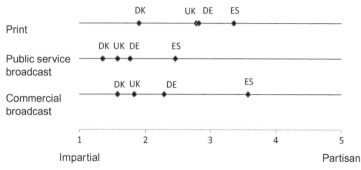

FIGURE 3.4. Impartial versus partisan role conceptions of political journalists working in Denmark, Germany, the United Kingdom, and Spain. *Note:* Figure shows mean scores on a scale from 1 (impartial) to 5 (partisan) for journalists working for print, public service broadcasters, and commercial broadcasters. Based on a survey among 425 political journalists (see Appendix to Chapter 2). Mean scores and standard deviations can be found in the Appendix to Chapter 3.

Spanish political journalists believe it is more acceptable for journalists to take sides in political disputes than their colleagues in northern Europe, who follow the journalistic watchdog model and aim to present balanced coverage (Blumler & Gurevitch, 1995).[7] These differences are significant for each type of news outlet, including public service media. The biggest country

me in how to do my work, and (2) in the news section my medium keeps a neutral position in partisan or policy disputes (reversely coded). The bivariate correlation of the two items is .42 across the four countries. Bivariate correlations per country: Denmark, .42; Germany, .29; United Kingdom, .48; Spain, .52. As an external validity check, the scores for different media types were compared. They showed that journalists working for press agencies scored lowest on this scale, while print journalists scored highest.

    The information-entertainment role is measured using the following question: How important are the following goals for you when you report on national politics: "Provide entertainment and relaxation"? Scale from 1 (completely unimportant) to 5 (very important).

[7] The impartial-partisan dimension used in this study only refers to the treatment of politicians in accordance with a particular medium's political line. This dimension is closely related to the neutral-partisan dimension used by Patterson and Donsbach (2004); instead of using *neutral*, however, we use *impartial*, given that *neutral* often indicates that personal remarks have been excluded or that one's own political leanings have not influenced content.

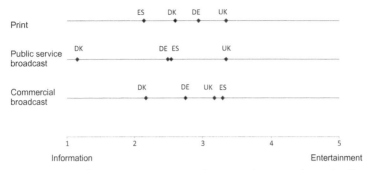

FIGURE 3.5. Information versus entertainment role conceptions of polit-ical journalists working in Denmark, Germany, the United Kingdom, and Spain. *Note:* Figure shows mean scores on a scale from 1 (Infor-mation) to 5 (Entertainment) for journalists working for print, public service broadcasters, and commercial broadcasters. Based on a survey among 425 political journalists (see Appendix to Chapter 2). Mean scores and standard deviations can be found in Appendix to Chapter 3.

variation is not in newspapers but in commercial broadcasting, and is mostly due to Spanish journalists working for commercial radio stations; they have the most partisan role conceptions of all journalists in the study. Two main reasons can be given for the wider acceptance of partisan role conceptions among Span-ish journalists. First is a partisan cleavage in Spanish society, which is deeper than in other countries. This cleavage is reflected in audience segmentation along partisan lines and the need for journalists to compete for partisan audiences. Second is the less autonomous position of Spanish journalists, with particular pres-sure coming from owners who want to use the media to affect the political process.

While Spanish journalists are the most sacerdotal and most partisan, British journalists are the most oriented toward enter-tainment (see Figure 3.5). British journalists working for all media types are on the entertainment end of the scale. The United Kingdom is also the country in which complaints about infotainment have been the loudest (McNair, 2009; Blumler & Kavanagh, 1999). The only other journalists on the enter-tainment side of the scale are Spanish journalists working for commercial broadcasters. There are clear cross-national differences in newspaper cultures: in Spain, where there are no tabloids and where newspapers mainly aim at an elite audience, the entertainment function is significantly less important than in the northern European countries. Journalists in the democratic corporatist media system prefer information over entertainment. The entertainment role is most clearly rejected by journalists who work for the Danish public broadcasting service.

CONCLUSION

Our descriptive account of the demographics, autonomy, and role conceptions of political journalists deflect or at least soften much of the criticism that has been directed at the political beat. Although political journalists have different demographic backgrounds than their audiences, the results do not suggest that they are "left-wing missionaries." Journalists believe that both political and commercial goals and spin doctors limit their autonomy. But these influences are not experienced by journalists in all four countries, and are generally less important than limitations related to journalistic routines and news formats. Journalistic role conceptions are first and foremost pluralistic. Spanish journalists stand out as the most partisan and British journalists as the most entertainment oriented. When we analyze political journalists on the basis of the three central concepts introduced in Chapter 1, we see that European journalists are still sacerdotal: in none of the countries do the journalists overtly or exclusively prefer a pragmatic, partisan, or entertainment role conception.

This chapter has thus provided a nuanced picture of political journalism, including important insights into cross-national differences. Political journalists in Denmark, Germany, Spain, and the United Kingdom have largely similar demographic backgrounds, but differ in perceived autonomy and role conceptions. These differences have their roots in the structural and historical contexts in which the political journalists work. While on the one hand our country selection thus nicely dovetails the typology of Hallin and Mancini (2004), our data do not *systematically* fit their model. This highlights the shortcomings of such classification systems and stresses the necessity to look more specifically at some of the dimensions in their model. In terms of conditions, the results in this chapter speak very clearly to the crucial importance of autonomy for political journalists. In the next two chapters we look at the consequences of these country differences. Chapter 4 will first show how perceived pressures from politicians and spin doctors lead journalists to take more cynical attitudes toward politics. In Chapter 5 the relationship between role conceptions and news content will be discussed.

4

Journalists and Politicians

A Troubled Relationship?

In this chapter we move beyond journalists only and turn to the interaction between journalists and politicians. This interaction is often under scrutiny. Political news has been criticized for reinforcing what has come to be known as "the spiral of cynicism." Because of negative reporting styles and cynical approaches toward politics, journalists are held responsible for decreasing levels of trust in government as well as increasing political cynicism among readers and viewers (Cappella & Jamieson, 1997; de Vreese, 2005). Critics condemn the "increasingly hostile and irresponsible tenor of political journalism" (Barnett in McNair, 2009, 244). Exposure to negatively framed news about politics is presumed to lessen not only trust but also political engagement (for example, see Patterson, 2000b). Empirical proof for this presumed causal relationship between negativity in political news and declining trust in politicians is, however, far from conclusive (see Adriaansen et al., 2011; Norris, 2000; de Vreese, 2005; Avery, 2009 for different findings). The impact of news on levels of trust seems to be contingent upon several factors; for instance, the type of news outlet, news content, and prior levels of trust.

Thus, evidence as to whether an increasingly negative reporting style influences voters' attitudes is inconclusive. Studies in different European countries, however, have indeed shown some

support for the claim that political news has become more critical – by using game frames and exposing the media strategies of
politicians, for example (see Brants & Van Kempen, 2000 for the
Netherlands; Schulz & Zeh, 2005 for Germany). Explanations
for the negative framing of politics have been sought in commercial pressures (Patterson, 2000b), political PR, adversarial
journalistic cultures (Esser & Spanjer, 2005), and differences in
political and media systems (Strömbäck & Shehata, 2007, 800).

Considering the interest in the spiral of cynicism and its
causes, it is surprising that there are almost no studies of one
particular possible cause – the attitudes of journalists. Do they
themselves have cynical attitudes toward politicians? How are
these attitudes influenced by their relationships with politicians?
The daily interactions between journalists and politicians are an
important antecedent of political information. Just as professional norms and routines within news organizations do, sources
shape journalistic output (Schoemaker & Reese, 1991). Blumler and Gurevitch (1995, 25) have described the relationships
between political journalists and politicians as "pivotal." Studies
that examine the relationships between the media and politics
often deal with agenda-setting power relations (e.g., Edwards &
Wood, 1999; Walgrave & Van Aelst, 2006; Van Aelst et al.,
2008) or political spin, especially during elections (e.g., Esser
et al., 2000, 2001; McNair, 2004; Moloney & Colmer, 2001;
Pfetsch, 2001). The daily contacts between political journalists
and politicians during routine periods, and the impact of these
contacts on the journalists' attitudes, have received considerably
less attention in political communication literature. The relative
absence of knowledge about this subject contrasts with the large
body of literature that has investigated the political leaning of
journalists as a possible antecedent of bias in political reporting (for example, Patterson & Donsbach, 1996; Henningham,
1995).

Studying the interactions between journalists and politicians
should be the first step toward understanding the complex relationships between the media and politics (Cook, 2005, 13).
Brants et al. (2010) argue that in order to understand the spiral of

cynicism between media content and audiences' political perceptions, researchers should focus on what comes before – and that is another kind of spiral, the spiral of mutual mistrust between politicians and journalists. The Brants study showed that Dutch politicians have a cynical attitude toward journalists and that the main sources of dissatisfaction were the media's portrayal of politicians and its agenda-setting power. By contrast, political cynicism among political journalists in the Netherlands was relatively low, and no discernable factors explained variation of political cynicism among journalists (Brants et al., 2010, 38, n7).

Studying the attitudes of political journalists from a comparative perspective might help identify independent variables that can explain variations in political cynicism. The democratic corporatist media system, to which the Netherlands belongs, is characterized by a strong public service tradition, a relatively high level of journalistic autonomy, and mutual consensus building, and may therefore be an unlikely breeding ground for high levels of cynicism among journalists (Hallin & Mancini, 2004b). A hyperadversarial journalistic approach toward politicians is still the exception rather than the rule in the Netherlands, and election coverage continues to focus mainly on substantive issues (Brants & van Praag, 2006). The relations between journalists and politicians might be less harmonious and journalists may be more cynical about politicians in countries belonging to the liberal media system, which has a more developed PR culture (Esser & Spanjer, 2005), or in countries belonging to the polarized pluralist media system, in which journalists experience more political pressure in their work (see Chapter 3). A comparative perspective is needed to study the influence of source professionalization and political pressure on the levels of cynicism among journalists, as these characteristics are strongly related to the political communication systems journalists work in.

In sum, explanations of negative framing and hyperadversarial reporting styles may be found not only at the level of the news organization or the journalistic beat, but also in the relationships between journalists and politicians. Before going deeper into the historical context of relations between media and politics in

Denmark, Germany, Spain, and the United Kingdom, we present a general framework for an understanding of the role relationships between journalists and politicians as part of our overall specification of the right mix of conditions that need to be present for political journalism.

AN AMBIGUOUS ROLE RELATIONSHIP

Working as they do on the political beat, parliamentary journalists have close contact with politicians on a daily basis (Gans, 2004).

Journalists and politicians meet each other not only in professional settings but also in less formal settings such as the German *Hintergrundkreise* (background circles) or the Lobby in the British House of Commons. Schudson (2003, 145) describes the environment in which politicians and journalists interact as a "common social world" or "microcosmos," emphasizing the extent to which their lives intertwine. Critics have claimed that when parliamentary journalism and politics become too closely interwoven, journalists may find it difficult to cover politics critically (Gans, 2004; Schudson, 2003; Sigal, 1986). Exchange relationships may develop in which journalists and politicians behave in ways that compromise the independent position of the journalist. Examples of such informal contacts include entering into a friendship with a politician, giving advice to a politician, or even simply lunching together.

Aside from this shared social world, the relationship between journalists and politicians is characterized by interdependencies (Neveu, 2002). The number of parliamentary journalists grew considerably in the last decades of the twentieth century, increasing competition among journalists. At the same time, politicians came to rely more heavily on the media to reach constituencies with weaker ties to political parties. Over time, the media became increasingly influential in the political process, forcing politicians to adjust their messages to a media logic (Brants & van Praag, 2006). These developments made parliamentary reporters and politicians more dependent on one another. Indeed, they are commonly regarded as mutually dependent actors (Blumler &

Gurevitch, 1995), whose behavior is guided by how they perceive their own roles as well as those of their counterparts. According to role theory, these actors continuously adapt their behavior to the expected behavior of the other. While each actor primarily acts to promote his or her own interests, journalists and politicians often have similar goals, and actually need each other. Politics without the media is no longer thinkable, and politicians need publicity to communicate with their peers and potential voters (van Aelst et al., 2008). Journalists working under increasing time pressure are dependent on politicians to fill the daily news hole (Cook, 2005).

Conflicting and simultaneously overlapping goals lead to an uneasy or ambiguous relationship, which can be classified according to its degree of harmony (Nimmo, 1964). In a cooperative relationship, the two actors share common goals and the level of conflict is low. This harmonious relationship can be described as symbiotic (Gans, 2004), with "two dissimilar organisms living in mutually beneficial relationship, each bringing something essential to the whole" (Merrit, 1995, 48). In a competitive relationship, journalists and politicians stand opposed to each other and pursue conflicting goals. Davis's (2009) study of the relations between UK MPs and parliamentary journalists confirms the complexity of the relationship in which antagonism and exchange exist side by side. This uneasy union reveals itself in the political coverage:

> For most interviewees, most of the time it was a relationship of cautious co-operation that benefited both sides. At the same time, conflict and mistrust were common and either side was capable of, and frequently did, damage to the other. This in turn was reflected in news coverage that could be either too compliant (. . .) or too aggressive (. . .). (Davis, 2009, 210).

Thus, in the relationship between journalists and politicians, we can see that trust is an important factor, which in practice translates into mutual understanding and respect for formal and informal rules (Mancini, 1993). According to Larsson (2002), interpersonal relationships in general, and relationships between journalists and politicians in particular, benefit from situations in which the relationship is balanced and both sides are willing to make an investment in and a commitment to the relationship. If journalists perceive that politicians lack respect for them and the work they do, the necessary relationship balance is challenged, and the relationship is guided by mutual suspicion, mistrust (van Aelst & Aalberg, 2009), and cynicism (Brants et al., 2010). On the basis of these observations, we discuss the influence of political pressure and source professionalization on political cynicism among journalists.

POLITICAL PRESSURE AND SOURCE PROFESSIONALIZATION

Worldwide, professional autonomy is one of the most important factors underpinning job satisfaction (Weaver, 1998). Although role perceptions among political journalists differ from one country to another (see Chapter 3), the watchdog function (holding government and other politicians to account), the forum function (providing a place for debate) and the function of expression (giving expression to public opinion) are generally perceived to be central to the media in all democracies (Graber, 2003; McNair, 2007). Political journalists' professional autonomy and their ability to fulfil their democratic function largely depend on the political context in which journalists work – in particular, on the level of political pressure (Mancini, 2000) and source professionalization (Esser & Spanjer, 2005).

Professional autonomy requires that political journalists do their work without political pressure (Hallin & Papathanassopoulos, 2002; see also Chapter 3). Autonomy is an essential element of journalistic professionalization. In countries with a tradition of journalistic professionalization, the journalists' work is defined by the professional goals of both the journalists and their news organizations (Schudson & Anderson, 2009; Deuze, 2002) rather than by the interests of other actors. Such an autonomous position can result from institutionalized self-regulatory mechanisms – including press councils, codes of ethics, and journalistic unions – or from a commercially profitable press that does not require financial support from actors outside the media (Hallin & Mancini, 2004b). When journalists have such an autonomous position, the relationships between journalists and politicians are based on equality.

When self-regulatory press mechanisms are not institutionalized, and the media are financially dependent on political actors outside the newsroom, the relationships between journalists and politicians are characterized by dependence rather than equality. In such a situation, political actors and other actors with a political agenda might have a direct influence on the work of journalists through instrumentalization. This can be seen, for example, in politicized public service broadcasting organizations that are under the influence of the governing party (Díez, Nicolas, & Semetko, 1995). Aside from direct influence by politicians, the work of journalists can also be exposed to the more subtle pressures of cliental relationships between media owners or chief editors and political leaders (Hallin & Papathanassopoulos, 2002). Dependency on, and pressures from, political actors can frustrate political journalists because in such situations they may find it difficult to work according to their own professional norms. We will therefore investigate whether the perceived political pressure as described in Chapter 3 makes journalists more cynical.

A well-functioning press requires that politicians be open in their communication and available for questions. Politicians' availability to journalists may vary considerably. In a highly competitive news environment, newsworthy politicians simply lack the time to address all journalists individually. In such cases, journalists are addressed in more controlled settings, such as press conferences, or they have to rely on spokespersons who act as gatekeepers. Limited availability to journalists may be a strategy applied by politicians reluctant to face critical journalists because they are fearful of possible missteps or blunders. One bypass strategy for politicians seeking to avoid answering weighty questions is to appear in entertainment or local media (Rosenstiel, 1993); instead, their spokespersons face critical questions from political reporters. Such tactics have resulted in an "irritated journalistic reaction" by traditional mass media political reporters (Brants, 1998, 331). Given the fact that political reporters do find that spin doctors limit their autonomy (Chapter 3), we study to what extent frustration with spin doctors leads to cynicism among political journalists.

The more open politicians are in their communication, and the more respect they have for the role of the journalist, the easier it is for journalists to hold politicians to account. Journalists may feel that they are not being taken seriously when politicians see publicity as an end in itself and seek to be the center of media attention. Media exposure is important to politicians at all times, not only during elections. Being able to communicate in a "media savvy" style and to transmit a positive image are important factors determining whether a politician can rise in the party hierarchy (van Aelst et al., 2008). In this regard, one can speak of permanent campaigning in non-election times. Politicians shape their messages, and to some extent their policies, according to media logic, and take a proactive approach toward journalists (Mazzoleni & Schulz, 1999). Journalists can benefit from such proactive politicians, particularly from those who are able to explain their political messages and decisions in short sound bites.

However, journalists may become cynical about politicians when their political work takes a backseat to their search for media attention. When politicians talk about their private lives in entertainment shows, frequently organize press events with little inherent news value, or walk out of a debate in parliament to give a live interview on television, then their motives are questioned. Are politicians appearing in the media to facilitate the democratic functioning of the press, or are they demonstrating their media salacity – that is, "the politician's repeated attempts and ultimate drive to get the camera's attention" (Brants et al., 2010, 30)? Journalists have reacted negatively to politicians who try to gain media attention by frequently organizing press conferences without providing real news (Ansolabehere et al., 1993, 123–5). Journalists generally become cynical about the political competences of politicians when politicians see media coverage as an end in itself, and everything else as secondary. We therefore study whether political journalists are more cynical toward politicians when they perceive those politicians to be driven by media salacity.

DIFFERENT CONTEXTS: DIFFERENT RELATIONS?

Political and media systems are integrated to varying degrees in different countries, and therefore the professionalization of news management by politicians also differs. These two factors mean that British, Danish, German, and Spanish journalists meet politicians in diverse contexts (Pfetsch, 2004). These differences are also likely to influence the role relations between journalists and politicians – and thereby the level of cynicism among journalists.

British newspapers traditionally had a partisan leaning, but economic and formal ties to political parties were less common than in southern and central Europe (Hallin & Mancini, 2004b, 221). The traditional journalistic approach toward politicians in Great Britain could be described as respectful and sacerdotal (Blumler & Gurevitch, 2001). Over the years, as a result of increased competition and technical developments, the environment in which political journalists work became much more dynamic. Audiences fragmented as the number of communication channels increased. The number of parliamentary journalists also increased substantially (Blumler & Kavanagh, 1999), and the link between voters and political parties became weaker. As the electorate became more volatile, the importance of election campaigns and the necessity to reach potential voters through the media increased. Countries belonging to the liberal media system were the front-runners in professionalizing political communication (Negrine et al., 2007). Indeed, the United Kingdom was the first European country in which communication by political parties and government became professionalized, often copying successful examples from the United States (Esser et al., 2001). In response to the increased professionalization of political communication in Britain, journalists have fought back by engaging in metacommunication, "self-referential reflection[s] on the nature of the interplay between political public relations and political journalism" (Esser et al., 2001, 16).

In the democratic corporatist media system, to which Denmark and Germany belong, the political and media systems were traditionally much more closely integrated than in the United Kingdom. Before 1970, "segmented pluralism" characterized most societies in the democratic corporatist media system (Lorwin, 1971, in Hallin & Mancini, 2004b, 152). It was not uncommon to find that the head of a political party was also at the head of a corresponding newspaper. Politicians belonging to one party often featured as sources in newspapers with the same political color (Brants, 2004, 145). According to Brants and van Praag (2006, 28), the approach taken by journalists toward politicians in those days was "obedient and even servile."

But as the importance of television grew and the audience became more unpredictable, the grip of political parties on the media diminished through the years. The media and political systems became less integrated, giving journalists a more independent position vis-à-vis politicians. Many newspapers became omnibus newspapers aimed at a general audience instead of a partisan audience. The idea that journalists should become influential by critically following developments in society and politics gained traction at the end of the 1960s (see, e.g., Djerf-Pierre, 2000, for Sweden). From then on, the relations between journalists and politicians were no longer dominated by political parallelism but rather by "critical professionalism" (Djerf-Pierre, 2000). As a result of this change, political color no longer defined the relationship between parliamentary journalists and their sources. Over time, just as in Great Britain, the general reporting style and approach of journalists toward politicians became less sacerdotal and more critical (Brants & van Praag, 2006).

As it has in the United Kingdom, doing well in the media has become more and more important for politicians in democratic corporatist countries. Tony Blair's successful political campaign and government communication inspired many political parties in democratic corporatist media system countries, which also professionalized their political communication (Esser et al., 2001). However, the strong corporatist tradition in these countries, combined with a multi-party system and a tradition of consensus, operates as a moderating factor that limits the extent to which politicians apply political communication practices (Brants & van Praag, 2006). Although the political communication systems in which Danish and German journalists work show great similarities, scale may have an impact. While the Danish parliamentary press corps consists of about 100 journalists, the number in Germany is more than six times greater, which might make politicians less easily accessible in Germany than in Denmark.

Of the four countries under study, the biggest differences appear to exist between journalists working in Spain and their northern colleagues. Spanish democracy and press freedom are still relatively young compared with that in Denmark, Germany, and the United Kingdom. The political and media systems in Spain are still closely integrated. The work of journalists continues to be characterized by dependence rather than autonomy and is very much shaped by persisting instrumentalism and close ties between editors-in-chief and political parties (Papatheodorou & Machin, 2003). The global trend of professional news management and the staging of tightly controlled news events has also been observed in Spain (Sampedro & Seoana Pérez, 2008). The reaction of journalists, however, has not been in line with the reaction in other countries, since the tone toward politicians remains sacerdotal rather than pragmatic, and news during political campaigns is more often based on events initiated by politicians than in other countries (Strömbäck & Luengo, 2008). In the face of increasingly professionalized news management in Spain on the side of politicians, political journalists have yet to find the right response.

In sum, we expect that the different contexts in which British, Danish, German, and Spanish political journalists work influence the role relations between journalists and politicians, with an associated impact on political cynicism among journalists. On the basis of the survey answered by 425 political journalists (see Chapter 2), we test whether political pressure on the one hand and a negative perception of the professionalization of political communication on the other hand can explain the levels of political cynicism among political journalists working in these four countries.

POLITICAL CYNICISM EXPLAINED

First, the influence of political pressure and source professionalization is tested on the aggregate level. To see how levels of political cynicism among journalists differ between countries with varying political communication contexts, we will first compare the mean scores of the political cynicism measure[1] for the four countries (Figure 4.1) and then compare these scores with the mean scores of perception of spin[2] and media salacity[3] for each

---

[1] To measure our dependent variable "political cynicism" we used a four-item scale used by Brants et al. (2010), which is based on a political cynicism scale used in several election studies. Respondents indicated on a five-point scale to what degree they agreed with the following statements: "(1) politicians promise more than they can deliver, (2) it is easier to become a member of parliament thanks to political friends than because of competence, (3) ministers are mainly focused on their own interests, (4) politicians do not understand what is happening in society" (overall scale α.70). Political cynicism scale per country: UK (United Kingdom), α=.58, M=3.16, SD=.57; DK (Denmark), α=.49, M=2.85, SD=.56; DE (Germany), α=.73, M=3.28, SD=.66; ES (Spain), α=.72, M=3.62, SD=.67.

[2] We measured the journalists' perceptions of the role of spin doctors in political communication by asking journalists to indicate on a five-point scale whether they disagree or agree with the statement that "spokespersons and other communication specialists inhibit journalists in their job." Mean scores of the spin-doctor variable per country (1 is positive perception, 5 is negative perception): UK, M=2.99, SD=1.09; DK, M=2.86, SD=1.10; DE, M=2.76, SD=1.04; ES, M=3.58, SD=1.02.

[3] We used two items measured on a five-point scale (Brants et al., 2010) to construct a media-salacity scale: "It is more important for a politician to get covered in the media than to work hard" and "Politicians would do anything to get attention from the media." Media-salacity scale per country (scale from 1 (low) to 5 (high), overall scale r.54): UK, r=.42, M=2.87, SD=.85; DK, r=.39, M=3.07, SD=.76; DE, r=.44, M=3.30, SD=.80; ES, r=.48, M=4.41, SD=.56.

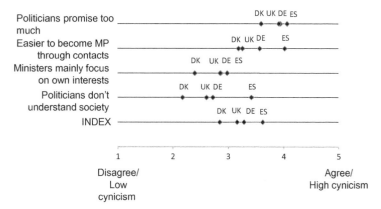

FIGURE 4.1. Political cynicism among Danish, German, British, and Spanish political journalists. *Note:* Figure shows mean scores on a scale from 1 (Disagree/low cynicism) to 5 (Agree/high cynicism). Based on a survey among 425 political journalists (see Appendix to Chapter 4). Mean scores and standard deviations can be found in the Appendix to Chapter 4.

of the four countries (Figure 4.2). The perception of political pressure[4] was already shown in Chapter 3 (Figure 3.2).

Denmark scores lowest of the four countries on each of the four items and on the combined political cynicism index (Figure 4.1). This score (M=2.85) is below the middle position of the index, indicating that levels of cynicism are not elevated. The mean scores of political cynicism in Germany (M=3.28) and the United Kingdom (M=3.16) are significantly higher than in Denmark, but not far from the middle position of the scale. The relatively low level of cynicism among British political journalists is noteworthy, since criticism about hyperadversarialism and a negative journalistic approach toward politicians is particularly common in the liberal media system (McNair, 2009; see the following discussion). The Spanish journalists are the most cynical: they

---

[4] To measure feelings of political pressure, journalists indicated "how much influence political pressure has on their daily work" on a scale from 0 (no influence) to 10 (large influence). Mean scores of the political-pressure variable per country (0 is low, 10 is high): UK, M=2.06, SD=2.12; DK, M=.87, SD=1.69; DE, M=1.69, SD= 2.03; ES, M=4.21, SD=2.92.

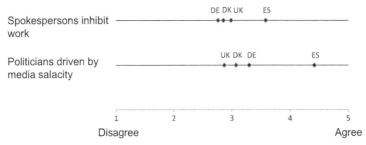

FIGURE 4.2. Perception of spin doctors and media salacity by Danish, German, British, and Spanish political journalists. *Note:* Figure shows mean scores on a scale from 1 (Disagree) to 5 (Agree). Based on a survey among 425 political journalists (see Appendix to Chapter 2. Mean scores and standard deviations can be found in the Appendix to Chapter 4.

score significantly higher on the combined scale than the three other countries (M=3.62). They agree significantly more than journalists in northern Europe with the statements that (1) politicians own their jobs because they know the right people, and (2) politicians do not understand what is happening in society.

Can differences in cynicism among journalists be explained by their relations with politicians? Before testing this on an individual level, we compare aggregated country scores. Danish political journalists experience fewest problems from political pressure and spokespersons. As indicated in Chapter 3 (see Figure 3.2), Spanish journalists report the most political pressure in their work. They are also most negative about political spokespersons, and believe that politicians are driven by media salacity (Figure 4.2). These opinions are expressed more concretely in some of the answers given by Spanish political journalists when asked about the most important limitations on their journalistic freedom: "the barriers put up by press offices," the "difficulty to access information and the constant battle against propaganda and the limitations that are established by the parties," or the "pressure of sources who temporarily silence themselves after negative news before giving information again."

German and British political journalists experience similar degrees of pressure from political parties and from spokespersons, but German journalists complain significantly more about politicians' media salacity than their British colleagues do. The frustration with the way politicians communicate is exemplified in the following answer from a German reporter to the question about the biggest limitation to his work: "The faint-heartedness of politicians not willing to 'stand by' their opinions. Instead, carefully defined packages are created, which are partly in contradiction with the real situation."

Comparing Figures 4.1 and 4.2, we see that on the aggregate country level, political cynicism is related to perceptions of political pressure and negative attitudes to the professionalization of political communication. Spanish journalists, who experience the most political pressure and are the most negative about the professionalization of political communication, are also most cynical about politicians. Danish journalists are significantly less cynical. They experience fewer problems concerning pressure from politicians and spokespersons, and are less suspicious of politicians' motives for initiating communication. But is this cynicism at the country level reflected at the level of the individual journalist? To answer this question, we run a regression analysis with the political cynicism index as a dependent variable. In this regression model, we include control variables that can potentially influence the attitude of journalists toward politicians, such as frequency of contact and journalistic experience.[5]

Figure 4.3 visualizes the various influences on political cynicism based on a regression model for the four countries combined. As expected, experiences of political pressure as well as negative perceptions of spokespersons lead to higher levels

---

[5] Contacts, based on one item from (1) never to (5) (almost) daily: "In an average month, how often do you have contact with a politician?." UK, M=4.29, SD=.87; DK, M=4.79, SD=.56; DE, M=3.77, SD=.91; ES, M=4.30, SD=1.08.

Medium type (print, broadcast, and press agency respectively): UK, 40.2%, 49.4%, 9.2%; DK, 66.2%, 26.8%, 7.0%; DE, 46.8%, 45.8%, 7.5%; ES, 33.3%, 42.4%, 24.2%.

Experience in journalism (measured in years): UK, M=19.40, SD=11.29; DK, M=13.70, SD=10.15; DE, M=18.67, SD=8.09; ES, M=18.23, SD=9.23.

Gender (% male): DK, 71.8%; DE, 70.5%; UK, 76.5%; ES, 59.0%.

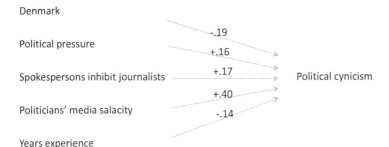

FIGURE 4.3. Explaining political cynicism among political journalists in the United Kingdom, Denmark, Germany, and Spain. *Note*: Entries are standardized beta coefficients (n=425, adjusted R² .31). Positive sign of beta-coefficient indicates positive association with political cynicism. Only significant indicators are shown in the figure. Controls were made for medium type, frequency of contact with politicians, and gender. Based on a survey among 425 political journalists (see Appendix). The full regression analysis is provided in the Appendix to Chapter 4.

of political cynicism. Political journalists who agree more that politicians are driven by media salacity are also more cynical about their political competence. Of the control variables, only job experience is significantly related to political cynicism, with more experienced journalists showing lower levels of cynicism (see the following discussion). Gender and frequency of contact do not have a significant influence on cynicism.

We seem to have identified important factors explaining cross-national differences in levels of political cynicism: the experience of political pressure and the reaction to the professionalization of political communication. After controlling for these variables, the difference between cynicism among British, German, and Spanish journalists is no longer significant. Only Danish journalists are still significantly less cynical than their colleagues abroad.

Table 4.1 studies the relationships in separate regression models for each of the four countries. This gives further support to our expectations. In each of the four countries, our models confirm that the perception that politicians are driven by media salacity breeds cynicism. Not all coefficients are statistically significant, however. In Denmark and Germany, more experienced political

TABLE 4.1. *Influence of Political Pressure, Spin Doctors, and Media Salacity on Political Cynicism in the United Kingdom, Denmark, Germany, and Spain*

Influence	Denmark	Germany	Spain	United Kingdom
Political pressure				++
Spokespersons inhibit journalists		++		
Politician's media salacity	+++	+++	+++	+++

++ significant influence p < .01,
+++ significant influence p < .001.Only significant influence is shown. Controls were made for medium type, frequency of contacts with politicians, experience, and gender. The full regression analyses are provided in the Appendix to Chapter 4.

journalists are significantly less cynical. Figure 4.4 gives a visual illustration of the estimates for media salacity provided in Table 4.1 and demonstrates the rise in political cynicism as a result of increasing media salacity per country. Figure 4.5 does the same for the relationship between political pressure and political cynicism.

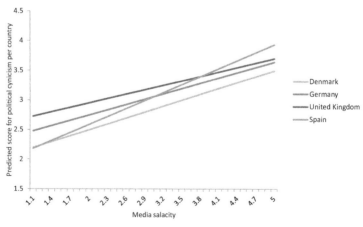

FIGURE 4.4. Influence of media salacity on political cynicism per country (other variables held constant).

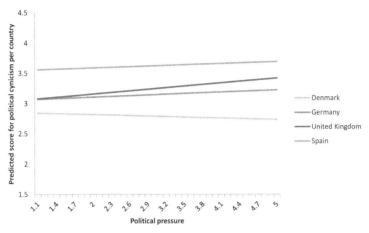

FIGURE 4.5. Influence of political pressure on political cynicism per country (other variables held constant).

DISCUSSION

In this chapter, we have investigated the relationship between political journalists and politicians to explain political cynicism among political reporters. Journalists who experience greater political pressure in their work are more cynical about politicians. Cynicism is also higher when spokespersons and communication specialists inhibit journalists in their work and when journalists believe that politicians see media attention primarily as an end in itself rather than as a side effect of their political function. On a more general level, cynicism touches on our distinction between sacerdotal versus pragmatic views of and approaches to politics (see Chapter 1). The more journalists feel under pressure, the more cynicism they express about politics, and the closer we get to a pragmatic approach to political reporting where caution and respect vis-à-vis politics is not guaranteed. In terms of the key indicators used by Hallin and Mancini (2004b), our results clearly speak to the benefits of low political parallelism for the way journalists view politics. In that sense, this chapter highlights one of the key conditions required for an optimal societal role for political journalism.

Our findings underline the importance of *historical* contexts for the understanding of the complex journalist/politician relationship. Corroborating the findings of Brants et al. (2010) in the Netherlands, these findings do not seem to indicate that the professional critical stance toward politicians in the democratic corporatist countries has turned into a cynical, mistrusting attitude. In Denmark and Germany, the overall level of political cynicism among political reporters is close to the middle position. While claims of hyperadversarialism and cynical reporting are mostly expressed in an Anglo-American context (McNair, 2009), the level of cynicism is highest in Spain, where journalists in their approach toward politicians remain much more cautious and sacerdotal (Strömbäck & Luengo, 2008; see Chapter 3). Compared with their British colleagues, Spanish journalists more often agree with the claim that politicians use the media to put themselves in the spotlight – perhaps because media salacity among politicians is a more recent phenomenon in Spain than in other countries. De Vreese and Elenbaas (2010) have shown that after a peak in about 1997, media coverage of spin doctors in the United Kingdom decreased dramatically. This decline seems to indicate that journalists in the United Kingdom have adapted to the professionalization of political communication and accept spin doctors and media salacity as a feature of political life.

An alternative interpretation for the relatively low levels of political cynicism among British parliamentary reporters might be that they have become too compliant. Members of the parliamentary press gallery in Britain have been accused of fostering overly friendly relations with the politicians they are supposed to cover critically (see Davis, 2009). The MP expenses scandal in the United Kingdom in 2009 was uncovered by journalists from outside the press gallery – perhaps proof that the close contacts between parliamentary journalists and politicians impair journalists' independence and capacity to be critical (Gaber, 2009). Additional analysis (not reported here) did not show a difference in levels of cynicism among members of the press gallery and other political journalists in Britain. The finding that cynicism is low among more experienced political reporters in Denmark and Germany might indicate that journalists working on the parliamentary beat lose their critical distance. On the other hand, higher levels of cynicism among younger reporters might show that a new generation of more distrusting journalists is emerging across Europe. This is a question that only future studies can answer.

As research on journalists moves ahead, it must address the extent to which journalists' cynical political attitudes influence their news content. This remains an empirical question. Applying psychological theories to decision making, Donsbach (2004) has argued that journalists' predispositions influence news decisions, especially when journalists working in packs share the same attitudes. Quasi-experimental studies have shown that attitudes toward subjects can influence the way individual journalists write about these subjects (Patterson & Donsbach, 1996; Starck & Soloski, 1977). Pack journalists often follow each other when facing uncertain situations, and tend to share similar attitudes, such that the effects of these attitudes on news decisions may even be "multiplied" (Donsbach, 2004, 152). Following this reasoning, cynicism should affect how politics are framed by journalists on the political beat. This chapter, showing that relationships between journalists and politicians engender cynicism among reporters, is a first step toward understanding the influence of these relations and the attitudes that are the result of them on political coverage. The influence of attitudes on behavior will be central in the next chapter, where we study the relationship between role conceptions and news content.

5

Do Role Conceptions Matter?

In this book, we try to specify the conditions under which political journalism is most likely to play a positive role in society. A number of conditions have been specified, and in Chapter 3 we saw that political journalists in Denmark, Germany, Spain, and the United Kingdom perceive their roles differently. This finding agrees with a growing body of comparative studies on journalistic cultures. Survey-based research addresses the different ways journalists see their roles (e.g., Donsbach & Patterson, 2004; Weaver & Willnat, 2012; Hanitzsch et al., 2010); a different line of research looks at the actual news content that is produced (e.g., Esser, 2008; Benson & Hallin, 2007). Whether there is a relation between these two factors, however, remains a disputed question, although several cross-national studies on content and others on role conceptions either speculate or presume that variations in role conceptions causes variations in content (Patterson, 1998, 30; de Vreese et al., 2001). For example, Donsbach (2008, 1) comments that role conceptions have "a strong influence on journalists' professional behaviour" and therefore provide an explanation for differences between news cultures.

Following recommendations by Esser (2008), this chapter studies cross-national differences in journalistic roles *in combination* with news content. In other words: what is the relationship between the way journalists in a particular country see their role and the way they do their work? This question is addressed by combining a survey of political journalists with the content analysis of political coverage during a routine period in 2007 (see Appendix to Chapter 2 for more details about the methods). We compare the journalistic role conceptions of British, Danish, German, and Spanish political journalists with the content they produce along the three dimensions introduced in Chapter 1 (pragmatic-sacerdotal, impartial-partisan, and information-entertainment).

ROLE CONCEPTIONS AND CONTENT

The study of journalistic role conceptions goes back to Cohen's (1963) study on foreign correspondents. Later studies by Johnstone, Slawski, and Bowman (1976) and Weaver and Wilhoit (1986, 1996) led to numerous survey projects, which describe the way journalists around the world see their professional tasks (see Vos, 2009; Weaver, 1998). Several studies extend beyond descriptive accounts by studying role conceptions as a dependent variable. Such studies have provided valuable insight into newsroom socialization and the professionalization of journalism, as well as the effects of personal values (Plaisance & Skewes, 2003), gender (Cassidy, 2008), education (Bjørnsen et al., 2007), and organizational context (Zhu et al., 1997) on role conceptions.

For most scholars, however, the relevance of role-conception studies goes beyond understanding socialization processes. As just mentioned, the rationale for studying role conceptions is based on the assumption that they influence journalists' work (see Vos, 2009, 2). Pritchard et al. (2005, 288) make this assumption explicit when they claim that "journalists who accord greater importance to disseminating the news quickly will generate different kinds of news stories from those who believe that the most important role is analysis." Donsbach (2008, 1) considers the role conception of individual journalists to be an intervening variable in the way they do their work. Journalists can, for example, let their personal feelings toward politicians influence their writing if they see their role to be that of a political activist rather than that of a common carrier.

More broadly, the relationship between attitudes and behavior is not only presumed theoretically, but also supported empirically. A meta-study of communication research on attitudes and behavior by Kim and Hunter (1993) convincingly showed an overall strong relationship between the two factors when controlling for methodological differences. The relationship was particularly strong when attitudes concerned a matter of great personal relevance. Since role conceptions define the professional identity of journalists, this condition is met.

In experiments, surveys, and studies combining surveys with content analyses of journalists' best work, several scholars have shown a relationship between what individual journalists say they do and what they actually do. An experiment by Starck and Soloski (1977) showed that articles by journalism students who have a participant role conception include more analyses and interpretations than articles by students who believe their role is to be neutral reporters. Culbertson (1983) showed a relationship between the role conceptions of newspaper journalists and the emphasis they place on particular journalistic practices. They found that journalists who preferred the role of providing interpretation also preferred investigative reporting over local news. Based on a survey of Danish journalists, Skovsgaard et al. (2012) showed that role conceptions influence the way journalists operationalize the objectivity norm. When comparing journalists' role conceptions and what they see as their best journalistic work, however, Weaver et al. (2007, 233) noted that a "journalist's support for a particular professional role occasionally seemed to have a modest association with the kind of story he or she chose." Replicating this study in Germany, Scholl and Weischenberg (1996) found a significant correlation between roles and content.

By aggregating their findings, Scholl and Weischenberg were even able to show a relationship between roles and content at the national level. Aggregating role conceptions to the national level can be justified since single-country studies of journalists generally describe a homogeneous journalistic profession, with limited variation between the role conceptions and ethical standards among journalists working for different news organizations (Skovsgaard et al., 2012; Deuze, 2002, among others). This homogeneity shows that socialization takes place across as well as within a nation's news organizations. Influences from competitors are especially strong among journalists covering the same subject (such as political journalists (Schudson, 2003)). Journalists working on a beat tend to report from the same point of departure and express similar points of view (Schudson, 2003, 139), a phenomenon previously described as "pack journalism" (Frank, 2003). Through the interaction with other journalists on the job and outside work, they develop "commonly shared perspectives" (Donsbach, 2004, 142) that influence news decisions.

Based on these considerations, we can expect to find a relationship between role conceptions and news content both at the level of individual journalists (micro) and when comparing across different journalistic cultures. Journalists' role conceptions are influenced by "journalism's majority culture" (Weaver & Wilhoit 1996, 138) – that is, the majority culture of the media system they work in. For the political journalists, who are central in this study, the relevant macro-level is the national level. Political journalists work on beats around the institutions of national government and parliament.[1] Media markets are still mainly organized nationally (Livingstone, 2003); newspapers and television channels compete for audiences within national borders. Although several scholars have claimed that cross-national differences in role conceptions and content are disappearing (for example, Hallin & Mancini, 2004b; Algarra & Gaitano, 1997), empirical studies show that both role conceptions (Donsbach & Patterson, 2004; Weaver & Willnat, 2012; Hanitzsch et al.,

---

[1] In countries that have different language regions, such as Belgium or Switzerland, the relevant macro-level may be regional rather than national. On the other hand, on beats that are organized around transnational political institutions, such as journalists covering the European Commission in Brussels, the most relevant macro-level may be at a transnational level.

2010; see also Chapter 2) and news content still vary considerably between nations (Esser, 2008; Benson & Hallin, 2007).

As with role conceptions, political news content shares strong similarities across news outlets within countries (Cook, 2005; Sparrow, 1999). Bennett (1996) speaks of a set of news rules that journalists across media outlets follow when they report about national politics, resulting in similarities in content. In the field of framing research, it has been shown that journalists are likely to frame stories as do other journalists (Scheufele, 1999, 117). Cook (2005, 64) summarizes the similarities in work practices by stating that the "transorganizational agreement of news processes and content suggest that we should think of the news media not as a set of diverse organizations, or even a batch of individual institutions, but collectively as a single social institution." Similarities in content will be strongest for news outlets that aim at similar audiences and rely on similar funding. In addition, previous research has shown that although content features are often similar across outlets, they vary across countries (Esser, 2008; Benson & Hallin, 2007). A content analysis by Esser (2008), for example, found that the use of sound and image bites in television news in France, Germany, the United Kingdom, and the United States differed more across countries than across television stations within countries.

Two pioneering comparative research projects on journalism went beyond studying the relationships between attitudes and behavior at the individual level; they convincingly showed that the same relationships were present when news cultures were compared. Using news scenarios, Köcher (1986) showed that differences between the journalistic roles of German and British journalists resulted in different news decisions. Paterson and Donsbach (1996) tested the relation with real-world news scenarios in no less than five different countries. The strong link that was established between the role conceptions of individual journalists and their decisions regarding news content could be replicated at the national level.

Because previous studies support the claim that both role conceptions and news content vary more across countries than within countries, this chapter examines whether the relationship between roles and content can be found on the national (macro) level. The studies by Köcher (1986) and Patterson and Donsbach (1996) have provided support for this relationship. We add to the external validity of these findings by measuring news decisions as they are expressed in news content. Given that a country's newspaper culture may differ from its television culture (Strömbäck & van Aelst, 2010), we compare the roles and content cross-nationally for print and television separately.

PRAGMATIC-SACERDOTAL

The first dimension along which role conceptions and content are compared concerns the status of political news. While journalists with sacerdotal role conceptions believe national politics and politicians have a sacred status, journalists with pragmatic journalistic role conceptions rarely attribute such a status to national politics (see Chapter 1). When deciding whether and how national politics should be covered, pragmatic journalists apply the same selection criteria and news values that they would apply to any other topic. As discussed in Chapter 3, Danish and Spanish political journalists have more sacerdotal role conceptions than their colleagues in Germany and the United Kingdom. These differences can be seen in the roles of print journalists and in journalists working in public service broadcasting but not commercial broadcasting.

Are these differences in role conceptions reflected in the reporting styles of national politics? To answer this question we look at the visibility of political news and the way political news is framed. First, in those countries where national politics has a special status, with journalists tending toward a sacerdotal role conception, political news will be covered more extensively and will often be visible on the front page.[2] Second, in countries where journalists have a more pragmatic role conception, news coverage

---

[2] For newspapers, the visibility of political news was operationalized as the proportion of stories on the front page covering national politics; for television news, it was operationalized as the share of stories in the news broadcast dealing with national politics.

will be based more on news values. Pragmatic journalists do not treat news about politics as inherently relevant, but will try to make political news attractive to the audience by framing politics in terms of conflict or by presenting it as a game[3] (Neuman et al., 1992, 64–6; Patterson, 1993; Cappella & Jamieson, 1997).

A comparative study of election coverage in the United Kingdom and the United States showed that U.S. journalists in the 1980s were more pragmatic in their approach and reported events "laced with drama, conflict, novelty, movement and anomaly" (Blumler & Gurevitch, 1991, 55). Revisiting the differences in campaign coverage between American and British television a decade later, Blumler and Gurevitch (2001, 389) concluded that the differences had decreased but were still present. "Despite some increased reliance on strategic scenarios, . . . British election coverage is still far less saturated with the 'horse-race' than is its U.S. counterpart." We expect these differences in focus regarding conflicts and games to be a consequence of each country's dominant role conception for journalists, whether pragmatic or sacerdotal. Apart from conflict and game framing, we also look at the use of human-interest frames.[4] In human-interest frames, journalists do not cover national politics with an emphasis on the political process, but instead focus on the impact of policy

[3] The coding instructions for these two frames were as follows: "Conflict news: does the story mention that one person, group, institution or organization reproaches/blames/criticizes another OR present quotes or paraphrases in which an actor criticizes or refutes claims of another actor?" Intercoder scores for newspaper: DK (Denmark), .74; DE (Germany), .90; UK (United Kingdom), .83; ES (Spain), .70. Intercoder scores for television: DK, .85; DE, .81; UK, .73; ES, .84 (Holsti's method of agreement). "Game news: does the story mention a national political actor winning and/or losing OR describe national politics using language from war/or games, e.g., gain, crush, defeat, strategy, and maneuver in a winning/losing context?" Intercoder scores for newspaper: DK, .89; DE, .87; UK, .77; ES, .76. Intercoder scores for television: DK, .85; DE, .76; UK, .80; ES, .89 (Holsti's method of agreement).

[4] The human-interest frame was measured with the following coding instructions: "Does the story provide a human example or human face to the story in order to illuminate developments in politics or society?" Intercoder scores for newspaper: DK, .95; DE, 1.00; UK, .89; ES, .97. Intercoder scores for television: DK, .69; DE, 1.00; UK, 1.00; ES, .95 (Holsti's method of agreement).

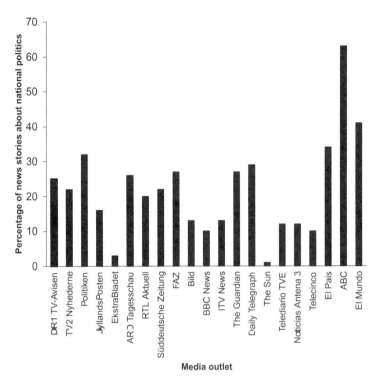

FIGURE 5.1. Visibility of political news (routine period). Percentage of stories on the front page (for newspapers) or percentage of stories in the news broadcast (for television) that deal with national politics. Based on the content analysis of two constructed news weeks during the routine period (see Appendix to Chapter 2).

decisions on ordinary citizens. Journalists with more sacerdotal role conceptions are less inclined to use this type of frame; rather, they cover policy decisions from the perspective of the politicians.

Figure 5.1 shows the visibility of news about national politics in newspaper and television outlets during the routine period in 2007. For newspapers, the visibility of national politics is highest in Spanish dailies compared with the other countries; this visibility is particularly striking in *ABC*, where more than 63 percent of the stories on the front page deal with national politics. The visibility of national politics in northern European newspapers is comparable: on average, one-fourth of all items on the front page of broadsheets deal with national news, while the share is lower for tabloids. For television, the countries can be divided into two groups. In the democratic corporatist countries (Denmark and Germany), national politics is twice as visible as in the United Kingdom and Spain. Differences in the visibility of political news between commercial and public service broadcasters are negligible.

The other indicators for a pragmatic versus sacerdotal reporting style also show that Spanish broadsheets stand out by comparison with northern Europe (Table 5.1). Spanish broadsheet outlets have the smallest percentage of news stories using the conflict and the game frame. The use of this frame hardly varies between Denmark, Germany, and the United Kingdom. The differences in the use of conflict framing between Spain and northern Europe are also present for public service broadcasting and commercial broadcasting. As the examples show, the conflict frame is used to highlight conflicts between a variety of political actors. In all countries, coverage of national politics on television is more likely to focus on the consequences of policy decisions for citizens than in broadsheet news. Again, sacerdotal Spain stands out as the country in which television reporters are least likely to use this type of framing.

EXAMPLES OF CONFLICT NEWS FRAMING

DENMARK

Exceptions split EU parties. *Forbehold splitter EU-partier* (Politiken, 8 January 2008)

New Year's speech provokes heads of unions. *Nytårstale provokerer fagbosser* (Jyllands Posten, 2 January 2008)

The opposition rages against the government's asylum agreement. *Oppositionen raser mod regeringens asylaftale* (Politiken, 17 January 2008)

GERMANY

Starting to slip. Bishops criticize Schavan in stem cell debate. *Ins Rutschen geraten; Bischöfe kritisieren Schavan in der Stammzell-Debatte* (Frankfurter Allgemeine Zeitung, 10 December 2007)

Roland the Weak. Hessen's penal system is more liberal than Populist Koch would like it to be. *Hessens Der weiche Roland; Hessens Strafvollzug ist liberaler, als es Populist Koch lieb ist* (Süddeutsche Zeitung, 4 January 2008)

Commotion in the FDP because of Gerhardt's attack. *Wirbel in der FDP um Gerhardts Vorstoß* (Süddeutsche Zeitung, 4 January 2008)

UNITED KINGDOM

Fury over Branson Rock 'deal' (The Sun, 21 January 2008)

Labour MPs threaten revolt over EU treaty (The Daily Telegraph, 21 January 2008)

Tory 'astonished' at Smith's fear of walking night streets (The Guardian, 21 January 2008)

SPAIN

Together, but without speaking or greeting each other. *Juntos, pero sin hablarse ni saludarse* (ABC, 21 January 2008)

Rajoy describes the latest unemployment data as "truly dramatic." *Rajoy califica de «auténtico drama» los últimos datos de desempleo* (ABC, 5 February 2008)

PSOE gets angry because Pizarro praises the voice of Sonsoles Espinosa. *El PSOE monta en cólera por una alabanza de Pizarro a la voz de Sonsoles Espinosa* (ABC, 5 February 2008)

TABLE 5.1. *Indicators of a Pragmatic versus Sacerdotal Reporting Style in Coverage of National Politics in Denmark, Germany, the United Kingdom, and Spain (routine period)[a]*

Country/Media Outlet (N)	Conflict Frame (%)[b]	Game Frame (%)[b]	Human Interest (%)[b]
Denmark			
JyllandsPosten (82)	65	27	5
Politiken (59)	54	27	15
EkstraBladet (21)	48	38	10
DR1 TV-Avisen (34)	71	35	26
TV2 Nyhederne (28)	82	32	46
Germany			
Frankfurter Allgemeine Zeitung (173)	64	25	2
Süddeutsche Zeitung (141)	72	26	3
Bild (88)	42	27	1
ARD Tagesschau (46)	61	20	0
RTL Aktuell (32)	47	16	31
United Kingdom			
The Daily Telegraph (75)	51	20	12
The Guardian (80)	49	24	4
The Sun (50)	52	22	8
BBC News (11)	91	45	27
ITV Nightly News (17)	71	35	18
Spain			
El Pais (144)	25	9	3
ABC (147)	36	5	4
El Mundo (134)	31	10	4
TVE Telediario 2 (40)	55	15	13
Antena 3 Noticias (38)	55	34	5
Informativos Telecinco (29)	41	21	10

[a] The indicators are based on the content analysis of two constructed news weeks during the routine period (see Appendix to Chapter 2).
[b] Percentage of news items using this type of framing.

On the basis of the different measures of pragmatic versus sacerdotal reporting styles, we can conclude that the sacerdotal role conception of Spanish journalists is reflected in newspaper and public service broadcast news content in Spain. The survey shows that Danish journalists have a more sacerdotal role conception than their colleagues in Germany and the United Kingdom, but this conception is not reflected in less conflict or human-interest framing in the Danish media. The survey reported in Chapter 3 does not show any significant cross-national differences in the role conceptions of those journalists who work for commercial broadcasters. However, when conflict and human-interest framing are used as indicators, Spanish commercial broadcasting also stands out as more sacerdotal.

IMPARTIAL-PARTISAN

Second, a relationship between journalistic roles and content is studied on the impartial-partisan dimension. Journalists who have a partisan role conception believe it is acceptable for journalists to take sides in political disputes, while impartial journalists aim to present balanced coverage. In the case of both newspapers and television, Spanish political journalists have more partisan role conceptions than journalists in northern Europe (see Chapter 3). To test whether these role conceptions are reflected in the news content, we compare the way newspapers and television outlets with different political profiles cover the largest left-wing and right-wing political parties.

Partisanship in news content can be reflected in either coverage bias or statement bias (D'Alessio & Allen, 2000, 135–6; Albæk et al., 2010). Coverage bias refers to imbalance in the visibility of politicians in the news. Coverage is biased toward a particular political party when its politicians systematically receive more coverage than politicians from other parties. Statement bias refers to the tone of coverage – either in favor of or against certain political parties. News is considered to be balanced when positive and negative evaluations are represented equally. Partisan bias should be distinguished from structural biases (Hoffstetter, 1976, 34): if all media outlets are consistently negative about one party or political bloc, the negativity is likely to be due to general news routines. In the four countries under study, broadsheet newspapers have distinct political profiles, which are expressed in the editorials, opinion pieces, and columns (Tresch, 2009; Steger, 1999). The newspapers' political profiles are reflected in their readers' political preferences (Seymoure-Ure, 1974; Hjarvard,

2007). Whether the political leaning of the newspaper is also visible in its news coverage is expected to depend on the dominant role conceptions of journalists. Impartial journalists in northern Europe will likely treat different politicians in the news section in a balanced manner, while more partisan journalists in Spain will let the political profile of the newspaper influence the way they report about politicians.[5] Taking into account the role conceptions of Spanish television journalists, we can expect Spanish commercial and public service broadcasters to give distinct treatment to left-wing and right-wing politicians.

Looking at the visibility of different parties (Table 5.2), we see no proof of a partisan bias in any of the four countries. The attention given to political actors is determined by structural bias rather than partisan bias. Within countries, left-wing newspapers did not differ from right-wing newspapers in their treatment of the largest parties on the left and right side of the political spectrum. In countries with strong governments, the news was structurally biased toward the party in power (van Dalen, 2012). In Germany, Spain, and the United Kingdom, the major left-wing party received more coverage than the major right-wing party. There was no indication of bias in the television news and tabloid newspapers; they divided their attention between candidates in much the same way as did the broadsheet newspapers.

In northern Europe, the tone toward most political actors was neutral. If politicians were evaluated, this evaluation was

---

[5] The presence of coverage bias was measured by comparing the visibility of political actors belonging to the largest left-leaning and right-leaning political party (Brandenburg, 2006). Intercoder scores for newspaper: DK, .79; DE .77; UK, .74; ES, .74. Intercoder scores for television: DK, .75; DE, .76; UK, .93; ES, .84 (Holsti's method of agreement). The presence of statement bias was measured by comparing the mean tone toward politicians of these two parties. Intercoder scores for newspaper: DK, .87; DE, .72; UK, .81; ES, .71. Intercoder scores for television: DK, .78; DE, .63; UK, .82; ES, .81 (Holsti's method of agreement). The tone can range from positive (when the emphasis in the story is on the actor's merits, successful solutions, solved problems, or abilities) to negative (when the emphasis is on the actor's failures, unresolved problems, or inabilities). Similar to Brandenburg (2006) and Schuck and de Vreese (2007), a scale was built measuring the mean tone, based on the news items in which politicians were either evaluated positively or negatively. The scale ranges from −1 (in the case where all evaluative statements about a political party are negative) to +1 (only positive evaluations).

TABLE 5.2. *Visibility of Largest Left-Wing and Right-Wing Parties in Danish, British, and Spanish Media Outlets (routine period)[a]*

Country/Media Outlet (number of politicians)	Left-Wing Party[b] (percentage of all politicians)	Right-Wing Party[c] (percentage of all politicians)
Denmark		
DR1 TV-Avisen (85)	15.3	23.5
TV2 Nyhederne (73)	20.5	20.5
Politiken (135)	20.7	23.7
JyllandsPosten (216)	22.2	23.1
EkstraBladet (45)	28.9	20.0
Germany		
ARD Tagesschau (122)	34.4	39.3
RTL Aktuell (70)	51.4	38.6
Suddeutsche Zeitung (272)	34.9	42.3
Frankfurter Allgemeine Zeitung (356)	33.1	39.3
Bild (145)	29.0	40.7
United Kingdom		
BBC News (35)	60.0	25.7
ITV Nightly News (34)	79.4	14.7
The Guardian (150)	64.8	25.5
The Daily Telegraph (196)	62.7	26.0
The Sun (110)	55.5	30.9
Spain		
TVE Telediario 2 (97)	43.4	38.1
Antena 3 Noticias (71)	54.9	39.4
Informativos Telecinco (69)	44.9	50.7
El Pais (320)	50.6	35.5
ABC (368)	50.5	43.2
El Mundo (279)	50.9	33.3

[a] The indicators are based on the content analysis of two constructed news weeks during the routine period (see Appendix to Chapter 2).

[b] Left-wing parties: Denmark: Socialdemokraterne; Germany: SPD; UK: Labour; Spain: PSOE.

[c] Right-wing parties: Denmark: Venstre; Germany: CDU/CSU; UK: Conservative Party; Spain: PP.

mostly negative (see Figure 5.2). In line with their impartial role conceptions, British, Danish, and German political journalists treated all parties equally: there were no significant differences in tone toward left-wing and right-wing politicians (independent

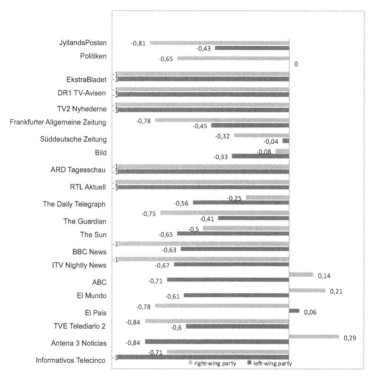

FIGURE 5.2. Tone toward largest left-wing and right-wing parties in Danish, German, British, and Spanish media outlets (routine period)·
Note: The mean tone toward a party is based only on news items in which politicians were evaluated positively or negatively, and can range from –1 (all evaluations negative) to +1 (all evaluations positive). Based on the content analysis of two constructed news weeks during the routine period (see Appendix to Chapter 2).

samples, t-tests). The tone was either negative toward all politicians (as in the British newspapers and television) or, on average, neutral toward both parties (for example, the German newspaper *Süddeutsche Zeitung*). The lack of significant differences in tone can also in some instances be explained by the low numbers of items in which politicians were actually evaluated (for example, as evident in the Danish newspaper *Politiken*).

The treatment of the largest left-wing and right-wing parties varied significantly for Spanish newspapers and for the Spanish television channel Antena 3. In Spanish newspapers, partisanship manifested itself in a slight increase in positive evaluations of the parties with which the newspapers are aligned and in an overtly negative bias toward opposing parties. Politicians belonging to the left-wing Spanish Socialist Workers' Party received almost neutral treatment in the left-wing newspaper *El País*, while they were presented predominantly negatively in the right-wing newspapers *ABC* and *El Mundo*. We see the opposite pattern in the case of politicians belonging to the right-wing People's Party. Commercial television station Antenna 3 reported positively about that party, while the other two broadcasters covered both the Left and the Right in a similar manner. The finding that a partisan bias in tone was only present in Spain but not in northern Europe is in line with previous research (see, e.g., López-Escobar et al., 2009, for Spain and Hopmann et al., 2011 for Denmark) and shows that there is a relationship between partisan role conceptions and partisan news coverage.

INFORMATION-ENTERTAINMENT

Lastly, the relationship between role conceptions and journalistic content is studied on the information-entertainment dimension. In their role conceptions, British journalists are clearly the most entertainment oriented. The only other journalists on the entertainment end of the scale are the Spanish commercial broadcasters. To test whether journalists who are more entertainment oriented produce different news content, we study the *privatization* of political news, which is operationalized by focusing on the private lives of politicians (see Chapter 7) and by covering scandals.

In the literature, scandal coverage has been connected to entertainment values and a tabloid style (Tumber, 2004). Entertainment orientation is thus expected to be reflected in more scandal coverage.[6] Media scandals are lively, dramatic topics, involving

---

[6] Scandal coverage is measured using the following question: "Is the main topic of the story an event or incident that is framed as if it constitutes a moral or political scandal? A scandal story involves allegations of wrongdoing, disgrace, or moral outrage." Intercoder scores for newspaper: DK, .95; DE, .100; UK, .91; ES, .97. Intercoder scores for television: DK, .85; DE, .86; UK, 1.00; ES, 1.00 (Holsti's method of agreement).

sex, money, and power, and appeal to broad audiences (Van Dalen & Skovsgaard, 2011). Scandals sell, especially those involving moral outrage over the behavior of politicians in powerful positions. Attention to scandals and an increased focus on drama and sensationalism have been criticized, as they are said to take attention away from more serious issues, such as economic or foreign policy (McNair, 2009, 242).

A second indicator of the information-versus-entertainment journalistic style is the focus on the private lives of politicians (see also Chapter 7).[7] Purely information-oriented journalists will not cover the private lives of politicians but will only portray them in their official capacity. But in journalistic cultures where entertainment is more important, politicians' private lives receive more attention in the news, be it their family life, their childhood, youth, and upbringing, or extra-marital affairs. Attention paid to the private lives of politicians is an example of 'soft' news. Critics argue that this type of news presentation is an increasing trend and a clear indicator that political information is turning into political infotainment (McNair, 2009, 242).

In the period under study, German and Spanish broadsheets and television stations barely touched scandals involving national politicians (see Figure 5.3). In "sleazy Britain," on the other hand, every fourth television item about national politics involved a political scandal. Denmark also had a larger share of scandal stories about national politicians (in particular, by the tabloid newspaper *EkstraBladet* and the commercial broadcaster TV2). As is shown in the examples, many of the scandals center around the possible misuse of public money. For the second indicator (the private lives of politicians), only the United Kingdom stands out (see Figure 5.4). In all the Spanish coverage there was only one newspaper article featuring the private life of a politician. In Denmark and Germany there is likewise only a limited focus on politicians' private lives – which is, in effect, a non-topic

---

[7] Coverage of private life is measured with the following question: "Does the story focus on the private life of politicians, rather than presenting them as spokespersons for certain policies or ideologies?" Intercoder scores for newspaper: DK, .89; DE, .97; UK, .97; ES, .91. Intercoder scores for television: DK, 1.00; DE, 1.00; UK, .87; ES, .95 (Holsti's method of agreement).

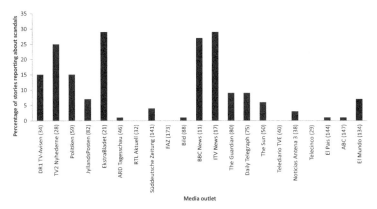

FIGURE 5.3. Proportion of news about national politics that reports about scandals. Total number of news items about national politics in parentheses. Based on the content analysis of two constructed news weeks during the routine period (see Appendix to Chapter 2). Percentages can be found in the Appendix to Chapter 5.

for television news. Other studies confirm that British political journalists have a special interest in politicians' private lives. Research on political scandals coverage has shown that scandals involving the private lives of politicians are much more common

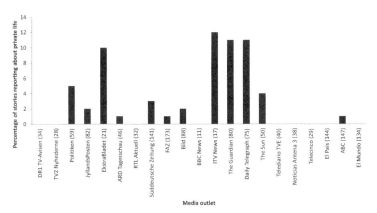

FIGURE 5.4. Proportion of news about national politics that reports about the private life of politicians. Total number of news items about national politics in parentheses. Based on the content analysis of two constructed news weeks during the routine period (see Appendix to Chapter 2). Percentages can be found in the Appendix to Chapter 5.

in the United Kingdom than in the rest of Europe (Canel & Sanders, 2006; Van Dalen & Skovsgaard, 2011; Holtz-Bacha, 2004). Combining these two indicators – scandals coverage and a focus on private life – we can conclude that the United Kingdom stands out as most entertainment focused, which is in line with their role conceptions.

EXAMPLES OF SCANDAL NEWS

DENMARK

Politicians attracted by Singapore. *Singapore trækker i politikere* (EkstraBladet, 13 January 2008, Hans Chr. Blem)

(Parliament's traffic committee wants to use more than 200,000 kroner for a trip to Singapore)

He signed as 'Oliver.' *Skrev under som 'Oliver'* (Ekstra Bladet, 7 February 2008, Jan Kjærgaard)

(An MP has been reported to the police for falsifying documents)

GERMANY

Jüttner attacks Wulff. *Jüttner greift Wulff an* (Suddeutsche Zeitung, 17 January 2008)

(The private life of politician Christian Wulff is criticized)

Ministry kept quiet about poisonous gas in the Baltic Sea. *Ministerium verschwieg Giftgas in der Ostsee* (Suddeutsche Zeitung, 1 February 2008)

UNITED KINGDOM

Speaker's wife spent 50,000 pounds on air travel. (The Daily Telegraph, 21 January 2008, Rosa Prince)

Tory MP 'rode quad bike on the road with child on back' (The Daily Telegraph, 4 January 2008, Richard Savill)

Nicholas Soames, the Conservative MP, has been pictured allegedly riding a quad bike on a public road with a child perched behind him.)

SPAIN

The passports of the former aide of the Ministry of Interior Affairs. *Los pasaportes del ex colaborador de Interior* (El Mundo, 10 December 2007)

(In the '90s, the Ministry of Interior Affairs gave three empty passports and other documents to one of its aides, and they were never returned)

The last parliamentary debate ended with great tension and disqualifications of PP by ERC. *El último debate de la legislatura acaba con gran tensión y descalificaciones de ERC al PP* (El Mundo, 12 January, p. 11)

(In the last parliamentary debate before the elections, the honorary president of one of the parties is accused of having blood on his hands due to his involvement with the former Fascist regime)

DISCUSSION

This chapter has studied the relationship between journalistic roles and news content cross-nationally to determine whether what journalists say they do influences what they actually do. Support for the relationship between role conceptions and news content is not consistently strong. Spanish political journalists are the most different from their colleagues in Denmark, Germany, and the United Kingdom. They see their role as sacerdotal rather than pragmatic, partisan rather than impartial, and view themselves as informers rather than entertainers. These distinct role conceptions are reflected in the reporting style of Spanish political news. British journalists stand out as the most entertainment oriented, both in their role conceptions and in the content they produce. The sacerdotal role conceptions of Danish journalists, however, are not reflected in their content, and a relationship between roles and content cannot be established for all media outlets in Denmark.

Three limitations of our study may have influenced these mixed results. First, although Spanish journalists are clearly outsiders, the cross-national differences in role conceptions and content between Denmark, Germany, and the United Kingdom are not very strong. Second, the absence of a clear relationship between roles and content might be the intervening influence of other factors in the political system or political culture. Alternative explanations are intrinsic to cross-national comparisons (Lijphart, 1971) and can only be addressed by repeating this study and conducting similar studies in more countries. Thus a possible third limitation, inherent in any cross-national comparative content analysis, is the use of standardized measures in order to make findings in different countries comparable. The trade-off in our study was that we needed to use indirect measures to classify reporting styles along the pragmatic-sacerdotal dimensions. Single-country studies can more directly observe the news values of certain stories or how issues in the news relate to the political agenda. Not being able to do so certainly complicated our analysis. In future studies, roles and content have to be compared in more, and more dissimilar, countries. Qualitative observational studies must also be integrated into the analysis to deepen our understanding of the relationship between journalistic ideals and practice.

Despite these limitations, the results give further support to the assumption already established in survey studies using news scenarios that journalistic roles and content are related at the national level (Köcher, 1986; Patterson & Donsbach, 1996). The finding that the role conceptions of Spanish journalists are distinctly different from those of northern European journalists contradicts the criticism that journalistic role conceptions cannot be studied by means of questionnaires (Josephi, 2005). Critics claim that journalists, when asked about their role (see also

Weischenberg et al., 2006), tend to see themselves as critical, objective watchdogs, but that these answers are idealized; they bear little relation to their actual work practice. It may be that when asked about their role conceptions, journalists do not describe their actual work practices but rather pay lip service to the researchers and give socially desirable answers. However, if that is true, our comparative journalism survey shows that what journalists presume researchers want to hear varies across countries and represents different normative ideals.

When asked about their role conceptions in this study, some Spanish journalists did indeed see their role to be that of impartial pragmatists. Spanish journalists who believe in the impartial-pragmatist model may find that their theory and practice is at variance. However, this chapter has shown that when the roles and news content of Spanish journalists are compared with the roles and content of journalists in northern Europe, Spanish journalists actually adhere least to this impartial-pragmatist model not only in practice (content) but also in ideals (roles). These conclusions highlight the fact that a *combination* of lower degrees of professionalization and higher degrees of political parallelism does not bode well for political journalism. Conversely, higher degrees of professionalization and lower degrees of political parallelism constitute part of the right *mix* of conditions that we set out to define (see Chapter 1). The conclusions also point to the fact that the world of political journalists and political journalism is less clear cut than what we might expect from classifications of the Spanish media system (e.g., Hallin & Mancini, 2004b). In this respect, the findings presented in this chapter are in line with Donsbach and Patterson (2004, 267), who argue, on the basis of their cross-national comparative survey in five Western countries, that "Western news systems are more alike than different, although their differences are important and consequential." It is precisely the consequences of the differences in news systems that are central in Chapters 6, 7, and 8.

6

What Type of Journalism Produces
Public Knowledge?

In the first part of the book, we focused mainly on the antecedents
and characteristics of political news in countries with different
media systems. In the second part we look at the *effects* of different types of political reporting on the public (see Figure 1.1,
Chapter 1). This part also serves to identify the right mix of
conditions for a positive role of political journalism. We move
from the effect of conditions on content to the effects of content
on users. The chapter will specifically investigate such effects
in relation to knowledge about politics. The news media is one
of the most important sources of information on politics and
is therefore a key contributor to citizens' political knowledge.
Previous literature has demonstrated that political knowledge is
a predictor of political involvement (McGraw & Pinney, 1990)
and electoral turnout (Neuman, 1986; Delli Carpini & Keeter,
1996), and also that greater political knowledge generates more
participation and greater tolerance of opposing viewpoints (Jerit,
Barabas, & Bolson, 2006). Moreover, political knowledge is a
key ingredient in virtually all models of democracy (Strömbäck,
2005). It is considered the "currency of citizenship," which can
be acquired over time and spent on various social goods, such
as voting, political action, and deliberating with and persuading
others (Delli Carpini & Keeter, 1996, 8).

Assuming that sound political knowledge is vital to the good health of a democracy, we might expect the media's impact on knowledge to have been exhaustively researched. Much of what we know, however, is based either on assumptions about news media content or on correlational evidence. In this chapter we focus on the impact that two of the most widely used news frames – human-interest and conflict – have on political knowledge. Both news frames are important indicators of a pragmatic journalistic approach to politics (see Chapter 1) and are used frequently in political news coverage (see Chapter 5). We develop an argument for the reason news coverage using this approach has a positive effect on knowledge acquisition, particularly for those with minimal interest in politics. We test the relationship between pragmatic news coverage and political knowledge by drawing on a combination of both the panel survey data and the content analysis between the two panel waves in Denmark, Spain, and the United Kingdom (see Appendix to Chapter 2).

LEARNING FROM THE NEWS

Evidence of knowledge gain from exposure to news media dates back to the Columbia studies: more than sixty years ago, Lazarsfeld and his colleagues found little proof that media exposure changes attitudes and opinions, but they demonstrated that people do acquire information from the mass media (Lazarsfeld et al., 1944). Since then, numerous studies have focused on the role of the news media in producing political knowledge (e.g., Brians & Wattenberg, 1996; Chaffee et al., 1994; McLeod et al., 1996; McLeod & McDonald, 1985; Neuman, 1986; Neuman, Just, & Crigler, 1992; Palmgreen, 1979; Robinson & Levy, 1996). After reviewing research on the effects of political communication, McLeod, Kosicki, and McLeod (2009, 231) concluded that "special forms of political communication, debates, and conventions, along with standard news coverage, convey discernible if modest amounts of information to their audiences." Research has shown that knowledge gain is the result of the combined influence of three factors: the availability of information, the nature of the medium, and individual motivations. Studies have thus focused on contextual/supply, medium-specific, or individual-motivational explanations.

Regarding supply, several studies have shown that the political information context, typically the country or the media market, matters if citizens are to learn from the news. Prior (2007) demonstrated that the changing mix of news and entertainment programs has influenced levels of knowledge among the U.S. population over time. Subsequent studies have shown that the opportunity for television viewers to see political news (a necessary precondition to learning) varies considerably across countries and is particularly influenced by the presence or absence of a tradition of public service broadcasting (Esser et al., 2011; Aalberg et al., 2010). Curran et al. (2009) found that the public service model of broadcasting gives more attention to public affairs and international news than the market model, thereby fostering greater knowledge in these areas. Wonneberger (2011) showed that citizens do not necessarily shy away from news and current affairs in situations of abundant choice. In general, however, the "trap effect" (Schönbach & Lauf, 2002) holds true for the relationship between information context and a knowledgeable population: when news is accessible but channel choice is limited, there is a greater likelihood that people will watch the news and learn from it.

In a pioneering study combining survey and content analysis, Iyengar et al. (2010) found that the importance of individual-level motivational factors for knowledge gain varies across contexts. In countries that have media systems with a strong public service tradition, hard news is more widely available, and individual motivation is less important in such countries than in information-deprived settings (Iyengar et al., 2010, 292). Jerit et al. (2006) employed a straightforward but underutilized approach to study the influence of the information environment on political knowledge: combining forty-one public-opinion surveys on different issues with content analyses, they showed that the attention the media pays to these issues increases policy-specific knowledge. They were furthermore able to show differences across media types: the highly educated learn more from newspapers than do the poorly educated, and both learn from television.

The ability to learn from television as opposed to newspapers has been a second key focus in the literature about political knowledge and the news. Both television and newspapers can contribute to political knowledge (e.g., Chaffee et al., 1994; Sotirovic & McLeod, 2004), although scholars have found newspaper readers to be more informed than television viewers (Robinson & Davis, 1990). This is consistent with Delli Carpini and Keteer's (1996) findings of positive effects on political knowledge for newspaper reading but no systematic effects for television. Weaver and Drew (2001) have shown that viewers learn from television news, although the effects are weaker than for newspaper news. For the less informed, television has been shown to be beneficial. Based on their study of learning from the mass media, Chaffee and Kanihan (1997, 427) describe television as a "bridging medium." Newspapers cover national politics in-depth, but television "brings news highlights to the less assiduous citizens."

The variation in effect on different types of people leads to the third main focus of research on gains of political knowledge from the news: individual motivation. At the individual level, education, existing knowledge, and political interest are key predictors for learning from the news (Price & Zaller, 1993; Tichenor et al., 1970). Prior knowledge facilitates learning because the more one knows, the easier it is to make sense of new information (Norris, 2000). Thus, people who are better informed are more likely to be aware of a topic when it appears in the mass media and are better equipped to understand it. A higher interest in, and attention to, news stories generates knowledge (e.g., Bennett, 1998; Chaffee & Schleuder, 1986; Chang & Krosnick, 2003).

In this chapter we bridge the gap between the three areas of knowledge explaining the relationship between news media and political knowledge – information availability, the medium, and individual motivation. Our cross-national study has ensured variation in the context and supply. Our analysis includes different media and assesses the impact of individual-level motivation. Our understanding to date of how political news affects political knowledge is largely based on self-reported media exposure measures, which are generally not combined with measures of news content (see Jerit et al., 2006, 267; Gaziano, 1997). Given this lack of evidence of actual media content, researchers are unable to say *what* it is about media coverage that influences learning (for exceptions, see Barabas & Jerit, 2009; Iyengar et al., 2010; de Vreese & Boomgaarden, 2006). When explaining the different effects of television and newspapers, differences in reporting style are generally assumed rather than measured explicitly. This chapter adds to the understanding of knowledge gain from political news by studying the effects of exposure combined with the characteristics of the news content.

THE EFFECTS OF NEWS FRAMES ON LEARNING

Differences in learning between different types of outlets are generally explained by the different characteristics of their formats (e.g., Graber, 2001). News media can be distinguished by the amount of information they convey (Kleinnijenhuis, 1991), the journalistic themes and angles that mold the news stories (see, e.g., Bennett, 1998; Gans, 1979), and the frames they apply (e.g., Rhee, 1997). Previous research on the influence of content characteristics has focused mostly on the distinction between television and newspaper news, and hard and soft news. While newspapers provide in-depth coverage of serious issues such as foreign news or public policy, television news is generally easier to digest and has more dramatic and emotional appeal (Neuman et al., 1992; Graber, 2001). Patterson (1980) believes that the differences in format and focus make television a less suitable medium than newspapers to convey political information. Others have argued that the more immediate and attractive style of television news makes news more accessible to people who are less informed in the first place (Graber, 2001).

While critics have been eager to debate the normative consequences of soft news, empirical assessment of soft news effects is rare (Prior, 2007; see also Chapter 1). Baum (2002, 2005) argues that soft news has the potential to expose uninterested citizens to relevant political information. Thus, an accidental by-product of programs such as daytime or late-night talk shows may be what viewers learn from them. Although there is empirical support for the view that soft news can attract inattentive audiences, evidence for knowledge gain from soft news is mixed, and seems to depend on the type of knowledge that is measured. While Prior (2007) found little support for the notion that a preference for entertainment programs increases factual knowledge, Baum and Jamieson (2006) showed that soft news helped the politically unsophisticated to vote consistently – that is, in line with their actual political preferences. What becomes clear from the debate about soft news is that an easily digestible style helps people attend to political information, particularly those who lack the motivation to attend to hard news. This attention-inducing style may help people with low political interest to learn from the news. In this chapter we investigate the way two prominent news frames that have the ability to attract an audience's attention – conflict and human-interest – affect knowledge gain (Semetko & Valkenburg, 2000).

The way news is packaged influences knowledge gain (Jerrit et al., 2006, 279). We focus in particular on conflict and human-interest framing because it is used frequently by newsmakers to entice audiences. Furthermore, these frames represent essential criteria for a news story to make it to the news (see Price, 1989; Valkenburg et al., 1999; de Vreese et al., 2001). Human-interest and conflict presentations often include a personal angle, either by treating politics as a series of discrete conflicts among individual politicians or parties (Bennett, 1998), or by adding an individual's story or an emotional angle to the presentation of an event, issue, or problem (Bennett, 1996; Valkenburg et al., 1999). This focus stems from the general assumption that audiences are naturally interested in learning about other people (Price et al., 1997, 484).

How does exposure to human-interest and conflict frames in the news affect knowledge acquisition? Research results are both fragmented and mixed. Some earlier studies suggested that highly emotional news stories diminish short-term recall (Mundorf et al., 1990). This is consistent with Valkenburg et al. (1999), who found no effects of exposure to the conflict frame, and negative effects of exposure to the human-interest frame, on readers' information recall. Further, conflict framing is conceptually related to the coverage of horse racing (Patterson, 1993), which has often been found to negatively affect learning from the news (e.g., Patterson, 1980). Graber (1990), Robinson and Levy (1986), and Gunter (1987) have shown that personalized and close-to-home news stories are more easily recalled.

Our study here argues that exposure to news containing human-interest or conflict elements may increase learning from the news for the following reasons: First, news stories using either or both elements are likely to attract the viewer's attention, which is then likely to increase exposure as well as enhance learning. According to Graber (2001), attention arousal is considered one of the first steps in information acquisition. Second, prolonged exposure should affect knowledge gain positively given the increased amount of information. Increasing the information flow, as some studies have noted, can positively affect knowledge acquisition, regardless of the frames employed. Third, Graber (2001) showed that people with low interest in, and exposure to, the news tend to focus more on soft news, such as human-interest stories, and that people who lack interest in politics pay more attention to human-interest stories and less attention to political stories. In fact, participants in Graber's study listed the relevance and emotional appeal of news stories as the primary considerations for preferring one news story over another. Finally, some earlier studies (e.g., Price & Czilli, 1996) found that personalizing the news increased learning.

THE MODERATING INFLUENCE OF POLITICAL INTEREST

Previous studies on learning from the news suggest a number of factors that condition knowledge gain. The "knowledge gap" hypothesis identified educational status as a dominant factor (see Tichenor et al., 1970). Most studies show that gaps in knowledge between groups with high and low levels of education are increased by news coverage (Tichenor et al., 1970; Eveland and Scheufele, 1995). "The rich get richer," since they have a better capacity to process new information: Kwak (1999), however, noted that this effect may be driven by motivational factors rather than by education, suggesting that these factors are the ones that moderate the impact of news exposure. We are particularly interested in individual-motivational factors in the context of abundant media choice (Prior, 2007). Of these factors, political interest is one of the most important and is empirically related to political knowledge (Bennett, 1995; Marcus & MacKuen, 1993; McLeod & Perse, 1994), media use (Lazarsfeld et al., 1944; Luskin, 1990), political discussion (Bennett et al., 2000; Myers, 1994), and news attention (Slater, 2004). Our study examines the way interest moderates the relationship between exposure to conflict and human-interest framing and political knowledge.

Previous framing research has focused on political knowledge as one of the most important individual-level moderators. The results of this research have been mixed, with some studies finding stronger effects of framing on less knowledgeable individuals (e.g., Schuck & de Vreese, 2006) and others the opposite (e.g., Nelson et al., 1997). Less knowledgeable individuals might be prone to a more significant immediate framing effect, but they are also less likely to integrate (and thus remember) the new information (e.g., Lecheler & de Vreese, 2011). A primary reason for the discrepancy in previous findings is the difference in the nature of the frame and in the outcome variable. Since we focus on knowledge gain as the outcome variable, we are concerned with motivational factors that might enhance or limit the impact of news frames – and as noted earlier, political interest is a key motivational factor. As succinctly noted by Prior (2010, 747), political interest is important because of "the effects of this kind of intrinsic motivation."

We specifically contend that individuals with low political interest are more susceptible to the effects of exposure to human-interest and conflict framing as regards knowledge gain. Since learning from human-interest and conflict framing may occur unintentionally through increased arousal (see Graber, 2001), we view this type of learning as an unintended by-product rather than an intentional activity. It follows that people with the lowest motivation, not the highest, will benefit the most in relative terms.

We also base our expectation on the study by Iyengar et al. (2010, 305), who showed that people with low motivation benefit most from situations that do not require them to "invest great effort to acquire information about current issues." Schönbach and Lauf (2002) demonstrated that those uninterested in politics gain the most from exposure to television news. Likewise, Liu and Eveland (2005) argued that the relationship between watching television and growth in political knowledge is strongest for people with low political interest. Baum and Jamison's (2006) empirical analysis showed support for the hypothesis that the attention-grabbing style of television is of particular benefit to those who lack motivation to follow the news. Jerit et al. (2006) offer a similar argument to explain why newspapers increase the knowledge gap between highly educated and poorly educated groups, while television does not. In relative terms, the latter groups learn more from television than do the former groups. Jerit et al. further relate this knowledge gain in poorly educated groups to the type of television content, which is one that can easily be comprehended and is attractive to these audiences. These groups clearly learn from the news as an unintended by-product: even though learning is "largely passive and unintentional . . . individuals may obtain enough information to function as monitorial citizens" (Jerit et al., 2006, 278).

KEY QUESTIONS

On the basis of these findings, we explore the dynamics of the relationship between media use and political knowledge. Our primary focus is to link the effects of news exposure to differences in content (see Slater, 2004 for a discussion). We will first examine how exposure to conflict frames and human-interest frames in the news affects knowledge gain. Based on the argument outlined earlier, we expect that exposure to news using these frames increases political knowledge gain.

Next, the chapter investigates how political interest moderates the relationship between exposure to conflict and human-interest frames and political knowledge. Previous research has shown that individuals with high political interest are more resilient to the influence of news exposure (e.g., Valentino et al., 2001). Concerning changes in knowledge, we expect individuals with low political interest to be more susceptible to the effects of exposure to conflict frames and human-interest news frames.

PREDICTING POLITICAL KNOWLEDGE

The dependent variable in this chapter is political knowledge. We chose to use knowledge about the U.S. presidential campaign and electoral system. This knowledge is expected to come mainly from the news media because it is a foreign issue for non-U.S. citizens. Therefore the issue is suitable for comparative research examining media effects triggered by exposure to news content in different countries. Finding questions that have an equal degree of difficulty poses a challenge in comparative research. By focusing on one international event, this study applies an inventive solution to that problem (see also Iyengar et al., 2010).

Knowledge was assessed using the following four multiple-choice questions (true, false, or don't know): "John McCain ran in the 2008 U.S. Presidential election for the Republican Party," "The U.S. President is elected to serve a term of two years," "American citizens elect the U.S. President directly," and "Party members who run for the U.S. Presidency are internally elected through their parties." Answers were recoded into dichotomous categories: 1 (correct) or 0 (incorrect or don't know) (Luskin & Bullock, 2005). The answers were combined into one knowledge scale.[1] We measured the time it took for respondents to answer the questions, and found no odd response-time patterns.[2] (See Appendix to Chapter 6 for mean political knowledge scores per single-outlet exposure.) To test for possible sensitization effects in the panel, a fresh sample from all three countries of about 200 respondents in total answered the same knowledge questions in wave II. The mean knowledge scores of the new sample did not differ significantly from the mean scores of respondents taking part in both panel waves.

The analysis consists of the following steps. First, we present the results of the content analysis, which show how much attention each medium paid to the U.S. election between the two panel waves and how their stories were framed. Second, we study the relationship between media use and knowledge about the U.S. elections in wave I of the survey. This shows whether people's knowledge differs depending on which medium they use. (In this part of the analysis we do not link news coverage to the change in knowledge, which is carried out in subsequent steps.) Third, we incorporate the results from the content analysis into the media exposure measure and use these figures to predict knowledge.

FRAMING OF THE ELECTIONS

The impact of news content on knowledge gain is examined by modeling knowledge gain dynamics, which is achieved by using an exposure measure. This measure estimates the exposure to conflict and human-interest frames at the level of the individual respondent between the two panel waves. The findings from

---

[1] An additive knowledge scale was formed ranging from 0 to 4 (wave I KR20=.56, wave II KR20=.57). Mean values: DK wave I, M=2.79, SD=1.11, DK wave II, M=2.98, SD=1.02; UK wave I, M=2.24, SD=1.16, UK wave II, M=2.36, SD=1.27; ES wave I, M=2.38, SD=1.22, ES wave II, M=2.53, SD=1.14.

[2] In all three countries, more than 90 percent of the respondents answered all questions in 90 seconds or less: more than 95 percent answered all questions in two minutes or less. The inclusion or exclusion of the remaining 5 percent does not alter the results.

the content analysis are used to identify the visibility of the U.S. elections in the different outlets in the three countries. To assess the visibility of the U.S. elections in the news, we collected and analyzed national broadcasts and newspapers from all sampled outlets in the period between the panel waves (see Appendix to Chapter 2).[3] The proportional amount (newspapers and television) and length (television) of U.S. election coverage are used to assess visibility.[4] To assess the presence of human-interest and conflict framing,[5] we looked at all news items in the relevant sections of the collected newspapers and broadcasts.[6] The Holsti indicator for intercoder reliability ranged from .69 to 1.00 for the different indicators in the different outlets.[7]

Figure 6.1 shows that the visibility of the U.S. elections (amount) is higher for public service than for commercial television in both Denmark and the United Kingdom. We find the

[3] The unit of analysis for television is the whole broadcast (172 news shows in total), and the unit of analysis for newspapers includes the front page and one randomly selected page (440 pages in total).

[4] A total of 1,378 newspaper articles and 2,965 TV news items was analyzed.

[5] The human-interest indicator is measured by the following item: "Does the article/story provide a human example or human face to the story in order to illuminate developments in politics or society?" (1 = yes, 0 = no). The conflict indicator is measured by the following item: "Does the story mention/portray the fact that one person, group, institution or organization reproaches/blames/criticizes another? Or does it present quotes or paraphrases in which an actor criticizes or refutes the claims of another actor?" (1 = yes, 0 = no).

[6] Special sections focusing on irrelevant topics (e.g., sports, advertising) were not analyzed. The single news item is the unit of analysis. A total of 3,994 TV and newspaper news items was screened to identify relevant news stories on the U.S. elections. The relevant items were then thoroughly analyzed for style. In total, 595 news articles and 272 news stories about the U.S. election were identified (see Appendix 2.3 for the number of news items per outlet).

[7] The intercoder reliability test was performed using a random sample of 67 news items on the U.S. elections. (The news items were collected from three different newspaper issues from each country, three news shows per outlet from Denmark and the United Kingdom, and two news shows per outlet in Spain.) Holsti scores range from .69 to 1.00 for the different indicators. Cohen's Kappa scores range from .40 to 1.00, except for the human-interest indicator on Danish television and the conflict indicator on British television. The Kappa score is sensitive to the number of cases, and most Kappa scores are above .60, which is considered solid.

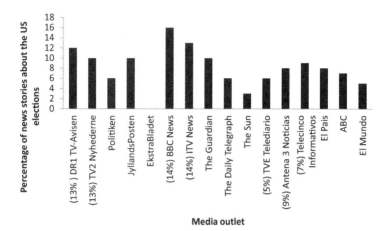

FIGURE 6.1. Visibility of news about the U.S. presidential elections per outlet. Percentage of stories on the front page (for newspapers) or percentage of stories in the news broadcast (for television) that deal with the U.S. elections. The duration of election news is given as a percentage of the total news duration in parentheses (television only). Based on the content analysis during the three weeks leading up to the presidential elections (see Appendix to Chapter 2).

opposite in Spain, with TVE about 2 percent behind Informativos and Antena 3. As for newspapers, differences in topic visibility are found between tabloids and broadsheets in Denmark and the United Kingdom, as well as among broadsheets in all countries. Election news stories were not visible in EkstraBladet and were barely visible (3 percent) in The Sun. Election coverage was more noticeable in The Guardian (10 percent) and JyllandsPosten (11 percent) than in Politiken and in the Daily Telegraph (7 percent and 6 percent, respectively). El Mundo had less visible coverage of the election than did ABC and El Pais.

Looking at conflict and human-interest framing (Figures 6.2 and 6.3), we find that commercial television coverage has less conflict and human-interest reporting in Denmark (26 percent on average) and Spain (22 percent on average) than public service broadcasts (31 percent on average per country). The BBC has more conflict-driven and less human-interest coverage than ITV. As for newspapers, the Danish tabloid has less conflict

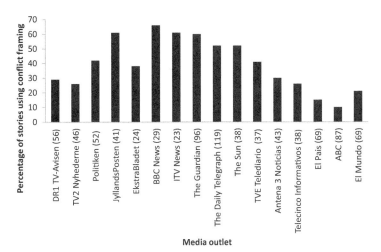

FIGURE 6.2. Proportion of U.S. election stories using conflict framing per outlet. Total number of news items about the U.S. elections in parentheses. Based on content analysis during the three weeks leading up to the presidential elections (see Appendix to Chapter 2).

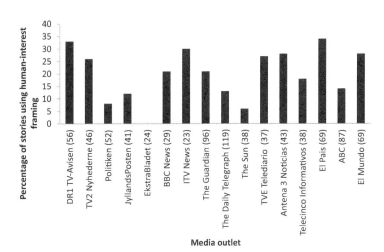

FIGURE 6.3. Proportion of U.S. election stories using human-interest framing per outlet. Total number of news items about the U.S. elections in parentheses. Based on content analysis during the three weeks leading up to the presidential elections (see Appendix to Chapter 2).

news than the two broadsheets, and does not focus on human-interest reporting at all. The tabloid versus broadsheet pattern holds in the United Kingdom with The Sun focusing less on human-interest coverage than the Daily Telegraph or The Guardian. Conversely, both the Daily Telegraph and The Sun have equal shares of conflict-driven coverage, though for The Sun this accounts for only seventeen stories compared with fifty-three stories in the Daily Telegraph. Conflict coverage is much more common in British and Danish than in Spanish broadsheets. In Spain, ABC differs from El Pais and El Mundo in that it focuses least on conflict and human-interest coverage during the last three weeks of the campaign. The content analysis does not show large cross-national differences regarding the attention devoted to the elections, but it does show that conflict framing is more prominent than human-interest framing. However, all countries used both types of frames, so we used pooled results in the analysis to assess the impact of exposure across the different contexts.

We next turn to predictors of political knowledge in Denmark, Spain, and the United Kingdom. In these analyses we look at political knowledge in the first wave of our panel data, and run prediction models using exposure measures at the outlet level. In the models, we control for gender (coded as female), age (in years), education,[8] and political interest (Delli Carpini & Keeter, 1996). We add a relative measure of preference for entertainment over information, which has been found to negatively affect political knowledge in some studies (e.g., Prior, 2003a) but not in others (e.g., research by de Vreese & Boomgaarden, 2006 showed no significant effects of preference for entertainment on levels of knowledge or on participation). The Appendix to Chapter 6 lists descriptives and specific wordings for the independent variables as well as the full regression analysis.

Figures 6.4–6.6 show these analyses by country and highlight the statistically significant independent variables. We see that

---

[8] The respondents' education levels were recoded due to differences in the education systems across the three countries. See Appendix 6.2.

FIGURE 6.4. Predicting political knowledge in Denmark at Wave 1.
Note: Entries are standardized beta coefficients (n=1539, adjusted R^2 .17). A positive sign of beta-coefficient indicates a positive association with political knowledge; a negative sign indicates a negative association. Only significant indicators are shown in the figure. Controls were made for age and exposure to DR1 TV Avisen, TV2 Nyhederne, Jyllands-Posten, and EkstraBladet. The full regression analysis is provided in the Appendix to Chapter 6.

gender (female) is negatively related to knowledge in all countries, while age, education, and political interest are positively related. Exposure to specific news outlets also correlate significantly with knowledge. Exposure to outlets such as ABC in Spain and The Sun and ITV in Britain is negatively correlated, while exposure to outlets such as Politiken in Denmark, The Guardian in Britain, and El Pais in Spain is positively correlated. While it might be tempting to draw various conclusions on the basis of these relationships, it would be hazardous to do so for two reasons. First, we are looking at correlations that cannot assess the direction of causality (are Guardian readers more knowledgeable because they read The Guardian? Or do knowledgeable people read The Guardian?). Second, we do not have content data from these media to substantiate the correlations. To overcome these two shortcomings, we rely on our panel survey data, which allows us to look at *change* in political knowledge. We also draw on our content analysis of the conflict and human-interest framing to explain this change.

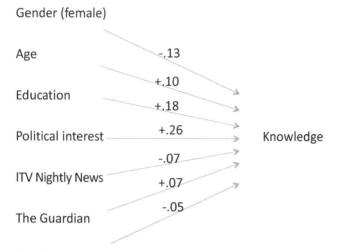

FIGURE 6.5. Predicting political knowledge in the United Kingdom at Wave 1. *Note:* Entries are standardized beta coefficients (n=1571, adjusted R^2 .21). A positive sign of beta-coefficient indicates a positive association with political knowledge; a negative sign indicates a negative association. Only significant indicators are shown in the figure. Controls were made for entertainment preference and exposure to BBC News and The Daily Telegraph. The full regression analysis is provided in the Appendix to Chapter 6.

PREDICTING CHANGE IN POLITICAL KNOWLEDGE

To test the effects of conflict and human-interest framing on political knowledge gain and the moderating function of political interest, we turn to our models of change (see Table 6.1). We incorporate the results of the content analysis directly into the exposure measure used in our change models. Individual respondents are assigned separate weighted scores determined by their frequency of exposure to the different news outlets in their countries, as well as by the average presence of the news frames in each news outlet during the period between the panel waves. We created our exposure measure by weighting the number of

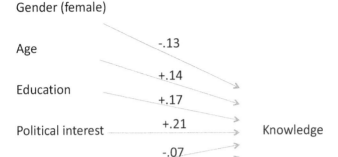

Gender (female)

Age — -.13

Education — +.14, +.17

Political interest — +.21 → Knowledge

ABC — -.07, +.05

El Pais

FIGURE 6.6. Predicting political knowledge in Spain at Wave 1. *Note:* Entries are standardized beta coefficients (n=1642, adjusted R^2 .15). A positive sign of beta-coefficient indicates a positive association with political knowledge; a negative sign indicates a negative association. Only significant indicators are shown in the figure. Controls were made for entertainment preference and exposure to TVE Telediario 2, Antena 3 Noticias, and Informativos Telecinco. The full regression analysis is provided in the Appendix to Chapter 6.

days per week that attention-inducing content[9] is present in each outlet. In our change models, we control for the attention paid to U.S. election news and for interpersonal discussion on the U.S. election during the last three weeks of the election campaign. Interpersonal communication is associated with political knowledge (e.g., Bennett et al., 2000; Delli Carpini & Keeter, 1996) and is considered both a conduit for gaining second-hand information from the news as well as a key antecedent to knowledge gain and political participation (Scheufele, 2002). Further, we control for political interest and use it as a moderator of the relationship under investigation (modeled as an interaction effect).

[9] The calculation is as follows: (number of days using medium 1) × (visibility + conflict framing + human interest) + (number of days using medium 2) × (visibility + conflict framing + human interest) +...

TABLE 6.1. Predicting[a] Change in Knowledge

| | Model 1 | | | Model 2 | | | Model 3 | | | Model 4 | | |
| | Unweighted Exposure | | | Weighted Exposure | | | Weighted Exposure (political interest as control) | | | Weighted (exposure × low political interest) | | |
	b[b]	SE	beta	b	SE	beta	b	SE	beta	b	SE	beta
Discussion	.034	.011	.051**	.034	.011	.050**	.027	.011	.041*	.027	.011	.041*
Attention	.073	.011	.105***	.072	.011	.104***	.058	.011	.084***	.058	.011	.084***
News exposure	.002	.002	.012	.005	.003	.019	.001	.003	.005	-.003	.004	-.011
Country (Denmark is baseline)												
United Kingdom	-.248	.036	-.099***	-.254	.035	-.102***	-.240	.035	-.096***	-.241	.035	-.096***
Spain	-.179	.034	-.072***	-.180	.034	-.073***	-.157	.034	-.063***	-.158	.034	-.064***
Political interest							.070	.010	.097***	.091	.012	.127***
News exposure × low political interest										.019	.006	.046**
Knowledge (t1)	.496	.012	.513***	.495	.012	.513***	.473	.012	.490***	.471	.012	.488***
Constant	1.01	.058		1.002	.057		.847	.061		.763	.067	
Adjusted R²			.3604			.3607			.3678			.3689
N			4751			4751			4751			4751

SE, standard error.
[a] Using OLS regressions.
[b] Unstandardized coefficients.
* p<.05, ** p<.01, *** p<.001.

We also control for country effects, as our sample comes from three different populations.[10] Finally, we include the lagged term of the dependent variable (i.e., political knowledge in wave I of the survey). This allows us to account for prior levels of knowledge (Price & Zaller, 1993) and to examine change between the panel waves (Markus, 1979). The Appendix to Chapter 6 lists descriptives and specific wordings for the independent variables.

After controlling for initial levels of political knowledge and country differences,[11] we find that media attention, discussion about the election, and political interest are positive predictors of political knowledge (Table 6.1, models 1, 3). Political knowledge is unaffected by unweighted news exposure (see model 1), but in line with our expectations, exposure to conflict and human-interest framing is a positive predictor for political knowledge (model 2).[12] The final model shows a significant interaction between low political interest and exposure to conflict and human-interest framing (model 4).[13] The significant predictors in this final model are visualized in Figure 6.7. This model shows that political interest moderates the relationship between exposure to conflict and human-interest framing and political knowledge gain. Exposure to these news frames is indeed beneficial to those who have low political interest.

Figure 6.8 further depicts the moderating effect of political interest. The effect of exposure to conflict and human-interest framing is shown for respondents with high and low political

---

[10] Country dummies serve as a comparative control. The type of medium (television versus newspapers), coverage type (public service television versus commercial television and broadsheet newspapers versus tabloid newspapers), and system level are presumed not to affect the relationship between exposure and political knowledge.

[11] The effects on knowledge of exposure to the news frames are not significantly moderated by country dummies.

[12] If the influences of exposure to conflict and to human-interest framing are presented separately in the same model, they result in multicollinearity because of repeated exposure frequency; therefore, we combine exposure to conflict and human-interest framing in one weighted exposure measure.

[13] The inclusion of age, education, and gender as controls in the final model does not change these results.

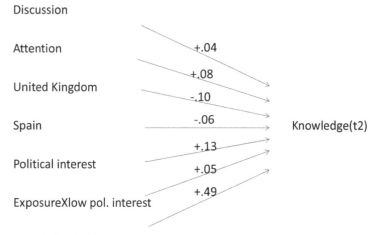

FIGURE 6.7. Predicting change in political knowledge. *Note*: Entries are standardized beta coefficients (n=4751, adjusted R^2 .37). A positive sign of beta-coefficient indicates a positive association with political knowledge; a negative sign indicates a negative association. Only significant indicators are shown in the figure. Controls were made for news exposure. The full regression analysis is provided in Table 6.1, model 4.

interest. The scores on the four-point knowledge scale change only marginally for people with high political interest when they are exposed to these frames. For people with low political interest, exposure to conflict and human-interest framing has a much larger impact. In the case of people with low political interest who are exposed maximally to this framing, they score almost one point higher on the four-point knowledge scale than do respondents with low political interest who are exposed minimally to this framing.

DISCUSSION

Most models of democracy stress the importance of an informed citizenry. The media's contribution to citizens' knowledge is the object of much research, and studies have produced mixed findings. In this chapter we have investigated the effects of the news

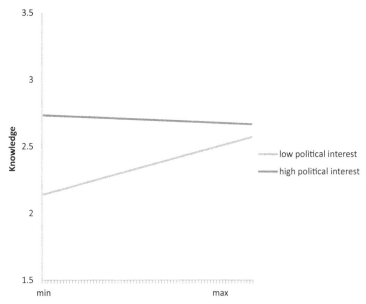

FIGURE 6.8. The effect of exposure to conflict and human-interest framing on political knowledge among respondents with low and high political interest.

media on change in political knowledge. The backdrop was the 2008 U.S. Presidential election, and the study was carried out in three countries, using two-wave panel surveys and media content analysis. We focused on the impact of exposure to conflict and human-interest news frames and found these to be conducive to learning from the news. This effect was particularly strong for those who were the least motivated to follow the news and who showed minimal interest in politics, suggesting that this kind of news reporting has the potential to entice individuals who might otherwise pay little attention to politics.

Our design looked at (1) the supply of political information framed in terms of conflict and human-interest, and (2) individual motivational factors. The content analysis showed that the elections were generally more visible in broadsheet newspapers and on public service broadcasters. These findings corroborate those of Iyengar et al. (2010), who found public broadcasting and broadsheet papers to include more hard news than their commercial and tabloid counterparts. The degree to which the conflict and human-interest frames were used differed somewhat between and within broadcasters and newspapers nationally, but the content analysis revealed it to be similar cross-nationally, other things being equal. Of the two frames, the conflict frame was the most frequently used, which dovetails with de Vreese et al.'s (2001) findings from their cross-national analysis of political news framing. The conflict frame is also important in light of the distinction between sacerdotal and pragmatic journalistic approaches to politics (see Chapter 1). Drawing on the conflict frame is a useful way for journalists to create a degree of autonomy from politics by highlighting a conflict rather than by approaching a political story in a passive manner. In this way, the use of conflict framing also bears on the journalistic attempts to offer impartial coverage (see also Chapter 1): a conflict frame will typically include two or more sides of an issue, and is a template for laying out differing views.

Our key interest was to assess the effects of these news frames on learning. Using the panel design we found a positive effect of exposure to the news frames on knowledge gain (see also Baum & Jamison, 2006). Human-interest and conflict reporting styles are often associated with soft journalism and a pragmatic journalistic approach to studying politics (Chapter 1). They are a way of ensuring that complex issues can reach the public, often drawing on entertainment elements (see van Dijk, 1988). Our analysis does not support previous research that shows a negative effect of the human-interest frame on readers' recall of information from the news. For example, Valkenburg et al. (1999) found such a negative effect – but only in regard to crime, not to the European economy. We interpret our positive finding on the human-interest frame as a function of making *political* news accessible through the use of personal, individual stories (see also Iyengar, 1991). No study until now has related the conflict frame to gains in political knowledge. A news story using the conflict frame is enticing and can foster a more broad-minded approach to an issue as well as boost political participation (de Vreese & Tobiasen, 2007). We can now posit that a conflict frame is conducive to political learning, which is especially helpful to those who are less interested in politics. Future experimental research should further disentangle what elements of the conflict and human-interest frames are most effective vis-à-vis political knowledge gain.

The moderating effect of political interest is an important finding in our study: those with lower levels of political interest gained most political knowledge. This finding is in line with evidence from previous studies showing individuals with low levels of interest in politics to be more susceptible to the influence of news framing (e.g., Iyengar & Kinder, 1987; Valentino et al., 2001). Some journalistic news frames, such as conflict and human-interest, are sometimes argued to have negative effects on political knowledge by distracting readers or viewers from facts. Our study suggests, however, that such frames can be effective for learning from the news, in particular for the less-interested segments of the population. In our theoretical overview we distinguished between supply and motivational factors affecting the learning process.

Our research points to the importance of considering information supply not only as the availability of news and current affairs programs, but as the availability of political information that is framed in accessible ways (see also Iyengar et al., 2010). Studies show that the availability of political informative indeed varies across media systems (Aalberg & Curran, 2011; Esser et al., 2012), but these differences can be augmented or mitigated depending on the way political news looks. In a high-supply system there might still be only limited news framing that facilitates knowledge, and conversely, in a low-supply system there might be sufficient enticing news from which learning is more likely to derive (see also the Discussion in Chapter 9). This supply of content is important for knowledge gain, in particular for those who might be less motivated. In fact, such content can help close the gap between the interested and the uninterested when they turn to the news. Of course, the actual implications will always be an interaction between contextual supply factors and individual motivational factors. It is therefore important to assess the scope of positive effects of learning from the news, but even if this positive spiral does not apply to all individuals, our finding has implications for the healthy functioning of any democracy and for framing and learning theory, in particular – and provides an important antidote to the often pessimistic conclusions about citizens' ability to learn from the news.

In the next chapter we will pursue our investigation of news media effects by demonstrating the way different kinds of political journalism matter in regard to our perception of politics.

7

Does Infotainment Journalism Lead to Political Cynicism?

THE EFFECTS OF PRIVATIZATION VERSUS
PERSONALIZATION IN THE NEWS

In the previous chapter we examined the effects of human-interest and conflict frames on political knowledge, and showed how especially those with lower levels of political interest may benefit from exposure to such political news. Along the same lines we will now examine the effects of infotainment coverage on citizens with various levels of political interest. Our key question is whether political journalism that draws on entertainment features in the news leads to political cynicism.

Journalists are often criticized for blurring the line between news and entertainment. This phenomenon, also known as "infotainment," is subject to continuous debate among political communication scholars regarding its causes, meaning, and most importantly its effects on citizens and democracy (see Brants, 1998). While differentiation between information and entertainment is much contested, it is important to note that news is never likely to be 100 percent entertainment. Traditionally, however, the expectation has been that news should be informative. In Chapter 1 we outlined the information-entertainment continuum as one of the core concepts of this book. We investigated the importance of this dimension for journalists' self-perceptions

(Chapter 3) and the content they produce (Chapter 5). In this chapter we turn to the effects of exposure to infotainment.

The effects of infotainment on the quality of a democracy have often been assumed, but rarely empirically tested. Scholars generally argue that in democracies the media perform vital functions regarding the political system and political information (see Strömback, 2005). The shift toward sensation, emotion, and scandal, however, is perceived to negate the type of journalism that is essential to democracy (Esser, 1999, 315) and to be a major cause of the crisis in public life. Scholars suggest that citizens' lack of information to make qualified decisions in elections is a result of journalism's focus on people and on politicians' non-political traits rather than issues and politicians' political qualities (see Adam & Maier, 2010). Some researchers expect that infotainment news will have a positive effect on democracy because it attracts audiences that would otherwise not be exposed to news at all (e.g., Baum, 2003).

Infotainment research has frequently focused on its potential effects on citizens' likelihood to participate in elections, among other things (see Adam & Maier, 2010). In this chapter we investigate the effects of exposure to infotainment news on citizens' attitudes toward the political system. We analyze the change in political cynicism among audiences in three media and political systems. Political cynicism is inversely related to efficacy (e.g., Craig et al., 1990) and trust in social, economic, and political institutions (e.g., Mishler & Rose, 2001). Cynicism influences key measures such as voter instability and political participation (e.g., Adriaansen et al., 2010). This chapter adds to the debate in the literature on whether infotainment approaches toward politics result in widespread cynicism about politics. We use the panel survey and content analysis data (see Appendix to Chapter 2) to investigate the relationship between political cynicism and news exposure in our three divergent media and political systems.

POLITICAL CYNICISM

The worst enemy of democracy is cynicism (Demers, 1998). The cynic tends to hold that the political system is corrupt, that its players are uninterested in the public good, and that its processes are driven by a concern with winning, not governing (see Cappella & Jamieson, 1997, 19). More specifically, scholars refer to cynicism in relation to candidates and institutions (Erber & Lau, 1990), the political process (Cappella & Jamieson, 1997), campaign perceptions (de Vreese & Semetko, 2002), and political debates (de Vreese, 2007). It is an open question, however, as to whether cynicism in one area carries over to another. Some researchers argue that citizens can become increasingly dissatisfied with the performance of representative institutions despite their faith in democracy as an ideal form of government (Norris, 2000). Others hypothesize that attitudes toward the authorities potentially affect belief in the legitimacy of the political system (Adam & Maier, 2010, 239).

The concept of cynicism is closely tied to an absence of trust (e.g., Mishler & Rose, 2001). Scholars believe, however, that measures of political trust should not be translated into approximations of political cynicism (e.g., de Vreese & Semetko, 2002; de Vreese, 2005) for two reasons: first, distrust does not correlate with several factors related to political cynicism, such as apathy, meaninglessness, and inefficacy. Second, trust comes fully into play only when a connection is established between the person who trusts and the object of that trust – particularly when actions at the highest levels of government are seen to affect daily life (see Cappella & Jamieson, 1997, 142). In Chapter 4 we addressed the relationship between politicians and journalists. In this chapter we turn to the relationship between media content and public cynicism. We contend that too much cynicism in either group is not beneficial. But as is the case with journalists and politicians, who must be mutually critical, citizens should also possess a healthy degree of skepticism vis-à-vis power holders. A healthy dose of cynicism is therefore little more than an expression of a critical citizenry.

INFOTAINMENT NEWS

Growth of infotainment reporting on politics has accompanied changes in the media and society. The modernization of political systems and the proliferation of market logic required a non-traditional media outreach to all relevant actors (see also Chapter 1). This new approach aimed to meet the needs and expectations of the average citizen through infotainment – with a focus on human-interest stories and emotions (van Zoonen & Holtz Bacha, 2000) – and thus blurred the boundaries that previously shaped political communication and that separated "quality" from "tabloid" coverage of politics (Blumler & Kavanagh, 1999). The development of infotainment news has not been uniform (see Brants, 1998). It has been shaped by media cultures and by economic and legal conditions in diverse political and media systems (see Hallin & Mancini, 2004b; Esser, 1999). Infotainment's motley growth is reflected in the varying popularity and availability of tabloid news in different countries.

In an attempt to define infotainment, reference is frequently made to "tabloidization" (see Brants & Neijens 1998). In the past, tabloidization referred only to changes in newspaper and broadcast formats, but nowadays it also encompasses changes in news content. Besides using format and content, scholars use style features to help define infotainment. Sparks (2000) describes infotainment as a trend of decreasing attention to politics, economics, and society compared with sports, entertainment, and scandals. To identify infotainment, Brants and Neijens (1998) refer to topic, style, and format, whereas Norris (2000) distinguishes between subject elements, style, and format. Some researchers propose an integrative examination of tabloidization that incorporates different levels of analysis, such as range, form, and mode of address (McLachlan & Golding, 2000).

Scholars tend to adopt one of two views of infotainment. Critics – who perceive it as a sensual form of news coverage (e.g., Grabe et al., 2001) – believe infotainment has resulted from a spillover of tabloid news values and topics to quality news (Sparks, 2000), which has entailed an overall decrease in journalistic standards (see Esser, 2009). Other researchers, however, disagree with this one-way assessment, and counter it with their own belief in convergence; public service stations tend to cover more entertainment, whereas commercial and entertainment stations strive to include more information in their coverage (Pfetsch, 1996). In this camp we find Brants (1998), who documented the emergence of infotainment trends in both the United States and the Netherlands, and Deuze (2002), who analyzed contemporary trends of infotainment in his study of the Dutch journalist profile. We, too, approach our study from this perspective, and accordingly analyze both types of news media – print (tabloid and broadsheet) and television (public service and commercial) – for the presence of infotainment content.

PRIVATIZATION VERSUS PERSONALIZATION

Despite the lack of a clear definition of infotainment, scholars generally mention personalization when they identify the presence of infotainment (see also Chapter 5). There is likewise minimal consensus on the exact definition of personalization. Some researchers describe personalization as both a focus on individuals and an improper understanding of large social issues in terms of individual actors (e.g., Bennett, 2001). For others, personalization means human-interest reporting (Brants, 1998), the presentation of public figures as private persons (e.g., Latimer, 1984), or the change in evaluation criteria for politicians from professional competence to non-political traits (Adam & Maier, 2010, 216). Van Santen (2009) proposes a definition of personalization that entails a focus on politicians' traits and skills (individualization), their competence (privatization), and their personal experiences and emotions (emotionalization). The increase in emotionalized stories is associated with both personalized (e.g., Valkenburg et al., 1999) and consumer-oriented news coverage (see McQuail, 2005).

Infotainment coverage is likely to contain soft rather than hard news. This type of news is typically more sensational, more personality centered, less time-bound, more practical, and more incident-based than other news (Prior, 2003b, 149). Infotainment content is more likely to sit within an episodic rather than a thematic frame. The thematic frame focuses on broader social trends and also places issues in a general context, whereas the episodic frame focuses on individual cases and depicts issues in terms of individual instances or specific events (see Iyengar, 1991). Unlike thematic framing, episodic framing emphasizes and fosters individual rather than government responsibility (see Adam & Maier, 2010, 239).

In this chapter we distinguish between two aspects of infotainment coverage that are often combined in the personalization literature: the personalization of politics and the "ordinary citizen" perspective. Personalization of politics refers to the shift in journalism toward covering individual political behavior and the private side rather than the public side of politicians. The ordinary citizen perspective refers to a news form that privileges the ordinary citizen's viewpoint whenever public issues are discussed. When infotainment of politics includes news coverage of politicians' private lives and scandals, we refer to it as *privatization*. Thus, privatization emphasizes candidates' personalities rather than substantive party issues (see e.g., Patterson, 1993). When news coverage from the ordinary citizen perspective includes human-interest and emotionalization, we refer to it as *personalization*. Unlike previous research, our suggested definition of infotainment is based on assumptions related to its effects on the public rather than its content features.

Privatization and personalization can be found in both the print press and on television, sometimes within the same news story. Their presence is expected to vary across different media and political systems (see Chapter 2 for a discussion on media system variations).

What we have defined as privatization in this chapter includes a focus on procedures above substance, which has been widely documented in the coverage of U.S. elections. Recent research shows that this form of election campaign coverage is gaining traction worldwide (Kaid and Strömback, 2008). Scholars suggest that the prominence of privatization is connected with journalists' increased treatment of campaigns as strategic games or horse races between candidates (Adam & Maier, 2010: 219). Strategic coverage has been found to increase cynicism. For example, Cappella and Jamieson (1997) showed that exposure to strategic news coverage during election campaigns makes citizens cynical and dissatisfied (see also Semetko & de Vreese, 2002).

EFFECTS OF INFOTAINMENT

The impact of infotainment on the public and on democracy is a controversial topic among political communication scholars. Exposure to infotainment news, with its increased attention to triviality, scandals, and entertainment, is argued to increase public cynicism and to negatively affect voting behavior, political participation, and cognitive processes. The damaging effects of the mass media have been dubbed "video malaise" (see van Santen, 2009). Theories of media malaise state that systematic patterns of political reporting discourage trust in political leaders, reduce active citizenship, and undermine confidence in the political system (see Robinson, 1976; Norris, 2000). Such theses arise in discussions about the relationship between commercialization and the declining quality of the democratic system (e.g., Pftesch, 1996; Hallin, 1996). Scholars generally argue that personalization of politics has negative consequences for the functioning of democracies (e.g., Kaase, 1994). Reducing the complexity of political processes to the achievements and standpoints of individual politicians weakens the impact of issues and party programs on voting decisions – neither national opinion building nor decision making are reinforced (Adam & Maier, 2010, 213). Several scholars suggest that the increased focus on scandals and private lives can undermine the public's involvement in the political process (Patterson, 1993), and may produce greater cynicism among readers (Norris, 2000, 73). In addition, infotainment shares several features with tabloidization, such as sensational reporting, which is believed to increase apathy and cynicism about the political system (see McNair, 2001; Schulz, 1998). Previous studies have further shown that sensationalism distorts comprehension and judgment (Vettehen et al., 2005) and may negatively affect the process of storing news messages (Grabe et al., 2000).

Few scholars mention the potentially positive influences that infotainment might have on citizenship and democracy. Brants (1998) argues that giving the citizen's voice a greater role is likely to increase involvement in politics; furthermore, personal characteristics of politicians can be important to democratic choices and evaluations in societies where differences and ideologies between political parties are less important and less visible. Similarly, Norris (2000) suggests that the characteristic style of tabloids may make politics more accessible to less informed readers. This is because, compared with citizens with significant political knowledge, less intelligent and less knowledgeable citizens may focus more on the non-political traits of politicians (see Adam & Maier, 2010). Infotainment coverage seeks to inform and entertain at the same time, and therefore can be very appealing to people who are unwilling to give up entertainment while watching the news (Prior, 2003b). Baum (2003) showed that consuming soft news influences the attitudes of politically inattentive individuals and that, in at least some fairly predictable contexts, it is associated with enhanced factual political knowledge. The claim that infotainment can be beneficial for the less educated or less politically interested seems to be consistent with studies that show a positive relationship between political sophistication and cynicism (e.g., Cappella & Jamieson, 1997). This relationship suggests that citizens can be interested in and knowledgeable about politics but still critical about politicians and their performance (de Vreese, 2005, 294).

KEY QUESTIONS

This chapter sets out to examine the effects of infotainment coverage on levels of cynicism among the public. Current arguments about the potential effects of infotainment on citizens do not usually distinguish between different aspects of infotainment. In this chapter, however, we examine the way privatization versus personalization affects political cynicism. The chapter builds on previous research predicting the antecedents of political cynicism through exposure to news (e.g., Cappella & Jamieson, 1997). Our main expectation is that exposure to infotainment elements in the news can both increase and decrease political cynicism. Specifically, we expect personalization to decrease cynicism and privatization to generate cynicism among the general public, because privatization is conceptually linked to strategic news coverage (which has consistently been found to increase public cynicism) (see Cappella & Jamieson, 1997; Semetko & de Vreese, 2002). This expectation is consistent with infotainment literature, which shows that news focusing on politicians' private lives and scandals may have a negative influence on the public and on democracy. In comparison, personalization of the news may render politics more understandable by increasing the relevance and vividness of political issues. This in turn might decrease citizens' cynical attitudes about the government and the political system.

Some scholars have suggested that infotainment may be beneficial to a democracy by increasing the political involvement of citizens with low interest in politics. We investigate this claim by examining the moderating effects of political interest in relation to both personalization and privatization. Previous research has shown that political interest is empirically linked to media use (Luskin, 1990) and news attention (Slater, 2004), and often moderates the effects of exposure to news media (Zaller, 1992). We expect political interest to only moderate the effects of personalized coverage on political cynicism; that is, those less interested in politics will become less cynical when exposed to personalization. This is because personalization, through emotionalization and human-interest stories, may make politics more understandable and relevant to people who are less politically engaged. Privatization coverage may attract public attention but at the expense of the public's trust in the political process. In other words, we expect privatization coverage to induce cynicism among the general public and personalization coverage to have the opposite effect, but only among individuals with lower levels of political interest.

MEASURING POLITICAL CYNICISM

The dependent variable is political cynicism. We looked at political cynicism directed at both national governments and political systems in general. Using a seven-point Likert agree-disagree scale, we measured individual responses in both waves to the following items: (1) "It is easier to become an MP due to political friends than to competence," (2) "Ministers and state secretaries are mainly focused on themselves," (3) "Politicians promise more than they can deliver," (4) Politicians don't understand what is happening in society. The items are inspired by previous work on political cynicism (e.g., Cappella & Jamieson, 1997; de Vreese & Semetko, 2002). The items formed a reliable scale.[1]

PREDICTING CHANGE IN POLITICAL CYNICISM

To explore the effects of media use on political cynicism, we measured news exposure by asking respondents in Denmark, the United Kingdom, and Spain to report how many days a week they use the sampled news outlets in each country[2] (see Appendix to Chapter 2 for the full list). These news outlets included commercial and public service broadcasts, and tabloid and quality press, which is consistent with our theoretical position that

---

[1] Political cynicism: (Cronbach's) DK wave I, *a*=.79, DK wave II, *a*=.79; UK wave I, *a*=.85, UK wave II, *a*=.86; ES wave I, *a*=.81, ES wave II, *a*=.83. A higher score reflects a higher level of cynicism. (DK wave I, M=4.6, SD=1.2, DK wave II, M=4.6, SD=1.1; UK wave I, M=5.2, SD=1.2, UK wave II M=5.2, SD=1.2; ES wave I, M=5.4, SD=1.2, ES wave II, M=5.3, SD=1.2). The items were randomly rotated in the two waves of the panel survey. Sensitization tests showed that political cynicism mean scores for the new sample (approximately 200 respondents per country) were not substantially different from cynicism mean scores calculated for respondents taking part in both panel waves.

[2] Media exposure (outlet level): number of days (per week) using each news outlet, ranging from 0 (none) to 7 (seven days). DK: DR1, M=3.23, SD=2.32; TV2, M=4.0, SD=2.4; Politiken, M=.91, SD=2.0; JyllandsPosten, M=.78, SD=1.81; EkstraBladet, M=.78, SD=1.76. UK: BBC, M=2.44, SD=2.32; ITV, M=1.33, SD=1.94; The Guardian, M=.46, SD=1.28; Daily Telegraph, M=.55, SD=1.54; The Sun, M=.66, SD=1.65. ES: TVE, M=2.21, SD=2.30; Antena 3, M=3, SD=2.47; Informativos, M=2.72, SD=2.37; ABC, M=.66, SD=1.56; El Pais, M=1.28, SD=2.07; El Mundo, M=1.20, SD=2.08.

infotainment is a result of the convergence of tabloid news and quality news. Several studies have considered media use as the source of political cynicism (e.g., Newton, 1999; Norris, 2000). However, "media consumption does not offer a very convincing explanation for the level of political trust" (Kleinnijenhuis et al., 2006, 88). Thus, we follow various studies – for instance, those by de Vreese and Semetko (2002) and by Patterson (1993) – and rely on the actual characteristics of the news to better understand the relationship between media consumption and political cynicism. We limit our analysis to political news because it is widely considered to be the most important source of political information (see Eurobarometer, 2001).

To measure the presence of infotainment in the news, we collected and analyzed the national broadcasts and newspaper issues for all sampled outlets in the period between the panel waves.[3] We looked at all news items in the major and relevant sections of the collected newspapers and broadcasts.[4] We drew on four indicators of infotainment news coverage (see also Chapter 5) that represent both personalization and privatization content. Privatization is operationalized as (1) the presence of moral or political scandal,[5] and (2) a focus on politicians' private lives rather than

---

[3] A total of 3,994 broadcast and newspaper items were analyzed to identify news on national politics. The unit of analysis is the single news item. Overall, 1,393 newspaper articles and 403 television stories on national politics were identified and then analyzed for the presence of infotainment elements. Adam and Mayer (2010) argued that the absolute amount of personalized politics can differ according to differences in the media and political systems. Curran et al. (2009) showed that British television news allocates significantly more time to soft news compared with Danish television news. They also found that the press in both Denmark and Britain prioritizes soft news. Their results suggest that a higher degree of commercialization may increase infotainment coverage even in public broadcasting (see also Adam & Maier, 2010).

[4] The pair-wise intercoder reliability test was performed using a random sample of news items on national politics. Intercoder reliability scores (Holsti's method) for scandal coverage, private life and human-interest framing were all above .69 (see Chapter 5). The intercoder reliability score for emotions is .65 and ranges from .49 for UK newspapers to .95 for Spanish television.

[5] A scandal story involves allegations of wrongdoing, disgrace, or moral outrage. A politician may be accused of engaging in various illegal, corrupt, or unethical

presenting them as spokespersons for certain policies or ideologies. Personalization is operationalized as the presence of (1) a human example or human face to the story in order to illuminate developments in politics or society (e.g., a citizen's experience is used to explain an event), and (2) explicit references to feelings or sentiments.[6] Two additive measures were formed (privatization versus personalization).[7] An overall additive exposure score was then calculated at the respondent's level and weighted by the content analysis findings for each outlet.[8]

Using multiple ordinary least squares (OLS) regression analysis, we first test a model investigating the effects of unweighted news exposure on change in political cynicism. We then examine the differential effects of the two arms of infotainment (privatization versus personalization) on the dynamics of political

practices. A political scandal can involve breaking the nation's laws or plotting to do so.

[6] Explicit references to feelings or sentiments may include words such as confused, excited, guilty, anxious, angry, sad, confident, embarrassed, happy, disgusted, frightened, cautious, smug, lonely, jealous, surprised, shy, and apathetic.

[7] A principal component factor analysis with varimax rotation on all infotainment items confirmed the presence of two divergent factors with eigenvalues exceeding 1, explaining 36% and 29% of the variance, respectively. Bartlett's test of sphericity reached statistical significance supporting the factorability of the correlation matrix. The eigenvalue for the first factor is 1.46, and for the second factor, 1.16. The two-component solution explained a total variance of 0.66. Items loading on the first factor (privatization): "scandal" = 0.84, "private life" = 0.84. Items loading on the second factor (personalization): "human interest" = 0.78, "emotions" = 0.74. The two additive measures (privatization versus personalization) were weakly correlated (r=.07, p>.05). Exposure to privatization: an additive scale of exposure to news weighted by the average presence of moral or political scandal and a focus on politicians' private lives. Exposure to personalization: an additive scale of exposure to news weighted by the average presence of human-interest and emotions.

[8] Exposure to privatization: DK, M=.51, SD=.49; UK, M=.98, SD=.91; ES, M=.60, SD=.39. Exposure to personalization: DK, M=4.48, SD=2.37; UK, M=2.34, SD=2.07; ES, M=2.44, SD=1.68. We incorporate the results of the content analysis directly into our change models (as discussed in Chapter 2) so that individual respondents are given separate weighted scores determined by their frequency of exposure to the different news outlets in their countries as well as the average presence of privatization and personalization indicators in each news outlet for three consecutive weeks.

cynicism. Finally, we test a model investigating the moderating effects of political interest on changes of cynicism levels. In our dynamic models, we control for a number of variables including gender (coded as female), age (in years), education,[9] political interest, interpersonal communication, and attention to national politics coverage. We also add a six-item index of political efficacy (Cronbach's a=0.60) (see de Vreese, 2005). Previous research has shown an inconsistent positive relationship between education and political cynicism (e.g., de Vreese, 2005) and a robust negative relationship between efficacy and political cynicism (e.g., Mishler & Rose, 2001; de Vreese & Semetko, 2002). We also account for country effects since our sample comes from three different populations.[10] Finally, we control for the lagged measure of cynicism in the first wave of the survey in order to examine change between the panel waves (see Markus (1997) for a discussion). See the Appendix to Chapter 7 for descriptives and specific wordings for the control variables.

PRIVATIZATION VERSUS PERSONALIZATION IN THE NEWS

We first look at the findings from the content analysis to assess the amount of national politics coverage and the presence of privatization and personalization elements at the medium, outlet, and country levels. Figure 7.1 (privatization) and Figure 7.2 (personalization) show that the news coverage of national politics varies substantially between newspapers in Denmark, Spain, and the United Kingdom. These findings dovetail with the data presented in Chapter 5. All three newspapers in the United Kingdom contain at least twice as many news items about national politics as do the Danish newspapers. For example, British papers ran 695 articles (226+324+145), while Danish papers ran 220 (99+84+37). The Spanish newspapers also have more national

---

[9] The respondents' level of education was recoded due to differences in the education systems across the three countries. See Appendix to Chapter 7.

[10] Country dummies serve as a comparative control. The system level is hypothesized not to affect the relationship between exposure to infotainment news and political cynicism.

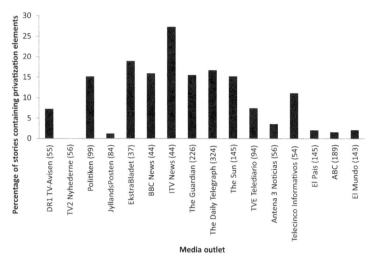

FIGURE 7.1. Proportion of news about national politics containing elements of privatization per outlet. Total number of news items about national politics in parentheses. Based on content analysis between the panel waves (see Appendix to Chapter 2).

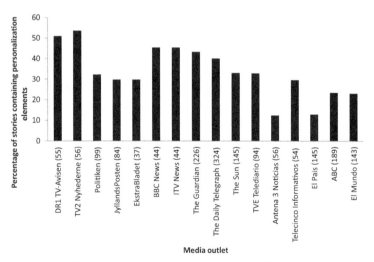

FIGURE 7.2. Proportion of news about national politics containing elements of personalization per outlet. Total number of news items about national politics in parentheses. Based on content analysis between the panel waves (see Chapter 2).

political coverage than the Danish newspapers, but the former also have more total pages than the latter. Of all print news, the two UK broadsheets personalize news coverage of national politics the most: The Guardian (43%) and the Daily Telegraph (40%). More generally, Spanish news outlets (print and television) personalize news coverage the least, whereas Danish news outlets personalize almost half of the news coverage. Overall, the personalization differential is more observable *between countries* than between media or news outlets.

The data show no consistent pattern to suggest differences in the privatization of news coverage (Figure 7.1), regardless of medium or newspaper type (i.e., broadsheet versus tabloid). Again, this outcome is in line with the analyses presented in Chapter 5. However, the share of privatization in the British commercial broadcast ITV (27 percent) is significantly higher than in the Spanish commercial broadcasts (7 percent on average), while the commercial news outlet in Denmark, TV2, did not include any privatization in its entire coverage of national politics. In Chapter 5, we provided examples of this from the actual privitization coverage. These are stories like "Speaker's wife spent 50,000 pounds on air travel" (Daily Telegraph, 21 January 2008) or "Tory MP rode quad bike on the road with child on back" (The Daily Telegraph, 4 January 2008), both focusing on private aspects of politicians' behavior. By and large, privatization is more prevalent in the United Kingdom than in either Denmark or Spain, which further implies that country differences are consistently related to the presence of personalization as well as privatization. Finally, the data show that news outlets in general include far more personalization than privatization, regardless of medium, newspaper type, or country differences.

EFFECTS OF EXPOSURE TO PRIVATIZATION VERSUS
PERSONALIZATION ON POLITICAL CYNICISM

Table 7.1 reports the results of three multiple OLS regressions investigating change in political cynicism. The first model shows that news exposure measures alone have no significant effect on

TABLE 7.1. *Predicting[a] Change in Political Cynicism*

	Model 1			Model 2			Model 3		
	b[b]	SE	beta	b	SE	beta	b	SE	beta
Gender (female)	-.06	.03	-.03*	-.06	.03	-.03*	-.07	.02	-.03*
Age (years)	.00	.00	.05***	.00	.00	.05***	.00	.00	.05***
Education	-.01	.01	-.01	-.01	.01	-.01	-.01	.14	-.01
Efficacy	-.34	.01	-.27***	-.34	.01	-.27***	-.34	.01	-.27***
Political interest	.03	.01	.04***	.03	.01	.04***	-.01	.01	-.01
News attention	.01	.01	.01	.01	.01	.01	.01	.01	.01
Interpersonal communication	.03	.01	.05**	.03	.01	.05**	.03	.01	.05**
Unweighted news exposure	-.01	.01	-.01						
Weighted exposure; privatization				.10	.04	.05**	.16	.09	.08
Weighted exposure; personalization				-.03	.01	-.06**	-.11	.03	-.20***
UK	.21	.04	.08***	.10	.04	.04	.08	.05	.03
Spain	.17	.04	.06***	.10	.04	.04*	.09	.04	.03*
Privatization × political interest							-.01	.00	-.02
Personalization × political interest							.01	.00	.16**
Political cynicism (t1)	.51	.01	.52***	.51	.01	.51***	.51	.12	.51***
Constant	3.12	.11		3.18	.11		3.36	.12	
Adjusted R²	.47			.48			.48		
N	4,752			4,752			4,752		

SE, standard error.
[a] Using OLS regressions.
[b] Unstandardized coefficients.
* p<.05. ** p>.01, *** p>.001

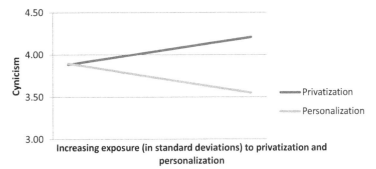

FIGURE 7.3. The change in cynicism with increasing exposure to privatization versus personalization features.

political cynicism. The model also shows a decrease in political cynicism among females and politically informed (i.e. "efficacious") respondents, but increased cynicism among elderly individuals. Higher levels of interpersonal communication and political interest among respondents also contributed to political cynicism. Model 2 demonstrates the main effects of exposure to privatization versus personalization on political cynicism. It shows that exposure to privatization in the news contributes to political cynicism, whereas exposure to personalization decreases cynical attitudes. This supports our expectations. Figure 7.3 illustrates the differential effects of exposure to privatization versus personalization on political cynicism by holding all variables constant at their mean. The slopes for the two lines are not significantly different statistically from each other: it appears that each additional "dose" of privatization and of personalization (of one standard deviation) is equal in strength, but opposite in effect, as regards political cynicism.

Model 3 in Table 7.1 is illustrated in Figure 7.4. It shows that levels of political interest moderate the relationship between exposure to personalization and change in political cynicism. For respondents with higher levels of political interest, cynicism increased after exposure to personalization. In other words, exposure to personalization decreases political cynicism only among those with lower levels of political interest. No

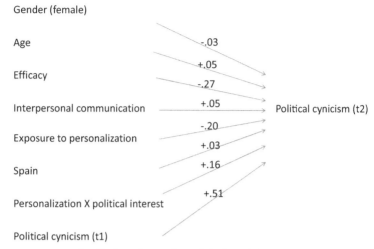

Gender (female)

Age

Efficacy

Interpersonal communication

Exposure to personalization

Spain

Personalization X political interest

Political cynicism (t1)

−.03

+.05

−.27

+.05   Political cynicism (t2)

−.20

+.03

+.16

+.51

FIGURE 7.4. Predicting change in political cynicism. *Note:* Entries are standardized beta coefficients (n=4752, adjusted R^2 .48). A positive sign of beta-coefficient indicates a positive association with political knowledge; a negative sign indicates a negative association. Only significant indicators are shown in the figure. Controls were made for education, political interest, news attention, exposure weighted by privatization, the United Kingdom, and privatization x political interest. The full regression analysis is provided in Table 7.1 (Model 3).

moderation effect is present for privatization. These findings support our expectation that privatization leads to an increase in political cynicism across the board and that the moderating function of political interest on the relationship between news exposure and political cynicism is only associated with personalization features.[11] The finding further shows that cynicism in individuals with higher levels of political interest increases with exposure to personalization features. Figure 7.5 shows that, over the whole range of data, the gap in political cynicism levels consistently widens between the politically sophisticated and the collective population samples. The columns demonstrate that an increase

---

[11] Exposure to personalization and privatization elements (combined) does not have significant effects on political cynicism. However, such exposure increases cynicism among the politically sophisticated group.

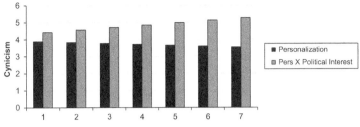

FIGURE 7.5. The change in cynicism with increasing exposure to personalization versus personalization by political interest.

in exposure to personalization of one standard deviation predicts a relatively modest decrease in political cynicism compared with a larger increase in political cynicism among individuals with high political interest. Finally, the three models show some significant country differences regarding respondents' change in cynicism.[12]

DISCUSSION

This chapter investigates the effects of exposure to infotainment news on political cynicism. The relationship is examined via two-wave panel surveys and a content analysis of national politics coverage in Denmark, Spain, and the United Kingdom. We distinguish between privatization and personalization in infotainment coverage. Privatization refers to the coverage of scandals and non-political traits of politicians, whereas personalization puts a human face on political issues by using emotionalization and focusing on human-interest stories. Our findings demonstrate that exposure to infotainment has both positive and negative effects on political cynicism, depending on the nature of the infotainment itself and on the public's interest in politics. Specifically, we found that exposure to privatized news generates cynicism among the general public, whereas exposure to personalized

---

[12] The effects of exposure to privatization and personalization frames on political cynicism are not significantly moderated by country dummies.

coverage has the reverse effect, but only among those who are less interested in politics. These results are generally consistent with research suggesting that news media effects are shaped by exposure to different types of news rather than news consumption as such (see Patterson, 1993).

Whereas previous studies have found little evidence that politicians' private lives and traits affect voting behavior (see Adam & Maier, 2010), our analysis shows that news focusing on these features increases cynical attitudes toward the political process. The privatization effect on political cynicism is seen across the board and is consistent with studies suggesting that the extensive coverage of scandals can increase disillusionment with public life (e.g., Esser, 1999). Our research coheres with strategic-framing research showing that exposure to news that deviates from public issues and that focuses on politicians' personalities induces public cynicism toward politics (e.g., Cappella & Jamieson, 1997). In the case of strategic news, focus on the political process takes priority over the focus on political substance, while in the case of privatization it is the focus on private lives that potentially drives out substance. Such findings indicate that privatization of news fails to play a positive role in a democratic system despite its potential to attract people's attention to politics.

But, personalization effects on political cynicism imply that infotainment is not necessarily a downgrading of journalistic standards. Our results show that focusing on human-interest stories and adding an emotional angle to the presentation of a political issue can have positive effects on attitudes toward the political system, at least for those with low interest in politics. Our evidence supports researchers arguing for positive influences of infotainment on citizenship and democracy (see Brants, 1998; Norris, 2000) – but we specify that these influences are limited to personalization coverage and politically less-engaged individuals. Infotainment's varying effects on political cynicism contribute to the ongoing discussion on soft news's potentially positive contribution to public life. The evidence we present (see also Chapter 6) suggests that soft news, despite its disputed effects on public knowledge about politics (see Prior, 2003b; Baum, 2002), does have the potential to contribute to the quality of democracy by making the politically less-engaged audience less cynical.

The moderating effect of political interest is evident. Cynicism increased among those who are interested in politics when they were exposed to privatization and personalization. This finding is consistent with previous research showing that political sophistication can be positively related to political cynicism (see de Vreese, 2004; Cappella & Jamieson, 1997), and demonstrates that those with higher levels of political interest are resilient to the positive effects of infotainment coverage. Personalization effects may not be particularly relevant to those who are already engaged in politics, because these citizens are more likely to be informed about politics and may have well-formed attitudes toward the political system. This may make them less able to distinguish between privatization and personalization. Both privatization and personalization exemplify episodic framing that depicts issues in terms of individual instances. Although concrete examples may encourage political reasoning and personal responsibility, they may also intensify political cynicism in those people who are already politically engaged and who are likely to have cynical attitudes about politics. Perhaps such an audience may be more inclined to judge the political system based on individual instances than those who are less interested in or less cynical about politics. Speculation aside, our research primarily suggests that the effects of episodic framing on cynicism can vary according to levels of political interest and the type of infotainment (personalization versus privatization).

Our analysis has shown that the differential presence of infotainment is more consistent among countries than between mediums or news outlets. The organizational influences on news content (see Shoemaker & Reese, 1996) should thus be seen in the light of macro-level factors related to the political and national media systems (see Hallin & Mancini, 2004b). No stark differences in infotainment coverage are found between commercial and public service television, suggesting that the latter may intersperse news with entertainment to increase the size of its "inadvertent" audience (see Curran et al., 2009). The same pattern is observed in tabloid and broadsheet newspapers; infotainment may indeed be spreading from the tabloid press into other outlets (see also Esser, 1999). The highest percentage of infotainment coverage appeared in the United Kingdom. The United Kingdom combines a classic majoritarian democracy – in which a two-party system allows the media to focus on two leaders only – with a highly commercialized system that prioritizes a more dramatized, personalized, and popularized style of reporting (see Adam & Maier, 2010). In contrast, soft news values seem to be least newsworthy in Spain. We should consider whether high degrees of political parallelism, as found in the Spanish case, also causes to journalists to be less adventurous in their reporting on politicians themselves. Finally, the content analysis demonstrates that far more personalization than privatization is present across all news outlets. This is illustrative of the "media logic" thesis, which entails a shift from news that identifies with politics and parties to news that identifies with people (see Brants, 2006).

Some concerns may be raised about our measurement of political cynicism. We measured cynicism toward politicians as individuals and not toward the political system as an institution, and the analysis showed minimal variation at the aggregate levels of cynicism.[13] We collected news content in a non-election period, which may have affected the relative presence of privatization features compared with personalization features.[14] We further limit our content analysis and exposure measures to infotainment features within different types of news media. Ideally, future studies may consider other infotainment sources, such as popular talk shows, to capture the range of this concept. Finally, relying on panel survey data makes it difficult to obtain a more nuanced interpretation of the results. Although weighting news

---

[13] Previous research has shown that trust in institutions depends largely on trust in persons (Min, 2004) and that individual-level variations are likely to shape variations at the aggregate level in the long term (e.g., Belndonet al., 1997).

[14] Analyses of election coverage have typically found that news tends to focus on candidates' strategies and personalities (e.g., Kaid & Strömbäck, 2008). This tendency may affect only the interpretation of the content data since we have used weighted exposure measures per respondent.

exposure by the share of personalized and privatized news frames produces significant main and interaction effects, it adds only little explanatory power to the model. What is the effect of being exposed to five personalization or privatization stories compared with ten? How does this effect differ among people with high and low political interest? Future research may help us find answers to such questions. This research would gain from considering the information-entertainment continuum that we set out in Chapter 1. It is evident from this chapter that some entertainment features may have less desired effects, but that other entertainment features appear harmless.

The debate about the implications of soft news for the public is widely referred to in the literature. As the lines between soft and hard news become increasingly blurred, the debate becomes even more relevant to the question of democracy. Until now, scholars have had very little empirical evidence regarding the consequences of soft news for the political process. Our findings in this chapter are a major step in this direction. We have investigated the effects of infotainment news on public political cynicism and shown that infotainment has positive effects as well as negative ones. We thus revise common overwhelmingly negative evaluations of infotainment. We propose a deconstruction of the concept and an inclusion of the political interest factor in subsequent studies addressing this debate. In the next chapter we will investigate the antecedents and dynamics of a different type of political perception – namely, satisfaction with political coverage.

8

Good Journalism, Satisfied Citizens?

HOW PERCEIVED WATCHDOG REPORTING AFFECTS
SATISFACTION WITH POLITICAL COVERAGE

Chapters 6 and 7 focused on the effects of specific content characteristics on citizens' knowledge and cynicism about politics. In this chapter we investigate the dynamics of citizens' satisfaction with political coverage. Media satisfaction is important since it is related to trust in other kinds of societal and political institutions and because the news media themselves have become an important political institution. The possible erosion in trust in media and politics has been addressed from a variety of perspectives in recent scholarship (Coleman, 2012; Quandt, 2012). We believe it is important to ground the discussion of satisfaction with political news in the practices of political journalism and the expectations that audiences have. In order to explore news satisfaction, we take a look at the watchdog journalism model and its relevance to the general public.

Central to this journalistic paradigm is the belief that journalists should carry out an investigative and watchdog role on behalf of the public (Waisbord, 2000), which finds expression in an objective, factual, and critical reporting style. An impartial approach to covering politics – focusing on factual information and balancing critique – is at the core of watchdog journalism.

In terms of our three guiding concepts (see Chapter 1) it is evident that watchdog journalism leans toward the pragmatic end of the sacerdotal-pragmatic continuum since it explicitly questions authority and the powers of politics. At the same time, however, the impartial approach and the emphasis on information places watchdog journalism toward the informative end of the information-entertainment continuum and toward the balanced end of the impartial-partisan continuum.

Although research has identified the watchdog role model as the most popular among journalists worldwide (see Weaver & Wu, 1998), the model has also been subject to much criticism regarding its applicability in journalism and its potential harm to the public. Some critics assume that the interdependence between media and politics challenges the media's ability to function as a counterweight to state power. They suggest that, by relying on officials, journalists' judgments are heavily influenced by elite sources (Entman, 2003); therefore, media coverage reflects the practices of those in power (Molotch & Lester, 1974, 111). Other critics believe that journalism has become indiscriminately critical and corrosively cynical of officials and candidates (Clayman et al., 2007, 24; see also Chapter 4). Too much critical reporting can lead to overemphasized sensational reporting that is argued to increase apathy and cynicism about politics (McNair, 2001) and to decrease news credibility (Wang & Cohen, 2009). It has been suggested that the watchdog journalism ideal may be far from universal and that its resonance with audiences varies across time and space. The rise of bloggers and social media has forced journalists in several countries to reconsider this ultimate journalistic goal – objectivity that is founded on verifiable facts (Singer, 2011). Several authors propose a more subjective journalistic style as a way to reconnect with audiences that have become used to a new, personal, journalistic style online (Rosen, 2005).

Empirical evidence supporting audience preference for neutral, factual watchdog journalism is scarce. The central goal of this chapter is to examine the effect of watchdog reporting on the dynamics of public satisfaction with political media coverage.

The chapter fills a gap in the media and communication literature by investigating the relationship between news satisfaction and some common concepts of the media's role in society. We utilize the cross-national panel survey data (see Chapter 2) to examine the antecedents and dynamics of satisfaction with political coverage. We compare Denmark, Spain, and the United Kingdom – three countries with different media systems and varying journalistic cultures (as we saw in Chapters 3 and 5) that help us to specify the mix of conditions needed for political journalism. This variation allows us to test (1) whether the differences in news content across the three countries (reported in Chapter 5) are perceived by the country's populations, and (2) whether watchdog journalism is rated as satisfactory in each of these three different contexts. If so, perceived watchdog journalism might be a key mediator between news media use and public satisfaction with political coverage.

NEWS SATISFACTION

Satisfaction has been widely studied in several social science disciplines, such as organizational communication, applied psychology, and market research, but remains a largely underexplored topic in media effects research. Communication scholars have rarely investigated satisfaction beyond the uses and gratification paradigm, which provides that "media and content choice is generally rational and directed towards certain specific goals and satisfactions" (McQuail, 2005, 424). Although satisfaction is an important antecedent to behavior (see Pinkleton & Austin, 2002), the communication field includes no satisfactory literature capable of advancing both theory and empirical research (see Patwardhan et al., 2008). Satisfaction with media coverage is described as "a general feeling of fulfillment as the result of repeated exposure to a particular content genre" (Palmgreen & Rayburn, 1985, 339), a definition that stems from consumer research, which perceives satisfaction as "a complex emotional response following experience with a product" (Oliver, 1981).

Media satisfaction has been used both as a dependent and an independent variable in media effects studies. Studies have shown that satisfaction is a significant predictor of newspaper reader-ship (Burgoon & Burgoon, 1980) and a more useful predictor of cynicism and negativism toward the media than the frequency of media use or measures of the perceived importance of the media (Pinkleton & Austin, 2002). Satisfaction is a positive predictor of using and revisiting Internet websites (Zhang & Gisela, 2000) and has been employed as a preliminary indicator for analyzing public perceptions about political balance in print and television news media (e.g., Albæk et al., 2010). Media researchers have found that higher levels of exposure affect satisfaction with tele-vision viewing (Perse & Ferguson, 1993) and that evaluations of media performance are strong predictors of overall satisfaction with cable service (Jacobs, 1995).

We conceive of news satisfaction as a response following media exposure (e.g., Perse & Ferguson, 1993; Papacharissi & Rubin, 2000; Palmgreen & Rayburn, 1985). News is a "product vested with public interest" rather than a "commodity prod-uct" (see McQuail, 2005), and an evaluation of media use is assumed to precede the feeling of satisfaction (see Patwardhan et al., 2008). This chapter first examines the effects of perceived watchdog reporting on the dynamics of news satisfaction and, second, analyzes the mediating role of watchdog reporting in the relationship between news media use and public satisfaction with political coverage.

WATCHDOG JOURNALISM

The watchdog function of journalism is at the heart of several news organizations today. The watchdog model has shaped the normative expectations we have of the media at the level of media structure (professional values and relations between the media and the state), conduct (the manner of operation), and performance (i.e., news content – what is actually transmitted to the audience) (McQuail, 2005, 192).

The watchdog model has important implications for the rela-tionship between the media and the state (media structure). This model is closely tied to the liberal press theory that emphasizes separation between media and government. While authoritarian theories hold that journalism should always be subordinate to the interests of the state in maintaining social order or achieving political goals, the liberal press theory expects the press to provide a marketplace of ideas, and sees the government as the primary (if not only) threat to press freedom. The primary duties of the press, according to the liberal theory, are to chronicle accurately the range of competing elite perspectives, to examine the character and behavior of elected officials, and to closely monitor their activities for corruption or incompetence. In other words, the press should adopt a critical, serious tone in covering public affairs, which encompass primarily the activities of government but also, in principle, those of business or other powerful social institutions (Benson, 2008, 3–5). The diffusion of power across highly differentiated political and journalistic institutions is necessary to guarantee the autonomy of journalists. Thus, major normative expectations regarding the media's role in a democracy are reflected in the watchdog ideal – including surveillance of relevant events, maintenance of media autonomy, and scrutiny of power (see Gurevitch & Blumler, 1990).

The watchdog model dominates the occupational ideology of journalists (news conduct). Even though full professionalization of journalism has been held back by the internal diversity of the media (McQuail, 2005, 288), comparative studies of journalists' profiles have identified the prevalence of common professional values that are closely related to the watchdog ideal. The degree, however, to which this model is embraced varies across journalistic cultures (van Dalen, 2012; Donsbach & Patterson, 2004; Hanitzsch, 2011). The watchdog journalist aims to contribute to the formation of an independent and democratic public opinion (Skovsgaard et al., 2013). In seeking to expose official corruption and government failures, the journalist carries weight as a player in the checks-and-balances system of a democracy (Norris, 2000). The watchdog function, also known as the "fourth estate," embodies an impartial and neutral role conception among journalists because it is based on factual reporting, and any connection between politics and journalism is weak (see Chapter 1 and Donsbach & Patterson, 2004). Watchdog journalism competes with lapdog journalism, which encompasses other journalistic paradigms that emphasize a subservient relationship with the state (see Bro, 2008; Clayman et al., 2007).

At the level of news performance (actual news content), the watchdog model has three classical elements: objectivity, factuality, and critical coverage. These news characteristics reflect the active-neutral dimension that is pivotal to the watchdog role conception among journalists.

Objectivity

The ideal of objectivity is central to journalists' professional self-perception (Weaver & Wu, 1998). Although no one can be value-neutral, journalists (and researchers) adopt like concepts, such as fairness, professional distance, or impartiality (Deuze, 2002, 12). Objective journalists are required to maintain detachment and neutrality toward the object of their reporting, to abandon partisanship and bias, and to maintain strict attachment to accuracy and other truth criteria, such as relevance and completeness (McQuail, 2005). Thus, the operationalization of objectivity often contains elements of factual reporting (Chalaby, 1998) and may be compromised by incomplete information (Austin & Pinkleton, 1999). Several newspapers conform to the concept of objectivity by distinguishing between news reporting and editorial pieces. Objectivity is often threatened by bias, which is defined as "any tendency in a news report to deviate from an accurate, neutral, balanced and impartial representation of the reality of events and [the] social world according to stated criteria" (McQuail, 2005, 548). Critics of the objectivity norm claim that it serves to hide personal bias, which journalists inevitably introduce into their writing (Shoemaker & Reese, 1996).

Factuality

Fact-centered discourse originated with the development of the commercial press, which emphasized news at the expense of political rhetoric and commentary (Hallin & Mancini, 2004b,

207). The watchdog journalist is, above all, a broker of relevant information with a distinctive, objective style of reporting based on facts (Donsbach & Patterson, 2004; see also Chapter 1). The watchdog role is meant to distinguish between factual coverage and commentary. The latter usually involves the exercise of judgments that are either normative (i.e., what is good or bad) or empirical (i.e., what is true or false) (see Benson & Hallin, 2007). Surveys across Europe on journalists' role perceptions have shown that journalists like to view themselves mostly as disseminators of news (see Weaver & Wu 1998). This specific role requires the quick reporting of hard facts to the public (see Deuze, 2002). For this reason, factuality is achieved through the "inverted pyramid" structure, which allows "the most important information" to come first, followed by progressively "less important information" (Thomson et al., 2008). In an effort to achieve factuality and to maintain an independent position, journalists emphasize the apparent objectivity of their sources – for example, by attributing facts to official sources (Ericson, 1998).

Critical Coverage

Critical reporting originates from a move in journalism toward critical professionalism, reflecting a social change: "affluence, political stability, and increasing educational levels led to a general cultural shift towards 'post-materialist' values of participation and free expression" (Hallin & Mancini, 2004b, 271). When journalists assume a critical stance toward the state, they become representatives of generalized public opinion, and their discourse is distinct from the discourse of parties and politicians (Norris, 2000). Watchdog journalists have often been adversarial and skeptical in their coverage (Patterson, 1998). In fact, several studies have shown that news content in recent years has become more critical of officials and their policies (e.g., Patterson, 1993). This development dovetails with the transition from more sacerdotal approaches to pragmatic approaches to politics (see Chapter 1). The aim of critical reporting is to safeguard effective political competition by ensuring that claims about a government's record or a candidate's qualifications for office are open to external scrutiny and evaluation (Norris, 2000, 29). Significant evidence exists today, however, that in pursuing this goal, journalists have become excessive in their critical coverage of the government (see Clayman et al., 2007 for a review).

IS WATCHDOG JOURNALISM SATISFACTORY JOURNALISM?

The main goal of this chapter is to examine the effects of perceived watchdog journalism on the dynamics of news satisfaction. Unlike previous studies that have looked at the relevance and importance of the watchdog model to journalists and media workers, the chapter takes a novel approach by evaluating the model's influence on the general public. The investigation fits in with media performance research. We strive to scrutinize some of the criticism aimed at the watchdog model as a journalistic ideal and to advance our understanding of the relationship between news media use and public satisfaction with political coverage.

First, we examine the effects of perceived watchdog reporting on news satisfaction dynamics. Since critics and political journalists generally uphold the watchdog model as the ideal one (e.g., Weaver and Wu, 1998), we expect the public to associate it with "good journalism" as well. Thus, we hypothesize that public perception of the fulfillment of watchdog criteria in political reporting is positively related to public satisfaction with political news.

Second, we investigate the influence of perceived watchdog reporting on the relationship between news exposure and satisfaction with political coverage. Scholars contend that focusing on media use as an independent variable usually has a significant impact on the outcomes of media research (see Pinkleton & Austin, 2002). Previous studies have shown a positive correlation between news exposure and public perceptions of media performance, such as those related to credibility assessments (e.g., Rimmer & Weaver, 1985). In this chapter we introduce perceptions of watchdog reporting as a mediator in the relationship between media use and news satisfaction. More precisely, we postulate that the potential effects of news exposure on satisfaction with political coverage can be partly explained by the perception of watchdog journalism.

Taking advantage of our cross-national design, we investigate whether differences in news satisfaction can be explained by the perceived presence (or absence) of watchdog journalism. Watchdog journalism originated in the United States (Challaby, 1996; Schudson, 1978). After the Second World War, commercialization and journalistic professionalization helped spread this Anglo-American news-making ideal throughout the world (Hallin & Mancini, 2004a). Several scholars, however, have argued that the watchdog ideal is not applicable as a journalistic model outside the West (Josephi, 2005). Mancini (2000) has argued that the watchdog model does not describe journalistic practice in Italy, which, like Spain, belongs to the polarized pluralist media system. Content analysis has indeed shown that in southern Europe, journalism is often characterized by partisanship (Roncarolo, 2009) and a more literary reporting style (Benson & Hallin, 2007), which are at odds with the watchdog ideal as described here. The content analysis presented in Chapter 5 confirms that Spanish journalism is less critical and more partisan than journalism in northern Europe. It remains an empirical question as to whether audiences in different countries are sensitive to these cross-national differences. If cross-national differences in watchdog journalism can explain differences in news satisfaction, we can conclude that the watchdog model travels well among audiences.

RESULTS

Perceived Watchdog Journalism and Satisfaction

We start our analysis by providing an initial insight into the perceived watchdog style in the three countries. To measure perceived watchdog reporting, we asked respondents to rate each news outlet (per country) according to the following watchdog criteria: objective, informative, and critical-of-government news reporting.[1] The question was: "Media are different in the way they operate and cover issues. Using the scale provided, please rate each of the following media." The scale ranges from (1) operating not according to "watchdog criteria" at all, to (7) operating very much according to "watchdog criteria." An additive measure of perceived watchdog reporting was then formed for respondents completing all items ratings.

In Chapter 5 we saw that the reporting style of Spanish journalists is more partisan and less pragmatic than that of their colleagues in northern Europe. These cross-national differences are recognized by the audience. Danes (M[mean]=4.5, SD=.72) and Britains (M=4.4, SD=.88) perceive the journalistic style of their media to be significantly more in line with the watchdog ideal than the does the general population in Spain (M=4.2, SD=.89).[2]

---

[1] The following are the mean scores per country on a scale from 1 (not satisfied at all) to 7 (very satisfied): DK wave I, M=4.41, SD=1.33, DK wave II, M=4.51, SD=1.35; UK wave I, M=3.99, SD=1.39, UK wave II, M=4.09, SD=1.35; ES wave I, M=3.71, SD=1.41, ES wave II, M=3.82, SD=1.42. To test for potential sensitization effects, fresh samples of approximately 200 respondents each in all three countries answered the satisfaction question in wave II of the panel. The mean scores for the new samples showed no substantial difference to mean scores calculated for respondents taking part in both panel waves.

[2] Media exposure (outlet level): number of days (per week) using each news outlet, ranging from 0 (none) to 7 (seven days). DK: DR1, M=3.23, SD=2.32; TV2, M=4.0, SD=2.4; *Politiken*, M=.91, SD=2.0; JyllandsPosten, M=.78, SD=1.81; EkstraBladet, M=.78, SD=1.76. UK: BBC, M=2.44, SD=2.32; ITV, M=1.33, SD=1.94; The Guardian M=.46, SD=1.28; Daily Telegraph, M=.55, SD=1.54; The Sun, M=.66, SD=1.65. ES: TVE, M=2.21, SD=2.30; Antena 3, M=3, SD=2.47; Informativos, M=2.72, SD=2.37; ABC, M=.66, SD=1.56; El Pais, M=1.28, SD=2.07; El Mundo, M=1.20, SD=2.08. The questions on rating news outlets are included only in wave II of the panel. The sample size changes according to the number of respondents who report reading or watching a particular news outlet. The sample size of respondents completing all watchdog ratings: DK, N=688; UK, N=735; ES, N=1,092. The scale includes a "don't know" option that is treated in the analysis as not answered. Observations for each watchdog criteria were stacked together, regardless of news outlet or country type, to form a single dataset (N=19,107). A principal component analysis with orthogonal varimax rotation was conducted for the three selected dimensions of watchdog reporting, and confirmed

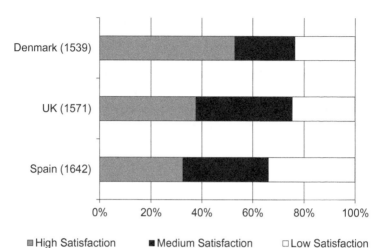

■High Satisfaction   ■ Medium Satisfaction   □ Low Satisfaction

FIGURE 8.1. Satisfaction with national politics coverage at the aggregate level.

The Spanish audience is also the least satisfied with media coverage. To measure audience satisfaction with political coverage, we asked the respondents to answer the following question: "How satisfied or not are you with the way in which national politics is covered by the media in general?"[3] Figure 8.1 shows aggregate news satisfaction per country. The chart shows that Denmark comprises the largest proportion of highly satisfied individuals (55 percent), followed by the UK (40 percent), then Spain (33 percent). Denmark also has the smallest proportion of dissatisfied respondents (20 percent), followed by the UK (26 percent) and Spain (34 percent). Figure 8.1 further shows that moderately satisfied to highly satisfied panelists outnumber

the presence of a single factor with an eigenvalue exceeding 1, explaining 60% of the total variance. Eigenvalue for the single factor: 1.81. Items loading on the watchdog factor: "objective" = 0.88, "informative" = 0.87, "critical to government" = 0.51.

[3] ANOVA showed a significant mean difference between these scales: $F(2, 2,530)=29.92$, $p<0.0001$. Multiple comparisons using the Bonferroni adjustment showed a significant mean difference only between Spain and the United Kingdom $(=-.21, p<0.0001)$ and between Spain and Denmark $(=-.30, p<0.0001)$.

dissatisfied panelists in the Danish and the British sample, while respondents in the Spanish sample are homogenously distributed over all three categories. On average, respondents in Denmark and the UK showed the highest levels of overall satisfaction with political coverage, and those in Spain the lowest.

On the aggregate level we find a relationship between perceived watchdog reporting and news satisfaction. The Spanish public, which judges the news to be least in line with the watchdog model, is also the least satisfied with news coverage. To see whether this relationship also holds at the individual level, we turn to multivariate analysis and run models predicting satisfaction with political coverage in the first wave of the survey. Table 8.1 reports the results of two multiple OLS regressions for each of the three countries (before and after accounting for perceived watchdog reporting in the analysis). In the models, we control for gender (coded as female), age (in years), education,[4] political ideology, and political interest, since these variables may potentially influence news satisfaction. The descriptives and specific wordings for the controls can be found in the Appendix to Chapter 8.

Model 1 shows that media use is a significant positive predictor of satisfaction with political coverage in all three countries. However, the significant effect of news exposure on satisfaction is indirect, which can be seen when controlling for respondents' watchdog-reporting perceptions. The effect of watchdog perceptions is significant in all three contexts (see model 2). The inclusion of watchdog perceptions into the model substantially increases our understanding of respondents' satisfaction levels. Model 2 explains variation in news satisfaction by 20 percent in Denmark, 16 percent in Spain, and 10 percent in the United Kingdom compared with model 1, which only accounts for 4, 2, and 1 percent, respectively, of the variation in the three countries. The relationship between perceived watchdog journalism and satisfaction of coverage that was found at the country level

---

[4] The respondents' education levels were recoded due to differences in the education systems across the three countries (see Appendix 8.1).

TABLE 8.1. Explaining[a] News Satisfaction at Wave I of the Survey

	Denmark				United Kingdom				Spain			
	Model 1		Model 2[b]		Model 1		Model 2		Model 1		Model 2	
	beta[c]	SE	beta	SE	beta	SE	beta	SE	beta	SE	beta	SE
Gender (female)	.05*	.07	.04	.10	.01	.07	.01	.10	.04	.07	−.05*	.08
Age (in years)	.04	.00	.04	.00	−.00	.00	−.07*	.00	.03	.00	.02	.003
Education	−.13***	.03	−.13***	.04	−.00	.04	.01	.06	−.08**	.04	−.07*	.05
Ideology	.11***	.01	.01	.02	.07**	.02	.07	.02	−.00	.01	−.03	.02
Political interest	.00	.02	−.05	.03	.05	.02	.06	.03	.10***	.02	.07	.02
News exposure	.09**	.03	.05	.04	.07**	.04	.03	.04	.07**	.02	.00	.03
Watchdog perceptions			.38***	.07			.29***	.05			.37***	.04
Adjusted R²	0.04		0.20		0.01		0.10		0.02		0.16	
N	1,425		673		1,292		673		1,545		1,048	

[a] Using OLS regressions.
[b] Model 2 includes only respondents who answered the watchdog perception items.
* p < .05, ** p < .01, *** p < .001.

154

is therefore confirmed at the individual level in a cross-sectional design.

Explaining Change in Satisfaction

Our panel design allows for an even stronger test to determine whether perceived watchdog journalism leads to news satisfaction. For this analysis we combine the data from the three different countries in one analysis. Between the two panel waves, the aggregate levels of news satisfaction have increased slightly. We use dynamic pooled OLS regression models to examine whether this change in satisfaction with political coverage is (at least partly) a function of watchdog reporting perceptions. Pooled OLS regressions allow us to establish a causal relationship between news satisfaction and the perception of watchdog reporting by controlling for respondents' initial levels of news satisfaction in the first wave of the panel survey (see e.g., de Vreese, 2005; de Vreese & Semetko, 2002 for similar analysis technique). In addition, we control for news attention and interpersonal communication. Political interest has been linked empirically to media use (Luskin, 1990) and news attention (Slater, 2004), while interpersonal discussion is considered a conduit for gaining second-hand information from the news (Scheufele, 2002). Finally, since our sample comes from three different populations, we control for country effects.[5] Similar control variables are used in the mediation analysis. The descriptives and specific wordings for the controls can be found in the Appendix to Chapter 8.

Table 8.2 displays the results of two multiple OLS regressions (before and after accounting for perceived watchdog reporting in the analysis). Model 1 shows that attention to the news increases satisfaction with political coverage, whereas interpersonal communication decreases news satisfaction. News exposure has no

---

[5] Bivariate regression models (per country) showed similar results in terms of direction and strength.

TABLE 8.2. *Predicting[a] Change in Satisfaction with Political Coverage*

	Model 1		Model 2[b]	
	beta[c]	SE	beta	SE
News satisfaction, wave I	.50***	.01	.40***	.01
Interpersonal communication	−.04**	.01	−.04*	.01
News attention	.11***	.01	.06**	.01
News exposure	.01	.01	−.02	.01
Denmark	.11***	.04	.02	.05
United Kingdom	.05***	.04	.00	.05
Watchdog perceptions			.36***	.02
Adjusted R²	0.304		0.42	
N	4,751		2,545	

SE, standard error.
[a] Using OLS regressions.
[b] Model 2 includes only respondents who answered the watchdog perception items.
[c] Standardized beta coefficient.
*** $p < 0.001$, ** $p < 0.01$, * $p < 0.05$.

effect on the dynamics of news satisfaction. The model also shows significant country differences for respondents' change in levels of news satisfaction. Model 2, also visualized in Figure 8.2, shows that perceived watchdog reporting is the strongest predictor of news satisfaction: the more the respondents perceived news reporting to be following the watchdog model, the more their satisfaction levels increased between the two panel waves. Including perceived watchdog reporting in the analysis increases our understanding of the variation in the dependent variable by more than 10 percent. The effects of news attention and interpersonal communication are reduced, but remain significant after controlling for watchdog-reporting perceptions. The differences between the countries, however, are no longer significant: differences in perceiving watchdog reporting seem to explain the difference in news satisfaction between Denmark, Germany, and Spain. These results support our expectation that perceived watchdog

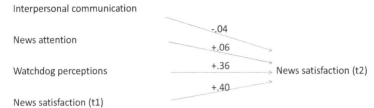

FIGURE 8.2. Predicting change in satisfaction with political coverage. *Note*: Entries are standardized beta coefficients (n=2,545, adjusted R^2 .42). A positive sign of beta-coefficient indicates a positive association with political knowledge; a negative sign indicates a negative association. Only significant indicators are shown in the figure. Controls were made for news exposure, Denmark, and the United Kingdom. The full regression analysis is provided in Table 8.2 (Model 2).

journalism is an important predictor of satisfaction with political news.[6]

We then turn to mediation analysis to test our second research question. A variable may be called a mediator "to the extent that it accounts for the relation between the predictor and the criterion" (Baron & Kenny, 1986, 1176). The traditional approach to testing mediation is the causal-step approach, in which all causal steps are tested separately. This approach requires a significant effect of the independent variable *(X)* on the mediator *(M)* and of the mediator on the dependent variable *(Y)*. In addition, a significant total effect of X on Y must be present initially, and Y should not cause M (Baron & Kenny, 1986). Figure 8.3 outlines the relationship we are interested in.

After controlling for the mediator in the model, the mediation is deemed to have occurred if the total effect has decreased

---

[6] We have relied on a generalized satisfaction measure for a comprehensive notion of this concept. The sampled news outlets are representative of some of the most important national news sources in each country. Future research may consider measuring news satisfaction per outlet to provide greater detail about the relationship between news satisfaction and watchdog-reporting perceptions. Our analysis has essentially shown that news satisfaction is largely dependent on public perceptions of political news coverage.

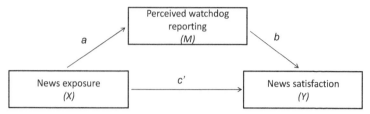

FIGURE 8.3. Model of the mediating influence of perceived watchdog reporting on the relationship between news exposure and news satisfaction.

to zero (perfect mediation) or to a non-trivial amount (partial mediation). The causal-step strategy has been criticized for having low statistical power, type I and type II errors, and for not yielding any point estimate or standard error of the mediation effect (Preacher & Hayes, 2004; 2008). Further, the literature is in disagreement on whether an initial total effect of X on Y should be significant (see Preacher & Hayes, 2008).

Instead of the causal step approach, we use Preacher and Hayes's (2004) methodology for indirect effects to test the role of perceived watchdog reporting as a mediator. This formal significance test utilizes a bootstrap method that addresses mediation effects more directly than the causal-step strategy. Several studies have used the bootstrap method to examine indirect relationships (e.g., Brandt & Reyna, 2010; Birnie et al., 2009; Buffardi & Campbell, 2008). The "bootstrapping" is achieved by taking a large number of samples from the data and computing the individual indirect effect for each sample (Preacher & Hayes, 2004). The distributions of these indirect estimates serve as empirical, non-parametric approximations of the sampling distribution of the indirect effect under study (Preacher & Hayes, 2008). In this chapter we calculated bootstrap estimates for the indirect effect of perceived watchdog reporting using 5,000 bootstrap samples and 90% bias-corrected and accelerated confidence intervals for those estimates – the equivalent of a one-tailed significance test. Interpretation of the bootstrap data is accomplished by determining whether zero is contained within the 90% confidence intervals (thus indicating the lack of significance).

TABLE 8.3. *Static[a] and Dynamic[b] Mediation of the Indirect Effect of Watchdog Perceptions on Satisfaction with Political Coverage*

	Point Estimate	BCa 90% CI	
		Upper	Lower
Static indirect effect			
Watchdog perceptions	0.0632	0.0481	0.0796
Dynamic indirect effect			
Watchdog perceptions	0.0454	0.0326	0.0590

BCa 90% CI, bias corrected and accelerated bootstrapping confidence intervals.
[a] Static model controls include gender, age, education, ideology, political interest, and country dummies. N=2,382; 5,000 bootstrap samples.
[b] Dynamic model controls include news attention, interpersonal communication, and country dummies. N=2,533; 5,000 bootstrap samples.

We use the OLS regression models investigating the antecedents and dynamics of news satisfaction (see Tables 8.1 and 8.2) for the mediation analysis. The separate prediction models of news satisfaction are pooled into a single model before undergoing static mediation analysis. Table 8.3 reports the estimates of the indirect effect of perceived watchdog reporting for the static and dynamic OLS regression models (see the method section for the list of controls), and the 90% bias-corrected and accelerated confidence intervals for those estimates. If zero is contained within the 90% confidence intervals, the indirect effect estimates are interpreted as non-significant. Table 8.3 shows that the 90% confidence intervals for the static and dynamic OLS regression models do not contain zero, thus confirming our second expectation that perceptions of watchdog reporting significantly mediate the effect of media use on satisfaction with political coverage.

DISCUSSION

In this chapter we explored the antecedents and process of news satisfaction. We looked at the relationship between perceptions of watchdog coverage, media use, and news satisfaction dynamics in three different media systems. Citizens in Denmark and Britain perceive their media to act more as watchdogs than do citizens in Spain. Danish citizens are by far the most satisfied with their media's coverage of politics, followed by the United Kingdom. In Spain, the satisfaction is the lowest, with more than one-third being outright dissatisfied. The analysis shows that perceived watchdog reporting increases satisfaction with political coverage; the more respondents perceive news media to perform according to the watchdog journalistic ideal, the more they are satisfied with the overall coverage of national politics. The analysis further shows that respondents' perceptions of watchdog coverage mediate the effects of news exposure on satisfaction with political coverage. These relationships were investigated through a two-wave panel survey. Likert-scale measures were calculated for respondents' personal evaluations of national news outlets according to the watchdog-model criteria.

Journalism researchers generally agree about the inadequacy of the watchdog model as an empirical journalistic standard (see Clayman et al., 2007). Objectivity, informational quality, and critical stances to power holders do not always go together. That said, the evidence provided in this chapter suggests a rather favorable public perception of that model. Perceived watchdog characteristics in the news proved to be important determinants of the viewers' qualitative media experience. Thus, the general public's appreciation of the watchdog model is evident, regardless of critics' fears that it may eventually lead to cynicism and disaffection with politics (see earlier discussion). The significance of perceived watchdog news is not merely confined to its positive influence on public satisfaction with political coverage; rather, watchdog news also explains the mechanism that underlies the observed effects of media use on news satisfaction dynamics. Critics have claimed that there is potential conflict between the ideal of objectivity and the need for the journalist to function as an active watchdog in the public interest. These critics argue that the watchdog model, because of its critical nature (see Entman, 1989), requires journalists to actively select and shape news information and that, in practice, the line between "reporting" and "interpretation" often becomes blurred (Norris, 2000). This chapter has shown, however, that being critical of government is not at odds with the objectivity norm in the minds of the public. The respondents had no problem evaluating news content as critical and, at the same time, as informative and objective. Previous survey research has shown a similar affinity between the watchdog role and the objectivity ideal among journalists; the watchdog role, it is argued, can motivate journalists to conform to the objectivity ideal so that they can defend themselves against accusations of political and ideological bias (Skovsgaard et al., 2013). Although journalists' role conceptions may differ in various countries (McQuail, 2005, 287), the effects of perceived watchdog reporting on people's news satisfaction dynamics do not differ. It is interesting to note that citizens seem to be able to combine the multiple dimensions in their evaluation. As argued in Chapter 1, political journalism flourishes mostly when the right mix of conditions is present. Arguably, the findings in this chapter are an indication that citizens can deal with multiple dimensions.

Some concerns may be raised about our measurement and analysis. We have used a generalized measure of news satisfaction, but our watchdog perception scales are drawn from evaluations of a limited number of news outlets.[7] Furthermore, the analysis in this chapter lacks model comparison. We have estimated the effects only of perceived watchdog reporting on news satisfaction dynamics; the relative impact of the watchdog model on those dynamics versus other news-reporting paradigms remains undecided.[8]

---

[7] We have avoided forced media estimates in this chapter by adding a "don't know" option to our evaluation scales so that only respondents who are familiar with the actual news coverage provide news performance judgments. Including this option, however, greatly reduced the size of our samples.

[8] Future research on the influence of several, competing news-reporting models on satisfaction with political coverage would further our knowledge about the relationships investigated in this chapter and would likely increase our understanding of the variation in news-satisfaction dynamics.

This chapter describes a cross-national approach to the examination of the relationship between perceived watchdog reporting and news satisfaction dynamics. The effects of perceived watchdog reporting on news satisfaction dynamics were highly positive in all three countries. Linking perceived watchdog journalism with the actual news content as presented in Chapter 5, we see that cross-national differences in content dovetail with cross-national differences in watchdog perception. The Spanish audience is significantly less satisfied with news content, which Spaniards (correctly) perceive as less critical and less objective. Our results show that the watchdog model is well received by audiences across Europe. The Anglo-American news-making ideal has spread through increasingly professional journalism education and an increasingly internationally connected media industry (Hallin & Mancini, 2004a). Through exposure to news on foreign channels, journalistic discourse, and movies (such as *All the President's Men* and other popular representations of watchdog journalists), the public has likewise come to recognize and appreciate objectivity, factuality, and critical reporting as synonyms of good journalism.

As is so often the case, high-minded concepts such as objectivity, factuality, and critical reporting can be understood differently by different people and can be used and abused. Consider the U.S. Fox News slogan, "Fair and balanced," for instance. Socialist newspaper readers will perceive their preferred newspaper as the most truthful, objective, and critical, while they will perceive a right-leaning newspaper as biased. Conservative newspaper readers might have exactly the opposite perception (Albæk et al., 2010; Christen et al., 2002). Even if the watchdog model, despite its critique, were to become a worldwide proxy "label" of good journalism, viewers and readers might perceive very different media outlets as living up to these standards. Therefore, one has to be wary of extrapolating what news people will actually watch or buy from their expressed preferred journalistic model. Hallin (2009), for example, found that certain newspapers in Italy that tried to adhere to the Anglo-American ideal failed to gain market share; this situation was reversed only when they started supporting a political party. De Miguel and Pozas (2009) showed how the Spanish newspaper El Mundo drew readers away from ABC by presenting more partisan coverage. Taking this line of selective self-exposure one step further, we can speculate that audiences may not only opt for media outlets that concur with their own political preferences (as the self-selection literature would predict), but perhaps the watchdog function is also a parameter influencing media choice.

Audience research is often conducted for commercial purposes, and has been used as a primary tool for close control and management (see McQuail, 2005). Because of the prevailing focus on commercial audience research, few studies have examined the relevance to the public of normative journalism models. This chapter analyzed the antecedents and dynamics of public satisfaction with political coverage. Although critics challenge the capacity of the watchdog model to shape the actual practice of journalism or to serve as an adequate counterweight to official power (see Clayman et al., 2007, 24), the fourth-estate ideal is apparently largely representative of international audience beliefs and expectations regarding the function of news media in democratic societies. Thus, cross-nationally, citizens have similar expectations of the media that determine their level of contentment with political news coverage. There are important differences, however, in what they actually get and in how satisfied they are. In the final chapter we turn to the lessons learned about the relationship between political journalism, political news coverage, and the effects on citizens and the specification of the right mix of conditions for political journalism.

9

Political Journalism

Today and Tomorrow

It is a truism that political journalism is not the same everywhere at all times. Political journalism is constantly developing; it has a reciprocal relationship with politics, it is highly responsive to changes in society, and it is itself responsible for social changes. Our starting point in Chapter 1 was that different conditions lead to differences in the content of political journalism, and these differences in content are likely to have different effects on different segments of the population. This starting point may seem tautologous, but our actual knowledge about the relationships between conditions and content, and content and its effects, is limited – particularly regarding the *dynamics* of these relationships.

In this book we investigate political journalism cross-nationally and test, reassess, and further develop a set of key propositions regarding the influence of news media on the general public, at a time when the nature of political reporting has changed. We refused to join a vocal chorus of pessimism and negativity about the quality of political journalism a priori. Instead, we expected that some types of journalism would be conducive to political knowledge, audience satisfaction, and engaged citizenship, whereas other types of journalism would have either less positive or no effects.

The book centers around three key concepts: the sacerdotal versus pragmatic journalistic approach to politics, the impartial versus partisan nature of political journalism and journalists, and the informational versus entertainment role of journalists. We look at how these concepts work out cross-nationally, how they affect the type and content of political reporting, and how they condition the effects of political news. In doing so, we explicitly aim to connect research on journalism and media sociology with research on political communication and media effects.

In this concluding chapter we ask if political journalism is ultimately similar or different in different media and political systems. How do journalists perceive themselves in different systems, and how does that self-perception affect their coverage? What effects does political journalism have in different countries? Are citizens satisfied with their political news? And if different conditions create different kinds of political journalism – including the kind that informs, entertains, and increases satisfaction with both democracy and political journalism – what can be done to facilitate this "virtuous circle"? First, we recap our most important findings. They are cast in the light of the broader trends in political communication that we outlined in Chapter 1. We then reflect on our research model and the extent to which journalistic practice is affected by differences in conditions. We conclude by linking our findings to a broader discussion of the media's role in democratic processes.

KEY FINDINGS

Our findings show, on the whole, a coherent picture with important ramifications for our understanding of the news media in Western democracies. Despite wide-ranging claims about the demise of political journalism, a worsening relationship between politicians and the media, and the decreasing quality of political news, we find that journalists and politicians can coexist when political control or market pressures are not all-pervasive. When news about politics is packaged in an accessible way, citizens can learn from it, and when the conditions are right, citizens are highly satisfied with the news media. Such conclusions differ from those of Curran and Seaton (2010) on the United Kingdom, the works of Fallows (1996) and Patterson (2000b) on the United States, and Mazzoleni and Schulz's (1999) warnings about mediatization. We are confident in our empirical findings. We have taken some important steps in regard to method and design: whereas most studies on media and democracy in different countries tend to rely on single-country studies, which are then examined side by side (e.g., Gunther & Mughan, 2000), truly comparative studies are few and far between. Those comparative studies that do focus on media content cross-nationally (e.g., Esser, 2008; de Vreese et al., 2006) do not include public opinion. The comparative study by Iyengar et al. (2010) and the collaborative project led by Aalberg (Aalberg & Curran, 2012) are two of the few exceptions because they rely on both survey and media content data. However, much as there is to admire in the latter study, it has the inherent shortcoming of relying on cross-sectional data. Cross-sectional data limits the inferences that can be drawn about the causality of relationships and the assessments that can be made of the extent of self-selection effects on outcomes (as the authors acknowledge, e.g., Jenssen, Aalberg, & Aarts, 2012, 156). We have extended and improved a similar design by incorporating panel survey data that enable us to study change while providing additional credibility to our conclusions about media effects. Many studies cannot fully assess whether they are picking up media effects or self-selection effects – for example, when politically interested and well-educated citizens select specific media outlets that are conducive to their level of political knowledge. We are in a position to offer more conclusive evidence due to the nature of the panel study and our exploration of the dynamics involved. In fact, previous research may have erroneously concluded that the media's impact is limited because too much credit was given to the self-selection hypothesis.

Our central claim is that different conditions lead to journalists' approaching politics differently, that these approaches shape their political coverage, and that the resulting political coverage has real implications for citizens' knowledge gains, political attitudes, and satisfaction with the news media. This corroborates and extends Aalberg and Curran's (2012, 189) conclusion: "How a nation organizes its television system influences its supply and consumption of news." We began by asking, "Who are the political journalists and how do they approach politics?" Contrary to popular belief, political journalists are not left-wing political missionaries (see also Albæk et al., 2010), and most reporters consider themselves politically centrist. The majority has a relatively sacerdotal approach to politics; although political events must meet conventional news-selection criteria to become news, journalists maintain an intrinsic respect toward politics and the belief that providing political information is a core function of the news media. Sacerdotalism in its pure form may not be the flavor of the day, but politics is still considered important per se. News values, however, determine which stories about politics are reported and how they are framed. While journalists share a belief in the importance of politics, there is little evidence of the singular, converged notion of political journalism predicted by Hallin and Mancini (2004a); important differences exist between the countries.

Cynical journalists? While political journalists have yet to abandon sacerdotalism, and are generally pragmatic when selecting news about politics, they may nonetheless have cynical attitudes vis-à-vis politicians. Our study shows that journalists are weary of media professionals and spin doctors who (along with politicians) attempt to manipulate the media. Our findings also suggest important cross-national differences: Spanish journalists are the most cynical, and Danish, the least. Political pressure is another key reason for political cynicism: autonomous journalists are less cynical. Thus, the media as a societal institution, and the way it is organized, contribute to the formation of journalists' attitudes toward politicians.

Believing and doing? A key question arising from our observations of journalists' attitudes is whether there is a relationship between "believing and doing." That is, do the role conceptions of journalists help mold their behavior and the actual journalistic products? While the relationship is not clear-cut, undoubtedly journalists' role perceptions and perceived constraints are reflected in their reporting. Specifically, Spanish news features less conflict and controversy than do both British and Danish news. Spanish journalists feel less at liberty to showcase political conflict and to use game frames. At the other end of the spectrum, Danish journalists feel the least political pressure and UK journalists entertain the most in their coverage. We do not find systematic political biases in the news, although the Spanish media tend to evaluate politicians according to partisan lines.

Learning from the news? Do these differences in political coverage have an impact on citizens' political knowledge? Political knowledge is an indispensable requirement for democracy, and one of the most important tasks entrusted to the media is to provide access to political information. While critics in the United States have suggested that citizens gain little from news media coverage that lacks contextualized political information (e.g., Bennett, 2003), we offer a different perspective. By means of our unique design (using two-wave panel survey data and media content analyses), we show how the news media, by presenting politics in an enticing way, can spark political learning. Contrary to common wisdom, we show that conflict and human-interest framing is conducive to knowledge gain, especially in those among the public with the least interest in politics.

Cynical citizens? Presentation styles in political journalism may not only affect knowledge but may also affect audiences' impressions of politics and politicians. In the literature, infotainment is often considered "bad for democracy." Many of these claims are based on arguments rather than on evidence. We disentangle the infotainment concept by distinguishing between personalization and privatization in the news. Privatization is a focus on politicians' private lives and scandals, and this type of coverage may indeed lead to increased levels of political cynicism. But personalization – providing human examples and a focus on individuals – does not. We contend that such features of news coverage are natural and integral to news journalism (see also Delli Carpini & Williams, 2001). They are neither unequivocally positive nor negative for democracy at large.

Happy citizens? Citizens are not always satisfied with their political news. Fallows (1996) boldly proclaims that "Americans hate the press," and Cook et al. (2000, 2) state that the "unpopularity of the news media is taken nowadays to be so obvious that it barely deserves discussion." We disagree. Granted, their observations pertain in particular to the United States, but what conditions have given rise to such conclusions? In the U.S. literature, market pressures and partisan media coverage are among the culprits that have been held responsible for citizens' negative attitudes toward the media (Cook et al., 2000; Iyengar & Kahn, 2008). In our study we find that political pressure and interference with the media are the biggest obstacles to public satisfaction with the news media – a situation exemplified by Spain, where satisfaction is the lowest and perceived political pressure the highest. In other words, the more political pressure, the less satisfaction. In contrast, when citizens perceive that journalists are fulfilling the watchdog function, they are more satisfied with media performance and the role of the media as a political institution.

LESSONS LEARNED

In Chapter 1 we argued that the conditions under which politicians, journalists, and audiences interact influence the type of contribution that political journalism can make to the democratic process. The three key concepts that guided our investigation of the production, contents, and effects of political journalism can help us to specify the mix of conditions that are most conducive to a positive role for political journalism.

Sacerdotal-Pragmatic. Our investigation shows that how political journalists view and approach politics matters for the attention devoted to politics in the news and the way in which the news is framed. The more pragmatic the approach to politics, for example, the greater the likelihood of applying news frames such as conflict and human interest. Spanish news features less conflict and controversy than do both British and Danish news, and Spanish journalists feel less at liberty to showcase political conflict and to use game frames. These frames in turn can effect what citizens learn from the news. As concluded earlier, sacerdotalism is replaced by pragmatism in many places, but even so there is only little evidence of the converged, universal notion of political journalism.

Impartial-Partisan. The relationship between politics and journalism and the extent to which political journalists perceive autonomy from, in particular, political pressure and political spin in their work was a core focus. Spanish media, for example, were more partisan in their news coverage than in the other countries. These differences in the coverage are observed by citizens, and the perception of objectivity and factuality affect how satisfied citizens are and how they rate their political news media.

Information-Entertainment. A final focus was on the degree to which political journalists see themselves as having informative or entertaining functions. We found that entertainment features in news can entice and excite audiences and help them learn about politics, but also make audiences turn cynical if there is too much focus on politicians' private lives, for example.

If we look across the empirical results of the different chapters, in relation to our key concepts, we identify *a high degree of professionalization in journalism, a low degree of political parallelism, a strong public broadcasting system, and moderate degrees of commercialization and competition as the right mix for political journalism.* The presence of one of these conditions is important and necessary, but not sufficient, for political journalism to play a positive role. It is the *combination* that provides the right mix.

Picking up from Chapter 1, we can also revisit some of the contextual trends that shape the conditions of journalism. First, our empirical findings confirm the influential role played by the *professionalization* of politics in the relationship between journalists and politicians in all the countries under study. Political PR and spin are among the most important limitations on the perceived freedom of journalists. About half of the political journalists in each country believe that spin doctors limit journalists in their work, and feel that politicians will do anything to gain the media's attention. Cross-national differences in political cynicism among journalists can be largely explained by their relationship with politicians and politicians' spin doctors. Our findings show that the professionalization of politics is a double-edged sword. In the short term, politicians may be successful in getting their message across to the public and keeping unflattering information out of the news. But this advantage comes at a price. Standing in front of cameras with insignificant and prefabricated messages, and limiting access to information, creates more cynical and skeptical journalists.

Although the professionalization of politics is a significant factor affecting journalistic attitudes and content in all countries, our study shows that the nature of its impact and the pace of its development vary widely across countries. The United Kingdom is generally seen as the front-runner in the professionalization of political communication (Esser & Spanjer, 2005). In Spain, the global trend of spin doctors has only been observed in more recent years (Sampedro & Seoane Pérez, 2008). Although the professionalization of political communication is less developed in Spain than in the United Kingdom, Spanish journalists are the most negative about politicians' and their spin doctors' communication, and the most cynical about politics. A possible interpretation of this state of affairs is that journalists are most cynical about professionalization when it is relatively new (Spain). Given time, as journalists learn to play the game (as in the United Kingdom) and the excessive attention to spin wears off (see Vliegenthart et al., 2011), the situation normalizes. Additionally, journalists in the United Kingdom can channel their negativity and disgruntlement into their political writings. Spanish journalists are more constrained in this regard, as is clear from their comments on autonomy and the content analysis presented in Chapter 5. The professionalization of politics is not a linear development – what happens in one country will not inevitably follow in all others.

The frequent use of strategy and game framing, and the attention paid (in some countries) to scandals and the private lives of politicians, is the price politicians pay for professionalizing their communication and yielding to media salacity (Holz-Bacha, 2004; Esser, 2001). But this cost is not borne by politicians alone; democracy suffers because news focusing on scandals and politicians' private lives increases political cynicism (Chapter 7). Tabloid media – in which scandals and details of private lives are highly visible – are the least appreciated by citizens. These results emphasize the impact that the professionalization of politics has on journalistic practice and journalism's effects. When professional relationships are maintained between politicians and journalists, journalists are less cynical and citizens are more satisfied with the news.

Moreover, our findings provide some antidote to the fear that, over the years, profit orientation has become an increasingly important factor in understanding how journalists work. Critics feared that the encroachment of entertainment values and the evolution of news into a commodity would spell the demise of political news. Our findings do not confirm this concern. In Denmark, Germany, and the United Kingdom, political journalists do not overtly perceive that audience figures, budget cuts, or competition with other media limit their work. In fact, we have shown that political journalists are shielded from commercial influences – unlike other reporters, such as foreign correspondents or general reporters (van Dalen & Skovsgaard, 2010). Since politicians are eager to be in the news, and political journalists work on a beat, the journalists' job is cost-effective. In addition, news media use political news to effectively brand themselves (McNair 2000); Kavanagh (2011) confirmed that the British political beat was actively upgraded at the beginning of the twenty-first century, while other beats were downgraded.

Strengthening the political beat at the cost of other beats might translate into more political news and more attention devoted to the work of government. Our content analysis confirms that political news features prominently on the front pages of the major newspapers and in the television news. Consolidating the political beat, however, may reinforce a top-down perspective on democracy – journalists report from within the political-media complex (Swanson, 1992) with a narrow focus on the topics raised within parliament, on the struggles taking place within parliament, and on scandals involving the personal lives of the people who work there. The bottom-up perspective, which relays the concerns of ordinary citizens to politicians, may be lost. And it is precisely these insider political news stories dealing with scandals and the private lives of politicians that make citizens cynical.

Commercialization has not only been linked to the amount of political news and the way it is presented, but also to the general decline of the party press and a universal move toward catch-all media. Despite claims of homogenization, this book has shown that the role conceptions and professional autonomy of political journalists vary across media systems. Spain – the polarized pluralist media system – stands out in particular. When the results presented in Chapter 3 are viewed in relation to an earlier study by Algarra and Gaitano (1998, 486), the gap between Spain and the rest of Europe seems to have widened. Algarra and Gaitano argued that younger generations of Spanish journalists had a neutral-adversarial role conception. They found that Spanish journalists positioned themselves closer to neutral than did German journalists and were more critical than British newspaper journalists. Based on the survey presented in this book, Spain is clearly an outlier on the sacerdotal-partisan end of the scale. This is confirmed in our survey, our content analysis, and the panel study.

Paradoxically, the divergence of journalistic cultures might be the result of commercialization, which is generally judged to cause convergence and homogenization. In the polarized pluralist media system, commercialization seems to have led to *more* partisan reporting and *more* political pressure. News organizations in Greece and Spain are often incorporated into larger companies, and owners exploit the influence of their news outlets to receive political favors that benefit their companies (de Miguel & Pozas, 2009; Papathanassopoulos, 2001). Competition for market share has led to more partisan reporting in some Spanish newspapers, as these newspapers try to appeal to various partisan audiences (de Miguel & Pozas, 2009). Our research suggests that the structural developments taking place in different media systems, though similar in nature, vary in their impact on the journalists working in these systems. This variation depends on, among other things, the relevant country's socio-demographic characteristics (political polarization in society) and cultural characteristics (e.g., rational-legal authority and clientalism). Thus, historical and cultural conditions must be taken into account when analyzing the way commercialization shapes journalism in any given country.

A third lesson ties in with the notion of *mediatization*. According to the mediatization thesis, the balance of power between politicians and the media has undergone a significant shift over the last five decades. In the past, politicians set the terms for media-politics relations; now, journalists have taken over. Liberated from political pressures, journalists have exchanged a partisan-sacerdotal journalistic approach for a non-ideological, pragmatic one. Many findings in this book are in line with this thesis, although they apply less to Spain than to the other countries. For example, in our study no Danish political journalist felt that political pressure limited his or her work. In northern Europe, a pragmatic role conception, albeit with sacerdotal sentiments, goes hand in hand with conflict and strategy framing. In each country, spin doctors help politicians configure their messages to media logic.

But the changes accompanying the power shift from politicians to the media need qualification. With the exception of Denmark, political pressure remains a notable influence on journalists' work. The prominence of spin doctors is evidence that politicians take the media into account as they go about their business, but such consideration does not mean that politicians cede to the media in all things. Mediatization has its downsides for journalists. Journalists' cynicism about politicians and their media salacity is one example; concern about negative media coverage on the part of governments is another. Such concerns can make governments extra secretive, less transparent, and sensitive about access to information (Fairbank, Plowman, & Rawlins, 2007). Secrecy and lack of transparency contributed to the dissatisfaction experienced by British parliamentary reporters in particular (Chapter 3). These examples demonstrate that, although politicians are mindful of the media, and often accommodate the media, the power balance between the two does not invariably tip in the media's favor.

Of course, pressure to tow a particular political line does not necessarily imply a dependence on politicians. Traditionally, political pressure was applied by governments and political parties that had firm control of the media. Our study identified several journalists who felt pressure coming from within the news organization itself. Such pressures may have become even stronger with the mediatization of politics.

Owners of media organizations have bargaining power. They can influence political decisions; politicians, in the belief that tabloid newspapers can make them win or lose the majority in parliament, place importance on positive media coverage in an attempt to achieve electoral success. As already mentioned, owners of news organizations in Spain that are incorporated into large media firms may use their media outlets to pressure politicians and to reward them for decisions that work to the benefit of their organizations (de Miguel & Pozas, 2009). Conversely, governments regulating against the owners' interests can be punished (Hallin and Papathanasopoulos, 2002). In the United Kingdom, prime ministers viewed Rupert Murdoch as a real threat and were fearful that he might turn his tabloid newspaper The Sun against them. Clearly, when politicians become more dependent on the media, journalists do not necessarily become independent of political pressures. Similar to the professionalization of politics and commercialization, the concept of mediatization and its dimensions is useful, but developments in this area vary widely and a one-directional shift from political to media logic is not evident.

Fourth, and finally, we need to consider the broader trend of *individualization*. An increase in news outlets and channels, as well as broader societal changes, have led to highly individualized patterns of media consumption. In the past, a country would have had only one television channel, and political and social status determined which newspaper one read. As television channels multiplied, one could *escape* the evening news, and today's media choice abundance makes patterns of news consumption less predictable. Our findings show that people have not overwhelmingly traded information for entertainment. The majority of the population regularly watches news on television. Many people still watch news on public broadcasters. Most users rely on more than one information source, and only a minority of the population does not follow the news at all. These findings are in line with Wonneberger's (2011) findings in the Netherlands.

VARIATION IN NEWS USE PATTERNS

Even though citizens may not have traded information for entertainment across the board, there are real and important differences in the degree to which citizens use news in the different countries. Based on our survey data, we find that only 3 percent of Danes consume no news at all (defined as the key daily newspapers and television news shows included in our study). The figure is 10 percent in Spain and 20 percent in the United Kingdom. Especially in the latter case, this is a sizable proportion of the population, and it creates a real distinction between news consumers and news avoiders. These cross-national differences are augmented by differences in the degree of consumption. In Denmark, 43 percent report using two sources of news a day, and an additional 17 percent use more than two sources a day. In Spain, 30 percent use two sources daily and 16 percent more than two sources. In the United Kingdom, these numbers are 20 and 5 percent, respectively. This means that in Denmark, a vast majority is exposed to multiple sources and contents every day; this is almost half the population in Spain, and in the United Kingdom about a quarter uses multiple sources. These figures are important because they show the variation in consuming any news at all, and the difference in the degree of news sources used. While our findings show that news contents, even of a sort that is often disregarded as not substantive, can be beneficial, we should also acknowledge that there is an important difference in the demand and use of these news sources between the countries.

In terms of news contents, competition from other types of programs seems to have prompted newsmakers to heed viewers' desires. By presenting the news in a more entertaining way and using conflict and human-interest frames and emotions, newsmakers are better able to connect with their viewers. While the abundance of choice has not resulted in a mass rejection of the news, it has led to more diverse news diets, making it harder to predict which type of outlets people read or watch. However, with the exception of tabloid newspapers, we found no obvious differences in the content of different media outlets. Neither did a clear pattern of differences emerge between commercial and public service broadcasters in terms of the amount of attention devoted to national politics and the way it was framed (Chapter 5). Although these outlets do not differ consistently in the way they present the news, they do attract different types of audiences. As the analysis in Chapter 6 shows, outlets vary widely in the number of viewers and readers they attract and in how knowledgeable their audiences are. This variation even extends to the effects of news exposure on audiences' political knowledge.

The self-selection of audiences raises questions about media effects in the future. Does such self-selection imply positive feedback loops where predispositions and media effects reinforce one another, increasing and solidifying the gap between the politically engaged and the politically ignorant, making only the knowledge-rich richer? Our findings on the effects of political news on knowledge gain suggest that, under certain conditions, the loops can be broken; in particular, the information-poor can get richer. It is precisely people with low political interest who learn from news that both grabs their attention and is presented in an easily digestible way. This group learns from watching the news as an unintended by-product. The public's preference for objective media outlets (Chapter 8) and limited political partisanship (at a minimum in hard news) suggests that, at least in northern Europe, a positive feedback loop with mutually reinforcing partisan media and partisan audiences will be less likely than in other more polarized and politicized media systems.

Conditions, Practice, Effects?

This book builds on the argument that different conditions create different kinds of political journalism, which in turn affect what people think and how they feel about politics. What did we learn about the relationship between context, practice, and effects? The comparative design showed marked differences in journalistic practice across countries, which we believe relate back to the conditions under which political journalists work. Our interpretation was based not only on our own theoretical suppositions and those garnered from previous studies (Chapter 3) but also on empirical evidence (Chapter 4). Previous comparative studies have pointed toward structural conditions, such as the presence of public service broadcasters (Aalberg & Curran, 2012; Iyengar et al., 2010) to explain differences in political news and the political information environment.

Our studies support the relevance of structural differences. For example, role conceptions differ between journalists working in public service outlets and journalists working in commercial outlets. In addition, many comparative differences that were identified in our study had a cultural explanation. For example, the political communication culture (Pfetsch & Mayerhöffer, 2011) between politicians, journalists, and spin doctors was a reason for political cynicism among journalists (Chapter 4). The differences in democratic traditions between Spain and northern European countries offer possible explanations for differences in role conceptions and political pressure (Chapter 3; see also Köcher, 1986). The different ways in which professionalization, commercialization, mediatization, and individualization play out across countries make it clear that the interaction between cultural and structural contexts shapes the conditions under which political journalists work.

The distinct role conceptions of Spanish and northern European journalists reflect the characteristics of the media systems they work in. We also found a relationship between role conceptions and news content. This connection supports the claim that role conceptions form a vital link between media systems and news content. Our results lend agreement to Donsbach (2008), who argued that role conceptions "can have a strong influence on journalists' professional behavior and thus can explain differences between news cultures."

In Chapters 6, 7, and 8, we looked at audiences' knowledge, cynicism, and satisfaction – in other words, at audience perception and cognition. Like journalistic practice and content, audience perception and cognition also vary cross-nationally. Differences in perception and cognition are related to differences in news content. Our statistical models explained more variance when we controlled for weighted exposure to news content, and in some cases cross-national differences between audiences could be explained entirely by news exposure; exposure to privatized news, for example, explained differences in political cynicism between Danish and British citizens. After controlling for watchdog perceptions, cross-national differences in satisfaction with political news were no longer significant. The effects of content on audiences were not bound only to specific countries; the countries did not moderate the effects. These findings support our argument that differences in citizens' perceptions and cognition in different countries can be partly explained by the different conditions under which journalists work and by the content they produce.

A possible objection could be raised to our argument on the importance of structural and cultural conditions of the media and political systems for content and the public. One might argue that we only focus on mainstream news media without reference to the changing media configuration, which has created a "post-broadcast democracy" (Prior, 2007) or "the era after broadcasting news" (Williams & Delli Carpini, 2011). Changing media configuration refers to significant changes in the patterns of news consumption. Williams and Delli Carpini (2011) document these changes, and in particular point out the decreasing importance of newspapers and broadcast television news for young citizens.

Although the *potential* of the Internet and non-mainstream news sources is widely debated, we are still only starting to learn about their impact in terms of information provision (Boulliane, 2009; Coleman & Blumler, 2009). In fact, according to recent studies, although a majority of citizens in Western democracies are active online, they spend this time on social activities and practicalities (e.g., banking, shopping, checking the weather) – not on politics (e.g., Bakker & de Vreese, 2011; Bakker et al., 2012). It remains to be seen if the supply of political information online is met by a sizable demand for it. But for now it has not diminished the relevance of the conditions under which political journalists work for news consumption and news effects.

Reflections on Design and Limitations: What Did We (Not) Learn?

This book set out to build a bridge between media sociology, journalism studies, and media effects research. These areas of research have long dealt with similar concepts but have largely remained separate (Benson, 2004). To build this bridge, we integrated journalism surveys, content analysis, and a panel study in one comprehensive research project. Cross-national projects are rare, and the combination of cross-nationally collected survey data and media content data even more so. Exceptions, such as Iyengar et al. (2010) and Aalberg and Currant (2012), rely on cross-sectional surveys rather than panel studies. However, even though we collected panel data, inevitably this pioneering effort has had its limitations. When interpreting our findings, the limitations must be taken into account; at the same time, they inspire new research questions and empirical approaches.

Using our cross-national comparative approach, we show how different conditions create variety in journalistic practice and content (Chapters 3–5). We find important differences between the four countries, but are not always able to pinpoint the exact condition (or combination of conditions) that led to these differences. Spanish media partisanships, for example, could be due to a strong influence of the state on the media, more recent democratic traditions, or deep political divides among the audience. Similarly, several explanations can be given for the entertainment orientation of political journalists in Britain, such as its tabloid tradition, competition within the media market, or even the theatrical nature of the British parliament.

Multiple explanations are inherent in comparative research. Small numbers of cases, in combination with several competing explanations, mean that dependent variables are often "overdetermined," which makes it impossible to eliminate all alternative explanations (Lijphart, 1971, 685). This problem could partly be dealt with by looking at lower levels of analysis. We study the causes of political cynicism both on individual and aggregate levels in Chapter 4. In Chapter 5 we compare role conceptions and content in different types of media outlets. But due to the importance of the structural characteristics of the media system and journalistic culture, differences within countries are often much smaller than cross-national differences.

A strategy that could be pursued to further address this problem would be to increase the number of countries (see Schuck et al., 2011). Adding more cases would also allow for a qualitative comparative analysis (or fuzzy set analysis), which could be applied to assess the (combined) influence of several competitive explanations (Ragin, 1994, 2000). Alternatively, a semi-experimental design could isolate single explanations for differences in journalistic practice across countries with strong historical, cultural, and structural similarities, such as the Baltic states or the Scandinavian countries. We recommend a longitudinal approach. The cross-national design we used meant that assumptions about historical developments could not be studied explicitly. This problem was partly addressed by comparing the findings with those of earlier empirical studies and theoretical discussions, but several questions remained unanswered. The finding that journalistic experience is negatively related to political cynicism, for example, could either be a cohort effect or a generational effect (Chapter 4), but this question cannot be answered by a one-shot survey. To answer this question, our study would have to be repeated in the future.

We argued that journalists' attitudes are crucial to our understanding of the link between the context in which journalists work and the news they produce. We found a relationship between role conceptions and content (Chapter 5), but this relation was not one-to-one. Other studies applying quasi-experiments to test the influence of role conceptions on news decisions have demonstrated stronger effects (Kocher, 1986; Patterson & Donsbach, 1996). Our design did not allow us to study the relationship between roles and content at an individual level. Due to privacy concerns, it was not always possible to match the news items included in the content analysis to the journalists filling out the survey. The tightening of privacy rules is increasingly problematic for journalism surveys (Weaver & Loffelholz, 2008, 6). A possible solution is to revisit the quasi-experimental approach and to study the relationship between role conceptions and content for the three central dimensions under study. Although this approach has lower external validity, it might show a stronger link between role conceptions and content.

Integrating our three central dimensions into content analysis, a journalism survey, and a panel study was a challenge to our operationalization. Since we could not rely on widely tested and accepted scales and measures, the reliability of some of the scales and content analytical indicators was not optimal. New scales were used for the survey, and the content analysis relied mostly on measures that have been used in various previous studies (both single country and cross-national). Nevertheless, no widely accepted standards exist to guide the operationalization of the key concepts of this study in a content analysis. Recent efforts have been made to establish such standards (Esser, de Vreese, & Strömbäck 2012), which are prerequisite to move the field toward more accumulative knowledge (Norris, 2009). In this book, however, the development of new scales and operationalizations is not an end in itself but a means to test hypotheses and make substantive claims about cross-national variation in political journalism. This study breaks new ground, and future studies should further refine the instruments used here. More attention needs to be paid to the concept of political knowledge and its measurement. Multiple-choice, exam-style measures are questioned regarding their broader relevance. Our choice of this measure over open-ended questions (e.g., Graber, 2001) or recognition questions (e.g., Valentino et al., 2001) was triggered by our interest in the relationship dynamics between framing and political knowledge. Future research may also need to take into account an additional factor: citizens' failure to recall particular items of information does not necessarily mean that they have learned nothing. They may have forgotten the details but grasped the meaning (see Graber, 2001).

Studying media effects by means of a panel study has clear advantages. By integrating content analysis data and the responses to the survey at the level of the individual respondents, we provide compelling evidence of media effects; we distinguish between reliance on a medium and exposure to a message, and between exposure in general and exposure to a particular message (see de Vreese & Semetko, 2004). Despite these advantages, our panel design is confined to investigating framing effects in the short term, which has undoubtedly influenced the relatively low increases of explained variance between the panel waves. Future researchers may choose to apply a broader longitudinal approach to trace the duration of these effects over time (see, e.g., Tewksbury et al., 2000; Druckman & Nelson, 2003; de Vreese, 2004; Lecheler & de Vreese, 2012). Studies should also preferably include a wider sample of media outlets. The outlets included in our study are among the most widely watched and read sources of political news in the country, but today these sources are not limited to newspapers and news shows – alternative news providers such as popular talk shows have also staked their claim. More research is needed to investigate the perceptual and cognitive influences of these infotainment genres on ordinary citizens.

Given the nature of our study, we were unable to assess the response to each individual news story. Experimental studies grapple less with this shortcoming as they allow for partial or complete manipulation of the stimulus material. We theorize that effects are linked to the accessibility of various frames and the arousal that these frames engender. Future experimental research should substantiate these theoretical expectations beyond what we are able to do here. Experiments are well suited to identifying and analyzing the mechanisms underlying knowledge gain through conflict and human-interest framing. Experimental studies would increase our understanding of the way journalistic styles affect cognition, and could also inform journalistic practice. As noted in Chapter 8, audience research is often confined to commercial purposes (McQuail, 2005). Journalists' ways of doing their work are based on presumed effects and traditions, rather than rigorously tested empirical evidence. Conducting experiments with the purpose of improving journalistic practice would complete the research cycle: linking practice with content, content with effects, and, ultimately, the understanding of these effects with practice.

Tomorrow's Journalism: Which Standards Do We Apply?

Will the political journalism of tomorrow do its job? In our concluding section we offer a number of considerations on the relationship between journalism, politics, and citizens. First of all, we contend that the *relationship between media and politics* (i.e., between journalists and politicians) is of crucial importance for a well-functioning democracy. Elsewhere we have argued that perhaps the real spiral of cynicism is between the mutually suspicious journalists and politicians rather than between politicians and citizens (Brants et al., 2010; van Dalen et al., 2011). However, this relationship is very much conditioned by structural issues that define its parameters: as we have shown, the absence of political interference and journalists' belief in their own autonomy are clear and necessary conditions for good political journalism. These conditions not only affect the practice and content of journalism but also citizens' satisfaction with the media, and are thus prerequisites for any well-functioning journalistic culture that is conducive to democratic processes.

For political journalism to fulfill its democratic role, a sufficient *supply of political information* must be available. Although dwindling political news is a frequently voiced criticism of the media, never before has so much news and political information been available – witness the number of newspapers (augmented by free papers), various television schedules (Aalberg et al., 2010; Esser et al., 2012), and the Internet. Thus, the supply of information is present – but what about the audience? When people do consume political information, what motivates them to do so and what type of political information do they prefer? In their study of news and democracy, Aalberg and colleagues (2012) put a premium on the role of public broadcasting in explaining why Europeans know more about politics and current affairs than their American fellow citizens do (see also Iyengar et al., 2010). Such findings are important because they emphasize the fact that structural investments in public news supply can influence the public's levels of knowledge in any given society.

When we attempt to answer as to whether tomorrow's political journalism will be doing its job, we need to go beyond an assessment of quantity and quality (on the supply side) and citizens' usage (on the demand side). Given that our question has a normative component, the answer largely hinges on the democratic standards by which one evaluates the media. And given that the notion of democracy is much contested, a brief exploration of the standards relevant to our research and conclusions will prove helpful.

Strömbäck (2005) offers reflections on four models of democracy and their (implicit) normative implications for political journalism. Each model has its own set of standards and expectations. In high demanding models, such as *participatory and deliberative democracy*, Stromback (2005, 341) suggests that the media are responsive to citizens' wishes and issues, that news journalism mobilizes and fosters civic and political engagement, focuses on problem solving, and stimulates discussions defined by rationality, impartiality, and equality. By the standards of a high-demanding model, the media and the political journalism we studied would probably fall short on a number of accounts. Online political sources might perform better on these criteria, but the usage of online political sources has yet to gain momentum outside short-lived political campaigns.

Without dismissing the models or the standards these online sources set for news journalism, we nonetheless question whether citizens and democracy are best served by mainstream media fulfilling the requirements of high-demanding models of democracy. Most citizens in today's world will find themselves, de facto, as part of what Strömbäck dubs the *procedural and competitive models of democracy*. In these models, political journalism is a watchdog vis-à-vis political elites and power holders, the fundamentals of democratic procedures are supported and respected, and political candidates and officeholders' records are scrutinized. Citizens are (critical) political consumers who make choices and invest elites with power in regular elections. These models are less demanding on both citizens and political journalists, and they corroborate some of the thinking of scholars such as Schudson, Graber, and Zaller on the role of the news media, political journalism, and citizens.

Schudson (1998) reviewed the implicit demands put on citizens in the United States from the era of the Founding Fathers through later periods, including, from the late nineteenth century onward, the expectations set by the ideal of the "informed citizen." Schudson concluded that this notion of the citizen was too unrealistic. Criticizing previous models for being too demanding and rigid, he describes his alternative model thus: "I propose that the obligation of citizens to know enough to participate intelligently in governmental affairs should be understood as a "monitorial" obligation. Citizens can be "monitorial" rather than informed. A monitorial citizen scans (rather than reads) the informational environment in such a way that he or she may be alerted on a very wide variety of issues for a very wide variety of ends, and may be mobilized around those issues in a large variety of ways. Print journalists regularly criticize broadcast media for being only a "headline service," but a headline service is what, in the first instance, citizens require."

The notion of the monitorial citizen is echoed in Zaller's (2003) *Burglar Alarm Standard*. Continuing the work of Converse (1964), he contends that citizens perform a cursory examination of the news, and – if necessary – the media will "alarm" them such that even the inattentive and politically uninterested citizen will be informed about major issues. This standard may seem far below the ideal of a fully informed, rational citizen, but Zaller (2003) suggests that in fact this behavior *is* rational since diving into deep and contextualized knowledge about most issues would neither empower the citizen nor yield anything in terms of political decision-making procedures. Therefore, a limited amount of news consumption suffices, while the (informed) decision making is delegated to elected officials and experts.

Critiques of Zaller's *Burglar Alarm* have focused on the problems that occur if the alarm rings too frequently or if it does not ring at all (Bennett, 2003). We also contend that it is too simplistic to pitch the burglar alarm against a full news model, and that we can ask more of political journalism that merely being an alarm. Journalism can rather be likened to surveillance cameras that filter out certain issues for citizens – not only those issues that merit immediate alarm ringing, but also those that may require it later – so as to provide continuous and contextualized news coverage. Alarm ringing alone impoverishes the diversity of news (Porto, 2007). In fact, proactive political watchdog journalism should develop and activate additional alarms and cameras. One of the most important lessons from our study is that *the people who are less interested in politics to begin with can learn from news that draws on entertainment features* – that is, news that uses the drama that Zaller (2003) also calls for. Similarly, in her book *Processing Politics: Learning from Television in the Age of the Internet*, Graber (2001) makes a plea for demanding less from the media and from citizens. She contends that television, at its best, does a good job in transmitting information and stimulating knowledge acquisition. The real need, according to Graber, is to lower the barrier even farther so that more people can benefit from this accessible news provision. Schudson, Graber, and Zaller – in more or less explicit terms – agree on a core set of standards for the news media and political journalism. As summarized by Strömbäck (2005), in a combination of the procedural and competitive models of democracy, the demands for political journalism are to (1) provide reliable information that can be acted upon, if necessary, (2) provide an overview of political events, (3) monitor and watch political elites and power holders, and (4) offer alternatives in political discussions.

Having identified some key standards, let us return to some of our key findings. News presented in terms of conflict and human-interest was found to be conducive to learning, especially for the least politically interested. Conflict and human-interest news framing explains political standpoints, contrasts options and opinions, and flags policies through the use of human examples. This type of presentation leads to learning. Although these news forms may not live up to the standards required by, for example, deliberative democracy models, the coverage and effects not only fulfill but exceed the minimum standards outlined here. Moreover, when political journalism is perceived as performing its watchdog function by monitoring political elites and power holders, citizens are even satisfied with their media.

These findings are sure to give rise to optimism, but it would be foolish to conclude that all essential standards are currently being met and that democracy is fully vibrant and needing no further improvement. Accessible political information leading to knowledge gain in the unmotivated does not cancel the need for highbrow, in-depth journalism; nor does it mean that information acquisition is impossible from news devoid of drama or human examples. However, given that accessible political information can engage inattentive audiences in political news, and that they can actually learn from it – but without arguing that limitless entertainment in the news is the only way forward – we must reconsider whether sweeping statements about the failings of either citizens or the news media are justified.

In this concluding chapter we have summarized our findings and viewed them from a broader perspective. We are aware that a good performance by the news media in one model of democracy might be a highly inadequate performance in another. We believe it important to stress that the subject matter discussed here is not free-floating, bound neither by time nor place: our research has centered on current political journalism in different European countries. Important differences were found between these countries, and our discussion could have been be more in-depth if we had looked yet further – to the United States, for example, or to transitioning or totalitarian regimes. Observers argue that the United States is at a critical juncture regarding the configuration and function of its media (Williams & Delli Carpini, 2011). In Europe, the situation seems less critical. However it may be, political journalism should not be treated complacently, and although our findings are mostly good news, we are well aware that the findings stem from a small part of the world. Yet this does not dismiss their importance and relevance to Western democracies. In fact, our findings clearly show that when the news media is the recipient of generous public funding, and when journalists are not tightly bound by commercial and political pressures, the news is more valued by the public.

Moreover, we should constantly keep in mind the standards against which we judge political journalism and citizens. The mass media and enlightened citizens are phenomena of the twentieth century. Neither appeared overnight. Neither was possible without policy making, public funding, and institutional arrangements. Both citizens and the media will continue to rely on all these things and on support from political elites to ensure the right conditions for political journalism and the "virtuous circle."

We started with the assumption that if conditions for political journalism differ, these differences will lead to different political news content, and are very likely to lead to different effects. And they did. We could have dwelt more on the negative implications of restricted journalistic autonomy, the cynical attitudes of some politicians and journalists, or the effects of some news features on public cynicism. But we have preferred to focus on our positive findings and observations. The glass is not only half full; sometimes it is more than that. When the conditions are right, there is more good news than bad news in our story. And the good news is that positive effects occur when journalists are autonomous and free from political pressure, when they are allowed to both inform *and* entertain, and when they are not cynical. Citizens living in a democracy are most satisfied when they perceive their political news media to be fulfilling a watchdog function. These may be uncertain times for Western democracies (as in other parts of the world), but we are confident that political journalism will continue to make a distinct and important contribution as we encounter future challenges.

Appendix to Chapter 2

To investigate how the personal backgrounds, role conceptions and perceived pressures vary across contexts, a survey was conducted among 425 political reporters in Denmark, Germany, Spain, and the United Kingdom (Appendix Table 2.1). The population under study consists of parliamentary journalists working in these four countries. The populations are defined as "journalists who report, analyze, or give commentary on national politics" and operationalized as members of parliamentary press galleries or of unions of parliamentary journalists. By focusing on parliamentary journalists rather than on general reporters, we have the advantage of functional equivalence, since parliamentary journalists all report on similar topics: government and members of parliament. Since the populations under study are quite small, we opted for approaching the whole population rather than taking a sample.

Between November 2007 and February 2009, the surveys were distributed in each of the four countries. We contacted the journalists by letter and email, inviting them to complete either pen-and-paper or online versions of the survey. Across countries most journalists completed the survey on-line. We used several strategies to increase response rates, such as incentives and

APPENDIX TABLE 2.1. *Characteristics of the Survey of Political Journalists in Denmark, Germany, the United Kingdom, and Spain*

Country	Denmark	Germany	United Kingdom	Spain
Population (N)	Presseloge (96)	Bundespresse-konferenz (620)	Press Gallery/ Register of Journalists Interests (281)	Asociación de Periodistas Parlamentarios (116)
Respondents	71	201	87	66
Response rate	74%	32%	31%	57%
Time of survey	November 2007–March 2008	April 2008–July 2008	June 2008–January 2009	October 2008–January 2009
Closest national elections	November 2007	September 2005	May 2005	March 2008
Remarks about repre-sentativeness	Representative for gender and type of medium	Representative for gender and type of medium	Representative for gender, type of medium, membership lobby, and press gallery	Representative for gender. Print journalists overrepre-sented, radio underrepre-sented

multiple follow-up contacts. In Spain and the United Kingdom, additional phone calls were made to increase an initially low response.

Response rates ranged from 31 percent in the United Kingdom, which is comparable with other journalism surveys (Donsbach & Patterson, 2004; Weaver, 1998), to 74 percent in Denmark, which is exceptionally high. Checks of representativeness showed that the characteristics of the respondent group are a good match with the characteristics of the full population. Not all characteristics were known for the populations of the different countries, so different representative checks were applied to each country. For all countries, we compared the distribution of the respondents' gender and type of medium with that of the whole population. These variables yielded comparable results in Denmark,

Germany, and the United Kingdom. In Spain, print journalists were more likely to answer the questionnaire than were radio journalists.

All surveys were carefully translated, and the wording of questions was discussed with researchers who were experienced in political communication in the respective countries. After the journalist surveys had been completed, tests were done to assess cross-national differences in response style (van Herk et al., 2004). No evidence was found of either differences in acquiescence bias (tendency to agree) or extreme response bias. We aimed for equivalence of scales by using mostly multiple-item scales (which were tested by factor analysis) and by performing reliability tests for the internal consistency of the scales used. Similar questions have been posed in numerous journalism surveys around the world (van Aelst et al., 2008; Weaver, 1998; Weaver & Willnat, 2012; Hanitzsch et al., 2010).

CONTENT ANALYSIS ROUTINE PERIOD

To study the relationship between role conceptions and reporting style (Chapter 5), we conducted a content analysis of political news in Denmark, Germany, the United Kingdom, and Spain during a routine period. The period of analysis was determined by a trade-off of three considerations. First, the period had to be comparable across countries in terms of real-world events (such as elections). Second, we had to take practicalities into account: it was not possible for us to gather news broadcasts and newspapers in the four countries for a whole year, therefore we limited the sample period to two weeks. Third, the sample had to be large enough to represent all the news within this period. Based on these considerations we sampled newspaper and television content over two constructed news weeks between December 8, 2007, and February 8, 2008 (see Riffe et al., 1993). The weeks before and after Christmas were excluded. This period started a month after the national elections in Denmark and finished one month before national elections in Spain. We tried to minimize the influence of the Spanish elections (March 9, 2008) on our content by completing the data collection before the hottest phase of the campaign (last four weeks).

In each country, news broadcasts of a public service and a commercial channel were included in the analysis, as well as a right- and a left-leaning broadsheet and a tabloid newspaper (see Appendix Table 2.2). Since Spain does not have the equivalent of a tabloid newspaper, we substituted an extra broadsheet for the Spanish tabloid. The content analysis covers news items from the main national news bulletins of the following public and private news broadcasts: BBC News at 22:00 and ITV Nightly News in the UK; DR1 TV-Avisen at 21:00 and TV2 Nyhederne at 19:00 in Denmark; ARD Tagesschau and RTL Aktuell in Germany; TVE Telediario 2, Antena 3 Noticias, and Informativos Telecinco in Spain; and the main news sections of the following broadsheet and tabloid newspapers: The Guardian, The Daily Telegraph, and The Sun in the UK; Politiken, JyllandsPosten, and EkstraBladet in Denmark; Suddeutsche Zeitung, Frankfurter Allgemeine, Zeitung, and Bild in Germany; ABC, El Pais, and El Mundo in Spain.

We analyzed news about national politics. National politics is considered the main subject of the news item when it receives the most attention in terms of duration or space, or when national politicians are the item's most prominent actors. Examples of topics on national politics are party politics, debates in parliament, legislation, and government actions. National politics is not necessarily related to a political event; it can also include subjects such as education, defense, immigration, and health when policy or politics are central, or when the main actor is a political actor. The minimum requirement is that at least one of the following terms is mentioned or visualized within a national context: "parliament, government, minister, ministry, and/or the name of a politician (Member of Parliament or member of government) and/or the name of a national political party or national party leader or member." Other indicators can be that the articles are written or presented by journalists who are explicitly labelled as "political editors," "political correspondents," and the like. In the design of the content analysis, efforts were made to limit the

APPENDIX TABLE 2.2. *Sample Size: Number of News Items in Routine and Panel Periods*

Country	News Outlet	Type of Outlet	News Items about National Politics (routine period)	News Items about National Politics (panel period)	News Items about the U.S. Election (panel period)
Denmark	JyllandsPosten	Right-leaning newspaper	82	84	41
	Politiken	Left-leaning newspaper	59	99	52
	EkstraBladet	Tabloid	21	37	24
	DR1 TV-Avisen	Public service broadcast	34	55	56
	TV2 Nyhederne	Commercial television	28	56	46
Germany	Suddeutsche Zeitung	Left-leaning newspaper	141	–	–
	Frankfurter Allgemeine Zeitung	Right-leaning newspaper	173	–	–
	Bild	Tabloid	88	–	–
	ARD Tagesschau	Public service broadcast	46	–	–
	RTL Aktuell	Commercial television	32	–	–
United Kingdom	The Daily Telegraph	Right-leaning newspaper	75	353	119
	The Guardian	Left-leaning newspaper	80	247	96
	The Sun	Tabloid	50	163	38
	BBC News	Public service broadcast	11	44	29
	ITV Nightly News	Commercial television	17	44	23
Spain	El Pais	Left-leaning newspaper	144	147	69
	ABC	Right-leaning newspaper	147	189	87
	El Mundo	Right-leaning newspaper	134	145	69
	TVE Telediario 2	Public service broadcast	40	94	37
	Antena 3 Noticias	Commercial television	38	56	43
	Informativos Telecinco	Commercial television	29	54	38
	Total		1469	1867	867

influence of cross-national differences in design on outcomes. To increase the comparability of the material, opinion pieces, letters to the editor, and editorials were excluded from the sample. The following types of news items were considered for the analysis: news stories, reportages, news readers, (brief) reports, and live reports, background/analysis stories, or bullets. By bullet we mean a short story which consists of a headline and a short summary (at least one sentence) that announces that a substantial article can be found inside the newspaper.

The variables in the codebook aim at providing a general descriptive account of the nature of political news and at operationalizing key theoretical concepts. The indicators provide insight into different types of political reporting. The specific operationalization of the different concepts is discussed in the relevant chapters. For each country, coders who were native speakers or had a high proficiency in the one of the four languages coded the material. The coders were trained and frequently supervised prior to and during the content analysis. The codebook was adjusted for newspapers and television analysis, and the coding procedure started with a training program during which the codebook was modified to prevent systematic errors (Riffe et al., 2005). Before the start of the coding, coder-trainer tests were done on the level of the news item in English (the working language) to assess whether coders with different language backgrounds had sufficient understanding of the English codebook (Peter & Lauf, 2002). After the coding was finished, intercoder reliability tests were done for coder pairs in each of the four countries with a sample of at least 10 percent of the material. Intercoder reliability scores are reported in Chapter 5.

PANEL SURVEY

Appendix Table 2.3 summarizes the main characteristics of the panel survey, which was conducted in Denmark, the United Kingdom, and Spain during the last three weeks of the 2008 U.S. elections. The first wave of the survey took place October 10–20, 2008; the second wave, November 7–14, 2008. The general

APPENDIX TABLE 2.3. *Characteristics of the Panel Study in Denmark, the United Kingdom, and Spain*

	Denmark	United Kingdom	Spain
Completed both waves	1539	1571	1642
Completed wave II only	215	204	201
Response rate wave I	75%	63.3%	74.7%
Response rate wave II	68.2%	74.4%	74.6%
Fieldwork wave I	October 10–17, 2008	October 10–20, 2008	October 13–20, 2008
Fieldwork wave II	November 7–14, 2008	November 7–13, 2008	November 7–14, 2008
Type of sample	Random sample	Light quota	Light quota
Remarks about representativeness	Representative for gender, age, and education	Representative for gender, age, level of education, and level of urbanization	Representative for gender, age, level of education, and level of urbanization

population targeted was 18–65 years old. All those who took part in the survey were existing members of TNS online panels. The panel surveys were conducted by TNS opinion. These online panels consist of several thousand members per country, with panel members receiving payment for each survey they participate in. The advantage of Internet panels over pen-and-paper surveys is that respondents can complete the questionnaire at their convenience and hence dedicate the necessary time to reflect on answers – thus presumably increasing the quality of the responses. In addition, Internet panels use self-administered survey modes, which yield less socially desirable answers compared with interviewer-administered survey modes (see Fricker, 2002). This situation is particularly advantageous when investigating issues related to domestic politics.

A quota system was used in the United Kingdom and Spain to ensure a well-distributed sample in terms of gender, age, level of education, and level of urbanization. A quota system was not needed in Denmark because the Danish TNS panel generates samples that are demographically well distributed. Survey-invitation emails were sent out at the start of the fieldwork. Respondents who did not respond to these emails (for example, through oversight) were sent another email invitation. To reduce potential bias, questionnaire scripting and layout were standardized, and invitations did not include the survey topic in order to avoid attracting only those with a particular interest in politics. The response rates in Denmark were 75 percent in wave I and 68.2 percent in wave II; in England, 63.3 and 74.4 percent, respectively; and in Spain 74.7 and 74.6 percent, respectively. A net sample of 1,539 respondents in Denmark, 1,571 respondents in England, and 1,642 respondents in Spain participated in both waves.

The questionnaire in each wave took about 15 minutes to answer. The panel survey included measures of media exposure and attention, perceptual and cognitive responses, and individual-level controls that are used to assess individual-level moderators of the effects. The source questionnaire was initially scripted and finalized in English, and then translated into Danish and Spanish. A strict translation procedure was applied, including proofreading and back-translation by experts operating as independent third parties. This procedure is essential for reliability in multilingual surveys in cross-national comparative research (see Werner & Campbell, 1970; van de Vijver & Tanzer, 1997).

Only respondents answering both panel waves were considered in the analysis. This approach was to ensure a balanced panel regardless of attrition between the panel waves. To test for possible sensitization effects in the panel – that is, whether second-wave responses are affected by respondents being surveyed twice within a short period of time – fresh samples of about 200 respondents in all three countries were probed for our dependent variables in wave II of the survey. The mean scores for the new sample were compared against mean scores for respondents taking part in both panel waves. The specific mean scores are reported in each chapter.

To establish the link between news content and media effects on the individual level, we content-analyzed Danish, British, and Spanish news coverage between the two waves of the panel study. For Denmark and the United Kingdom, this period fell between October 10 and November 4, 2008, and for Spain, between October 13 and November 4, 2008 (since the first wave of the panel survey was fielded there on October 13). In the panel period, news items about both national politics and the 2008 U.S. presidential elections were included, and the same outlets were analyzed as during the routine period (see Table 2.2). The U.S. election is the main subject of the news item if it receives the most attention in terms of duration or space, and if at least one of the following actors is mentioned once: Barack Obama, John McCain, Joe Biden, Sara Palin, Republican Party, and Democratic Party. Coding instructions and intercoder reliability scores for this content analysis are reported in Chapters 6 and 7.

Appendix to Chapter 3

APPENDIX TABLE 3.1. *Characteristics of Surveys of Political Journalists in Denmark, Germany, the United Kingdom, and Spain*

	Denmark	Germany	United Kingdom	Spain
Mean political leaning[a] (sd)	4.90	4.37	4.51	3.68
	(1.43)	(1.36)	(1.58)	(1.27)
Mean political leaning of medium[a] (sd)	5.80	5.38	4.97	5.36
	(1.63)	(1.37)	(1.27)	(1.81)

sd, standard deviation.
[a] Scale from 0 (completely left leaning) to 10 (completely right leaning).

APPENDIX TABLE 3.2. *Influence of Political and Commercial Pressure on the Work of Political Journalists in Four European Countries*

	Denmark	Germany	United Kingdom	Spain
Political pressure	0.87_a $(1.69)^a$	1.69_b (2.04)	2.06_b (2.12)	4.21_c (2.92)
Potential/actual budget cuts	1.69_a (2.59)	2.36_a (2.95)	2.45_a (2.70)	4.25_b (3.27)
Advertisers	0.23_a (0.83)	1.09_b (1.99)	0.34_a (0.83)	1.86_c (2.67)
Audience figures	3.32_a (2.85)	4.48_a (3.28)	4.12_a (2.95)	4.55_a (3.69)
Competition with other media	6.57_a (2.93)	6.20_a (2.61)	6.95_a (2.26)	7.22_a (2.61)
N (minimum)	70	197	82	63

[a] Mean score on scales from 0 to 10 with standard deviations in parentheses. In each row, means that do not share subscripts differ at $p < .05$ in the Tukey honestly significant difference comparison.

APPENDIX TABLE 3.3. *Pragmatic versus Sacerdotal Role Conceptions of Political Journalists Working in Denmark, Germany, the United Kingdom, and Spain*

Medium Journalist Works for	Denmark	Germany	United Kingdom	Spain
Print	$3.35_a\,(.85)^a$ N=46	$2.71_b\,(1.00)$ N=94	$2.66_b\,(.97)$ N=35	$3.73_a\,(.94)$ N=22
Public service broadcast	$4.08_a\,(.76)$ N=13	$2.77_b\,(1.19)$ N=64	$3.28_b\,(.94)$ N=25	$3.86_a\,(1.10)$ N=14
Commercial broadcast	$3.17_a\,(.75)$ N=6	$2.50_a\,(1.00)$ N=28	$3.11_a\,(1.18)$ N=18	$3.64_a\,(1.15)$ N=14

[a] Mean score on scales from 1 to 5 with standard deviations in parentheses. In each row, means that do not share subscripts differ at $p<.05$ in the Tukey honestly significant difference comparison.

APPENDIX TABLE 3.4. *Role Conceptions of Political Journalists Working in Denmark, Germany, the United Kingdom, and Spain*

Medium Journalist Works for	Impartial [1] – Partisan [5]			
	Denmark	Germany	United Kingdom	Spain
Print	$1.90_a\,(0.83)^a$ N=46	$2.78_b\,(0.80)$ N=92	$2.82_b\,(1.00)$ N=33	$3.36_c\,(1.04)$ N=22
Public service broadcast	$1.35_a\,(0.47)$ N=13	$1.77_a\,(0.69)$ N=64	$1.58_a\,(0.72)$ N=25	$2.46_b\,(0.95)$ N=14
Commercial broadcast	$1.58_a\,(0.38)$ N=6	$2.29_a\,(0.87)$ N=28	$1.83_a\,(0.79)$ N=18	$3.39_b\,(1.04)$ N=13

	Information [1] – Entertainment [5]			
	Denmark	Germany	United Kingdom	Spain
Print	$2.60_a\,(1.04)$ N=47	$2.94_a\,(0.95)$ N=93	$3.34_b\,(1.00)$ N=33	$2.14_c\,(1.13)$ N=22
Public service broadcast	$1.15_a\,(0.38)$ N=13	$2.49_b\,(0.91)$ N=64	$3.36_c\,(0.81)$ N=25	$2.57_b\,(0.94)$ N=14
Commercial broadcast	$2.17_a\,(0.98)$ N=6	$2.75_b\,(0.89)$ N=28	$3.17_b\,(1.04)$ N=18	$3.29_b\,(1.20)$ N=13

[a] Mean score on scales from 1 to 5 with standard deviations in parentheses. In each row, means that do not share subscripts differ at $p<.05$ in the Tukey honestly significant difference comparison.

Appendix to Chapter 4

APPENDIX TABLE 4.1. *Political Cynicism Among British, Danish, German, and Spanish Political Journalists*

	Denmark	Germany	Spain	United Kingdom
Politicians promise more than they can deliver	3.59_b (0.81)	3.94_a (0.82)	4.06_a (0.72)	3.91_a (0.68)[a]
Easier to become MP through contacts than through competence	3.19_a (1.02)	3.57_b (0.89)	4.02_c (0.84)	3.26_a (0.88)
Ministers are mainly focused on their own interests	2.40_b (0.85)	2.87_a (0.95)	2.98_a (1.03)	2.86_a (0.95)
Politicians do not understand what is happening in society	2.18_b (0.83)	2.73_a (0.88)	3.42_c (0.98)	2.61_a (0.87)
Index	2.85_b (0.56)	3.28_a (0.66)	3.62_c (0.67)	3.16_a (0.57)
N (minimum)	67	196	62	85

[a] Mean score on scales from 1 (completely disagree/low) to 5 (fully agree/high) with standard deviations in parentheses. In each row, means that do not share subscripts differ at $p<.05$ in the Tukey honestly significant difference comparison.

APPENDIX TABLE 4.2. *Perception of Spin Doctors, and Media Salacity by Danish, German, British, and Spanish Political Journalists*

	Denmark	Germany	United Kingdom	Spain
Spokespersons and other communication specialists inhibit journalists in their job (scale from 1 to 5)	2.86_a (1.10)	2.76_a (1.04)	2.99_a (1.09)	3.58_b (1.02)
Politicians driven by media salacity (scale from 1 to 5)	3.07_a (0.76)	3.30_a (0.80)	2.87_b (0.85)	4.41_c (0.56)
N (minimum)	63	199	85	62

[a] Mean score with standard deviations in parentheses. In each row, means that do not share subscripts differ at $p < .05$ in the Tukey honestly significant difference comparison.

APPENDIX TABLE 4.3. *Explaining Political Cynicism among Political Journalists in the United Kingdom, Denmark, Germany, and Spain in One Combined Regression Model*

	b^a	SE	beta
Country (baseline = United Kingdom)			
Denmark	−.337	.092	−.194***
Germany	.020	.073	.015
Spain	−.178	.105	−.100
Medium type (baseline = press agency)			
Print	−.119	.092	−.092
Broadcast	−.104	.092	−.079
Political pressure	.044	.013	.162***
Spokespersons inhibit journalists	.100	.026	.166***
Politicians' media salacity	.294	.036	.402***
Frequency of contacts	−.012	.030	−.018
Years of experience	−.009	.003	−.137**
Gender: male	.021	.059	−.014
Intercept	2.276	.216	

Adjusted $R^2 = .31$; N=425.
[a] Unstandardized coefficients. Missing values are replaced by mean values.
* $p < .05$, ** $p < .01$, *** $p < .001$.

APPENDIX TABLE 4.4. *Explaining Political Cynicism among Political Journalists in the United Kingdom, Denmark, Germany, and Spain in Four Separate Regression Models*

	Denmark	Germany	Spain	United Kingdom
Medium type (baseline = press agency)				
Print	−.072 (.227)	−.028 (.160)	−.223 (.190)	.012 (.201)[d]
Broadcast	−.181 (.241)	.135 (.160)	−.363 (.180)*	−.063 (.193)
Political pressure	−.028 (.035)	.039 (.021)	.033 (.027)	.087 (.026)**
Spokespersons inhibit journalists	.068 (.056)	.119 (.041)**	.096 (.078)	.059 (.050)
Politician's media salacity	.332 (.084)***	.297 (.056)***	.448 (.135)**	.249 (.065)***
Frequency of contacts	.041 (.112)	−.006 (.047)	−.010 (.069)	−.029 (.064)
Years of experience	−.014 (.006)*	−.016 (.005)**	.004 (.008)	−.007 (.005)
Gender: male	.179 (.132)	−.048 (.090)	−.119 (.153)	−.013 (.139)
Intercept	1.625 (.702)*	2.209 (.317)***	1.431 (.729)***	2.391 (.385)***
Adjusted R^2	.24	.23	.22	.26
N	71	201	66	87

The coefficients represent unstandardized betas with standard errors and their significance in four separate ordinary least squares regression models predicting the political cynicism index. Missing values are replaced by mean values.

* $p<.05$, ** $p<.01$, *** $p<.001$.

Appendix to Chapter 5

APPENDIX TABLE 5.1. *Coverage of Scandals and the Private Life of Politicians in Danish, German, British, and Spanish Media Outlets (routine period)*[a]

Country/Media Outlet	News Items (N)	Scandals (%)	Private Life (%)
Denmark			
JyllandsPosten	82	7	2
Politiken	59	15	5
EkstraBladet	21	29	10
DR1 TV-Avisen	34	15	0
TV2 Nyhederne	28	25	0
Germany			
Frankfurter Allgemeine Zeitung	173	0	1
Süddeutsche Zeitung	141	4	3
Bild	88	1	2
ARD Tagesschau	46	1	1
RTL Aktuell	32	0	0
United Kingdom			
The Daily Telegraph	75	9	11
The Guardian	80	9	11
The Sun	50	6	4
BBC News	11	27	0
ITV Nightly News	17	29	12
Spain			
El Pais	144	1	0
ABC	147	1	1
El Mundo	134	7	0
TVE Telediario 2	40	0	0
Antena 3 Noticias	38	3	0
Informativos Telecinco	29	0	0

[a] This analysis is based on the content analysis of two constructed news weeks during the routine period (see Appendix to Chapter 2).

Appendix to Chapter 6

APPENDIX TABLE 6.1. *Knowledge Scores per Outlet in the Two Waves*[a]

Country	Media Exposure	Wave I M[b]	Wave I SD[b]	Wave II M	Wave II SD	N
Denmark	DR1 TV-Avisen	2.81	1.09	3.01	1.01	1280
	TV2 Nyhederne Politiken	2.79	1.10	2.96	1.03	1359
	JyllandsPosten	3.14	.95	3.30	.88	354
	EkstraBladet	2.94	1.01	3.14	.90	352
		2.77	1.16	2.88	1.05	375
United	BBC News	2.39	1.15	2.54	1.17	1070
Kingdom	ITV Nightly News	2.24	1.18	2.40	1.19	725
	The Guardian	2.67	1.08	2.69	1.15	269
	The Daily Telegraph	2.60	1.00	2.72	1.10	273
	The Sun	2.01	1.27	2.05	1.29	311
Spain	TVE Telediario2	2.49	1.17	2.61	1.13	1076
	Antena3 Noticias	2.41	1.19	2.55	1.13	1253
	Informativos Telecinco	2.40	1.19	2.53	1.13	1232
	ABC	2.36	1.20	2.51	1.13	370
	El Pais	2.59	1.15	2.72	1.09	673
	El Mundo	2.51	1.16	2.62	1.12	562

[a] The first wave took place three weeks before the 2008 U.S. presidential elections, the second wave in the week after the elections.

[b] Mean scores and standard deviations of a scale from 0 (low) to 4 (high) measuring knowledge about the US presidential campaign and the US electoral system.

OVERVIEW OF INDEPENDENT VARIABLES

Gender: female = 1; male = 0

Age: in years

Education: recoded into four categories, comparable across the three countries, ranging from 1 (primary school), 2 (high school or equivalent [about 13 years' training]), 3 (BA or three years of vocational training or equivalent [16 years]), and 4 (master's or postgraduate training [19+ years]).

Political interest: one item scale response from 1 (not interested at all) to 7 (very interested).

Question wording: "How interested or not are you in politics?" DK, M=4.96, SD=1.46; UK, M=4.30, SD=1.65; ES, M=4.36, SD=1.68.

Entertainment preference: respondents were asked: "Of all the following programs available on TV, which one would you choose first? and which one would you choose second? (1) national news, (2) local news, (3) film, (4) game show, (5) documentary, (6) soap opera, (7) political show.". Respondents' first choices were recoded into a dummy variable [0] (news/politics preference) or [2] (entertainment preference), which includes the categories from (3) to (6). Second preference responses were recoded into a binary variable [0] (news preference) or [1] (entertainment preference). A combined index of both variables (ranging from 0–3) was constructed: DK, M=1.58, SD=1.09; UK, M=2.30, SD=.90; ES, M=1.67, SD=1.09.

Interpersonal discussion of the U.S.election: a seven-point scale ranging from 1 (never) to 7 (very often). Question wording: "How often did you discuss the U.S. elections in the last three weeks?" DK, M=5.01, SD=1.68; UK, M=4.33, SD=1.87; ES, M=4.69, SD=1.69.

Media exposure (outlet level): number of days (per week) using each news outlet, ranging from 0 (none) to 7 (seven days). DK: DR1, M=3.23, SD=2.32; TV2, M=4.0, SD=2.4; Politiken, M=.91, SD=2.0; JyllandsPosten, M=.78, SD=1.81; Ekstra-Bladet, M=.78, SD=1.76. UK: BBC, M=2.44, SD=2.32; ITV,

M=1.33, SD=1.94; The Guardian, M=.46, SD=1.28; Daily Telegraph, M=.55, SD=1.54; The Sun, M=.66, SD=1.65. ES: TVE, M=2.21, SD=2.30; Antena3, M=3, SD=2.47; Informativos, M=2.72, SD=2.37; ABC, M=.66, SD=1.56; El Pais, M=1.28, SD=2.07; El Mundo, M=1.20, SD=2.08. Attention to U.S. election: a seven-point scale ranging from 1 (no attention at all) to 7 (a great deal of attention). Question wording: "How much attention did you pay to the U.S. elections in the last three weeks?" DK, M=5.45, SD=1.53; UK, M=4.58, SD=1.77; ES, M=4.71, SD=1.66.

Table [8.2]. Predicting Knowledge at Wave 1

	Denmark			United Kingdom			Spain		
	b[b]	SE	beta	b	SE	beta	b	SE	beta
Gender (female)	-.239	.053	-.108***	-.329	.058	-.131***	-.320	.057	-.131***
Age (in years)	-.003	.002	-.030	.010	.002	.103***	.014	.002	.142***
Education	.162	.025	.160***	.261	.035	.176***	.268	.037	.170***
Political interest	.234	.019	.308***	.195	.019	.257***	.151	.017	.208***
Entertainment preference	.054	.026	.053*	-.038	.033	-.027	-.045	.027	-.041
News exposure									
DR1 TV-Avisen	.017	.013	.035						
TV2 Nyhederne	-.022	.012	-.047						
Politiken	.035	.013	.066**						
JyllandsPosten	-.008	.015	-.014						
EkstraBladet	-.002	.0156	-.003						
BBC News				.036	.014	.048			
ITV Nightly News				-.048	.016	-.074**			
The Guardian				.073	.023	.074**			
The Daily Telegraph				.008	.019	.010			
The Sun				-.040	.019	-.052*			
TVE Telediario 2							.020	.014	.038
Antena 3 Noticias							.001	.012	.002
Informativos Telecinco							-.007	.013	-.014
ABC							-.056	.021	-.072**
El Pais							.031	.015	.053*
El Mundo							.021	.016	.036
Constant	1.433	.160		.558	.177		.664	.172	
Adjusted R²			.167			.212			.153
N			1539			1571			1642

[a] Using OLS regressions.
[b] Unstandardized coefficients.
SE, standard error.
* p<.05, ** p<.01, *** p<.001 (two-sided tests).

Appendix to Chapter 7

OVERVIEW OF CONTROL VARIABLES

Gender: female = 1; male = 0

Age: in years

Education: recoded into four categories, comparable across the three countries, ranging from 1 (primary school), 2 (high school or equivalent [about 13 years' training]), 3 (BA or three years of vocational training or equivalent [16 years]) and 4 (master's or postgraduate training [19+ years]).

Political interest: one item scale response from 1 (not interested at all) to 7 (very interested).

Question wording: "How interested or not are you in politics?" DK, M=4.96, SD=1.46; UK, M=4.30, SD=1.65; ES, M=4.36, SD=1.68.

Interpersonal communication: a seven-point scale ranging from 1 (never) to 7 (very often). Question wording: "How often did you discuss domestic politics in the last three weeks?" DK, M=3.92, SD=1.64; UK, M=3.52, SD=1.82; ES, M=4.49, SD=1.70.

Attention to national politics coverage: a seven-point scale ranging from 1 (never) to 7 (very often). Question wording: "During the past three weeks, how much attention did you pay to news on television/newspapers about domestic politics?" DK, M=4.64, SD=1.41; UK, M=4.35, SD=1.62; ES, M=4.77, SD=1.54.

Efficacy (six standard items): (1) Politics can be so complex that people like me don't understand what is going on (r). (2) People like me don't have a say in what the government does (r). (3) I think that I am better informed about politics than others. (4) MPs want to keep in touch with the people. (5) Parties are only interested in people's votes, not their opinions (r). (6) The political parties are so similar that it does not matter who is in government (r). Items marked by (r) are recoded to form an index of political efficacy (Cronbach's a=.0.60). DK, M=3.95, SD=.99; UK, M=3.51, SD=.92; ES, M=3.49, SD=.97.

Appendix to Chapter 8

Gender: female $= 1$; male $= 0$

Age: in years

Education: recoded into four categories, comparable across the three countries, ranging from 1 (primary school), 2 (high school or equivalent [about 13 years' training]), 3 (BA or three years of vocational training or equivalent [16 years]) and 4 (master's or postgraduate training [19+ years]).

Political interest: one item scale response from 1 (not interested at all) to 7 (very interested). Question wording: "How interested or not are you in politics?" DK, M=4.96, SD=1.46; UK, M=4.30, SD=1.65; ES, M=4.36, SD=1.68.

Interpersonal communication: a seven-point scale ranging from 1 (never) to 7 (very often). Question wording: "How often did you discuss domestic politics in the last three weeks?" DK, M=3.92, SD=1.64; UK, M=3.52, SD=1.82; ES, M=4.49, SD=1.70.

Attention to national politics coverage: a seven-point scale ranging from 1 (never) to 7 (very often). DK, M=4.64, SD=1.41; UK, M=4.35, SD=1.62; ES, M=4.77, SD=1.54.

Political ideology: respondents are asked: "In politics, people sometimes talk of "left" and "right." Where would you place yourself on a scale from 0 to 10, where 0 means the extreme left and 10 means the extreme right?" DK, M=4.7, SD=2.16; UK, M=5.1, SD=1.83; ES, M=4.59, SD=1.8.

References

Aalberg, Toril, and James Curran, eds. 2012. *How media inform democracy: A comparative approach.* London: Routledge.

Aalberg, Toril, Peter van Aelst, and James Curran. 2010. Media systems and the political information environment: A cross-national comparison. *International Journal of Press/Politics* 15:255–71.

Adam, Silke, and Michaela Maier. 2010. Personalization of politics – towards a future research agenda: A critical review of the empirical and normative state of the art. *Communication Yearbook* 34:213–58.

Adriaansen, Maud, Philip Van Praag, and Claes H. De Vreese. 2011. Substance matters. How news content can reduce political cynicism. *International Journal of Public Opinion Research* 22:433–57.

Albæk, Erik, David N. Hopmann, and Claes H. de Vreese. 2010. *Kunsten at holde balancen; dækningen af folketingsvalgkampe I tv-nyhederne på DR1 og TV2 1994–2007* [The art of keeping balance: Coverage of parliamentary election in television news on DR1 and TV2 1994–2007]. Odense: University Press of Southern Denmark.

Albæk, Erik, Arjen van Dalen, and Claes H. de Vreese. 2008. Den representative politiske journalist? [The representative political journalist?]. In *Et løfte til journalistikken* [A promise to journalism], eds. T. Mylenberg and P. Bro. Odense: University Press of Southern Denmark.

Algarra, Manuel M., and Norberto G. Gaitano. 1997. The political role of the Spanish journalist. *Political Communication* 14:481–95.

Ansolabehene, Stephen, Roy Behr, and Shanto Iyengar. 1993. *The media game: American politics in the television age.* New York: Macmillan.

Austin, Erica W, and Bruce E. Pinkleton. 1999. The relation between media content evaluations and political disaffection. *Mass Communication & Society* 2:105–22.

Avery, James M. 2009. Videomalaise or virtuous circle? The influence of the news media on political trust. *International Journal of Press/Politics* 14:410–33.

Bakker, Tom P., and Claes H. de Vreese. 2011. Good news for the future? Young people, internet use, and political participation. *Communication Research* 38:451–70.

Bakker, Tom P., Klaus Schönbach, and Claes H. de Vreese. 2012. The people still known as the audience: The limited political use of online participatory platforms. (On file with authors.)

Barabas, Jason, and Jennifer Jerrit. 2009. Estimating the causal effects of media coverage on policy-specific knowledge. *American Journal of Political Science* 53:73–89.

Baron, Reuben M., and David A. Kenny. 1986. The moderator-mediator variable distinction in social psychological research: Conceptual, strategic, and statistical considerations. *Journal of Personality and Social Psychology* 51:1173–82.

Baum, Matthew A. 2002. Sex, lies, and war: How soft news brings foreign policy to the inattentive public. *American Political Science Review* 96:91–109.

Baum, Mathew A. 2003. Soft news and political knowledge: Evidence of absence or absence of evidence? *Political Communication* 20:173–90.

Baum, Matthew A. 2005. Talking the vote: Why presidential candidates hit the talk show circuit. *American Journal of Political Science* 44:213–34.

Baum, Matthew A., and Angela S. Jamison. 2006. The Oprah effect: How soft news helps inattentive citizens vote consistently. *Journal of Politics* 68:946–59.

Bennett, Stephen E. 1995. Americans' knowledge of ideology, 1980–1992. *American Politics Quarterly* 23:259–78.

Bennett, Stephen E., Richard Flickinger, and Staci Rhine. 2000. Political talk over here, over there, over time. *British Journal of Political Science* 30:99–119.

Bennett, W. Lance. 1996. An introduction to journalism norms and representations of politics. *Political Communication* 13:373–84.

Bennett, W. Lance. 1996. *News: The politics of illusion.* 3rd ed. White Plains, New York: Longman.

Bennett, W. Lance. 2001. *News: The politics of illusion.* 4th ed. White Plains, New York: Longman.

Bennett, W. Lance. 2003. *News: The politics of illusion.* 5th ed. White Plains, NY: Longman.

Bennett, W. Lance. 2003. The burglar alarm that just keeps ringing: A response to Zaller. *Political Communication* 20:131–8.

Bennett, W. Lance, Regina G. Lawrence, and Steven Livingston. 2007. *When the press fails: Political power and the news media from Iraq to Katrina*. Chicago: University of Chicago Press.

Benson, Rodney. 2004. Bringing the sociology of media back in. *Political Communication* 21:275–92.

Benson, Rodney. 2008. "Normative theories of journalism." In W. Donsbach, ed., The Blackwell International Encyclopedia of Communication, 2591–2597.

Benson, Rodney, and Daniel C. Hallin. 2007. How states, markets and globalization shape the news: The French and U.S. national press, 1965–97. *European Journal of Communication* 22:27–48.

Birnie, Carolyn, M. Joy McClure, John E. Lydon, and Diane Holmberg. 2009. Attachment avoidance and commitment aversion: A script for relationship failure. *Personal Relationships* 16:79–97.

Bjørnsen, Gunn, Jan Frederik Hovden, and Rune Ottosen. 2007. Journalists in the making: Findings from a longitudinal study of Norwegian journalism students. *Journalism Practice* 1:383–403.

Blach-Ørsten, Mark, and Peter Bro. 2009. Inde på Christiansborg: den synkroniserede journalistik [Inside Christiansborg. Synchronized journalism]. In *Hvor kommer nyhederne fra? Den journalistiske fødekæde i Danmark før og nu* [Where does the news come from? The journalistic food chain in Denmark before and now], eds. Anker Brink Lund, Ida Willig, and Mark Blach-Ørsten, 19–28. Århus, Denmark: Forlaget Ajour.

Blendon, Robert J., John M. Benson, Rich Morin, David E. Altman, Mollyann Brodie, and Maria Brossard. 1997. Changing attitudes in America. In *Why people don't trust government*, eds. Joseph Nye Jr, Philip D. Zelikow, and David C. King, 205–16. Cambridge, MA: Harvard University Press.

Blumler, Jay G., and Michael Gurevitch. 1991. The election agenda-setting role of journalists: Comparative observation at the BBC and NBC. In *The formation of campaign agendas: A comparative analysis of party and media role in recent American and British elections*, eds. Holli A. Semetko, Jay G. Blumler, Michael Gurevitch, and David H. Weaver, 33–61. Hillsdale, NJ: Lawrence Erlbaum.

Blumler, Jay G., and Michael Gurevitch. 1995. *The crisis of public communication*. London: Routledge.

Blumler, Jay G., and Michael Gurevitch. 2001. "Americanization" reconsidered: U.K.-U.S. campaign communication comparisons across time. In *Mediated politics. Communication in the future of democracy*, eds. W. Lance Bennett and Robert M. Entman, 380–406. Cambridge: Cambridge University Press.

Blumler, Jay G., and Denis Kavanagh. 1999. The third age of political communication. *Political Communication* 16:209–30.

Bouliane, Shelley. 2009. Does internet use affect engagement? A meta-analysis of research. *Political Communication* 26:193–211.

Brandenburg, Heinz. 2006. Party strategy and media bias. A quantitative analysis of the 2005 UK election campaign. *Journal of Elections, Public Opinion & Parties* 16:157–78.

Brandt, Mark J., and Christine Reyna. 2010. The role of prejudice and the need for closure in religious fundamentalism. *Personality and Social Psychology Bulletin* 36:715–25.

Brants, Kees. 1998. Who's afraid of infotainment? *European Journal of Communication* 13:315–35.

Brants, Kees, Claes H. de Vreese, Judith Möller, and Philip van Praag. 2010. The real spiral of cynicism? Symbiosis and mistrust between politicians and journalists. *International Journal of Press/Politics* 15:25–40.

Brants, Kees, and Peter Neijens. 1998. The infotainment of politics. *Political Communication* 15:149–64.

Brants, Kees, and Hetty van Kempen. 2000. The uncertain watchdog. In *Political journalism: New challenge*, eds. Raymond Kuhn and Erik Neveu, 168–85. London: Routledge.

Brants, Kees, and Philip van Praag. 2006. Signs of media logic: Half a century of political communication in the Netherlands. *Javnost/The Public* 13:25–40.

Breed, Warren. 1955. Social control in the newsroom: A functional analysis. *Social Forces* 33:326–35.

Brians, Craig L., and Martin P. Wattenberg. 1996. Campaign issue knowledge and salience: Comparing reception from TV commercials, TV news, and newspapers. *American Journal of Political Science* 40:172–93.

Bro, Peter. 2008. Normative navigation in the news media. *Journalism* 9:309–29.

Buffardi, Laura E., and W. Keith Campbell. 2008. Narcissism and social networking web sites. *Personality and Social Psychology Bulletin* 34:1303–14.

Burgoon, Judee K., and Michael Burgoon. 1980. Predictors of newspaper readership. *Journalism Quarterly* 57:589–96.

Cappella, Joseph, and Kathleen Hall Jamieson. 1997. *Spiral of cynicism: The press and the public good*. Oxford: Oxford University Press.

Chaffee, Steven H., and Stacey F. Kanihan. 1997. Learning about politics from the mass media. *Political Communication* 14:421–30.

Chaffee, Steven H., and Joan Schleuder. 1986. Measurement and effects of attention to media news. *Human Communication Research* 13:76–107.

Chaffee, Steven H., Xinshu Zhao, and Glenn Leshner. 1994. Political knowledge and the campaign media of 1992. *Communication Research* 21:305–24.

Chalaby, Jean. 1998. *The invention of journalism.* New York: St. Martin's.

Chang, Lin C., and Jon A. Krosnick. 2003. Measuring the frequency of regular behaviors: Comparing the "typical week" to the "past week." *Sociological Methodology* 33:55–80.

Christen, Cindy T., Prathana Kannaovakun, and Albert C. Gunther. 2002. Hostile media perceptions: Partisan assessments of press and public during the 1997 United Parcel Service strike. *Political Communication* 19:423–36.

Clayman, Steven, John Herritage, Mark Elliott, and Laurie L. McDonald. 2007. When does the watchdog bark? Conditions of aggressive questioning in presidential news conferences. *American Sociological Review* 72:23–41.

Cohen, Bernard C. 1963. *The press and foreign policy.* Princeton: Princeton University Press.

Coleman, Stephen. 2012. Believing the news: From sinking trust to atrophied efficacy. *European Journal of Communication* 29 (3): 35–45.

Coleman, Stephen, and Jay G. Blumler. 2009. *The Internet and democratic citizenship: Theory, practice, and policy.* Cambridge: Cambridge University Press.

Colomer, Josep M., ed. 2008. *Comparative European politics.* 3rd ed. London: Routledge.

Converse, Philip E. 1964. The nature of belief systems in mass publics. In *Ideology and discontent*, ed. David E. Apter. New York: Free Press.

Cook, Timothy E. 2005. *Governing with the news. The news media as a political institution.* 2nd ed. Chicago: University of Chicago Press.

Craig, Steven C., Richard G. Niemi, and George E. Silver. 1990. Political efficacy and trust: A report on the NES pilot study items. *Political Behavior* 12:289–314.

Crigler, Ann, and Klaus Bruhn Jensen. 1991. Discourses on politics: Talking about public issues in the United States and Denmark. In *Communication and citizenship. Journalism and the public sphere in the new media age*, eds. Peter Dahlgren and Colin Sparks. London: Routledge.

Culbertson, Hugh M. 1983. Three perspectives on American journalism. *Journalism Monographs* 83:1–33.

Curran, James, Shanto Iyengar, Anker Brink Lund, and Inka Salovaara-Moring. 2009. Media system, public knowledge and democracy: A Comparative Study. *European Journal of Communication* 24:5–26.

Curran, James, and Myung-Jin Park, eds. 2000. *De-westernizing media studies*. London: Routledge.

Curran, James and Jean Seaton. 2010. *Power without responsibility*. London: Routledge.

D'Alessio, Dave, and Mike Allen. 2000. Media bias in presidential elections: A meta-analysis. *Journal of Communication* 50:133–56.

Dahlgren, Peter. 1995. *Television and the public sphere: Citizenship, democracy and the media*. London: Sage.

Davis, Aeron. 2009. Journalist-source relations, mediated reflexivity and the politics of politics. *Journalism Studies* 10:204–19.

De Miguel, Juan Carlos, and Víctor Pozas. 2009. Polarización ideological o económica? Relaciones entre los medios y el poder politico y corporativo [Political or economical polarization? Relations between the media and political and economic power]. *Viento Sur* 130 (Mayo):43–52.

De Vreese, Claes H. 2001. Election coverage – new directions for public broadcasting: The Netherlands and beyond. *European Journal of Communication* 16:155–80.

De Vreese, Claes H. 2004. The effects of strategic news on political cynicism, issue evaluations, and policy support: A two-wave experiment. *Mass Communication & Society* 7:191–214.

De Vreese, Claes H. 2005. The spiral of cynicism reconsidered: The mobilizing function of news. *European Journal of Communication* 20:283–301.

De Vreese, Claes H. 2007. A spiral of euroscepticism: The media's fault? *Acta Politica* 42:271–86.

De Vreese, Claes. 2009. Campaign communication and the media. In *Comparing democracies 3*, eds. Lawrence LeDuc, Richard Niemi, and Pippa Norris, 118–49. London: Sage.

De Vreese, Claes. 2012. Comparative political communication research. In *Oxford handbook of political communication*, eds. Kate Kenski and Kathleen Hall Jamieson. Oxford: Oxford University Press.

De Vreese, Claes H., Susan A. Banducci, Holli A. Semetko, and Hajo A. Boomgaarden. 2006. The news coverage of the 2004 European parliamentary election campaign in 25 countries. *European Union Politics* 7:477–504.

De Vreese, Claes H., and Hajo G. Boomgaarden. 2006. News, political knowledge and participation: The differential effects of news media exposure on political knowledge and participation. *Acta Politica* 41:317–41.

De Vreese, Claes H., and Matthijs Elenbaas. 2010. Spin and political publicity: Effect on news coverage and public opinion. In *Challenging the primacy of politics. Political communication in postmodern democracy*, eds. Kees Brants and Katrin Voltmer. New York: Palgrave Macmillan.

De Vreese, Claes H., Jochen Peter, and Holli A. Semetko. 2001. Framing politics at the launch of the Euro: A cross-national comparative study of frames in the news. *Political Communication* 18:107–22.

De Vreese, Claes H., Andreas R.T. Schuck, Rachid Azrout, Hajo Boom-gaarden, Matthijs Elenbaas, Joost Van Spanje, and Rens Vliegenthart. 2010. The 2009 European parliamentary elections: (In)visible? European? Exciting? Results from a twenty-seven country study. Paper presented at the 3rd international conference of the European Communication Research Association, Hamburg.

De Vreese, Claes H., and Holli A. Semetko. 2002. Cynical and engaged: Strategic campaign coverage, public opinion, and mobilization in a referendum. *Communication Research* 29:615–41.

De Vreese, Claes H., and Holli A. Semetko. 2004. News matters: Influences on the vote in a referendum campaign. *European Journal of Political Research* 43:699–722.

De Vreese, Claes H., and Mette Tobiasen. 2007. Conflict and identity. Explaining turnout and anti-integrationist voting in the Danish 2004 elections for the European Parliament. *Scandinavian Political Studies* 30:87–111.

Delli Carpini, Michael X., and Scott Keeter. 1996. *What Americans know about politics and why it matters*. New Haven, CT: Yale University Press.

Delli Carpini, Michael X., and Bruce A. Williams. 2001. Let us infotain you: Politics in the new media age. In *Mediated Politics: Communication in the Future of Democracy*, eds. W. Lance Bennett and Robert M. Entman, 160–81. Cambridge: Cambridge University Press.

Demers, David. 1998. Spiral of cynicism: The press and the public good. *Mass Communication and Society* 1:107–9.

Deuze, Mark. 2002. Journalists in the Netherlands: An analysis of the people, the issues and the (inter-)national environment. Amsterdam: Aksant Academic.

Díez Nicolas, Juan, and Holli A. Semetko. 1995. La television y las elecciones de 1993 [Television and the 1993 elections]. In *Comunicación política*, eds. Alejandro Muñoz-Alonso and Juan Rospir, 243–304. Madrid: Editorial Universitas.

Dimmick, John, and Philip Coit. 1982. Level of analysis in mass media decision making: A taxonomy, research strategy, and illustrative data analysis. *Mass Communication Review Yearbook* 4:361–90.

Djerf-Pierre, Monika. 2000. Squaring the circle: Public service and commercial news on Swedish television 1956–99. *Journalism Studies* 1:239–60.

Dobek-Ostrowska, Bogusława, Michał Głowacki, Karol Jakubowicz, and Miklós Sükösd, eds. 2010. *Comparative media systems: European and global perspectives.* Budapest: Central European University Press.

Donsbach, Wolfgang. 2004. Psychology of news decisions: Factors behind journalists' professional behavior. *Journalism* 5:131–57.

Donsbach, Wolfgang. 2008. Journalists' role perception. In *The international encyclopedia of communication.* Oxford: Blackwell.

Donsbach, Wolfgang. 2010. The global journalist: A professional structures being flattened? In *Comparative media systems: European and global perspectives,* eds. Bogusława Dobek-Ostrowska, Michał Głowacki, Karol Jakubowicz, and Miklós Sükösd, 153–70. Budapest: Central European University Press.

Donsbach, Wolfgang, and Thomas E. Patterson. 2004. Political news journalists: Partisanship, professionalism, and political roles in five countries. In *Comparing political communication: Theories, cases, and challenges,* eds. Frank Esser and Barbara Pfetsch, 251–70. Cambridge: Cambridge University Press.

Druckman, James N., and Kjersten R. Nelson. 2003. Framing and deliberation: How citizens' conversations limit elite influence. *American Journal of Political Science* 47:729–45.

Edwards, George C., and Wood, B. Dan 1999. Who influences whom? The president, congress, and the media. *American Political Science Review* 93:327–44.

Entman, Robert M. 1989. Democracy without citizens: Media and the decay of American politics. New York: Oxford University Press.

Entman, Robert M. 2003. Projections of power: Framing news, public opinion, and U.S. foreign policy. Chicago: University of Chicago Press.

Erber, Ralph, and Richard R. Lau. 1990. Political cynicism revisited: An information-processing reconciliation of policy-based and incumbency-based interpretations of changes in trust in government. *American Journal of Political Science Review* 34:236–53.

Ericson, Richard V. 1998. How journalists visualize fact. *Annals of the American Academy of Political and Social Science* 560:83–95.

Esser, Frank. 1999. Tabloidization of news: A comparative analysis of Anglo-American and German press journalism. *European Journal of Communication* 14:291–325.

Esser, Frank. 2008. Dimensions of political news culture: Sound bite and image bite news in France, Germany, Great Britain, and the United Kingdom. *International Journal of Press/Politics* 13:401–28.

Esser, Frank, and Paul D'Angelo. 2003. Framing the press and the publicity process: A content analysis of meta-coverage in campaign 2000 Network News. *American Behavioral Scientist* 46:617–41.

Esser, Frank, Claes H. de Vreese, Jesper Strömbäck, Peter van Aelst, Toril Aalberg, James Stanyer, Günther Lengauer, et al. 2012 Political information opportunities in Europe: A longitudinal and comparative study of 13 television systems. *International Journal of Press/Politics* 17, 3, 247–274.

Esser, Frank, and Thomas Hanitzsch, eds. 2012. *Handbook of comparative communication research*. New York: Routledge.

Esser, Frank, and Barbara Pfetsch, eds. 2004. *Comparing political communication: Theories, cases, and challenges*. Cambridge: Cambridge University Press.

Esser, Frank, Carsten Reinemann, and David Fan. 2000. Spin doctoring in British and German election campaigns: How the press is being confronted with a new quality of political PR. *European Journal of Communication* 15:209–39.

Esser, Frank, Carsten Reinemann, and David Fan. 2001. Spin doctors in the United States, Great Britain, and Germany: Metacommunication about media manipulation. *Harvard International Journal of Press/Politics* 6:16–45.

Esser, Frank, and Bernd Spanier. 2005. News management as news. *Journal of Political Marketing* 4:27–57.

European Commission, Directorate-General for Education and Culture. 2001. *Eurobarometer: Public opinion in the European Union. Report No. 54*. Brussels, Belgium: Office for official publications of the European communities, 2001.

European Science Foundation. 2009. *Political communication cultures in Western Europe – a comparative study*. (Accessed February 3, 2012, at www.esf.org/publications/social-sciences.html.)

Eveland Jr., William P, and Dietmar A. Scheufele. 1995. Connecting news media use with gaps in knowledge and participation. *Political Communication* 17:215–37.

Fairbanks, Jenille, Kenneth D. Plowman, and Brad L. Rawlins. 2007. Transparency in government communication. *Journal of Public Affairs* 7:23–37.

Fallows, James. 1996. Breaking the news: How the news media undermine American democracy. New York: Pantheon.

Frank, Russell. 2003. "These crowded circumstances:" When pack journalists bash pack journalism. *Journalism* 4:441–58.

Frees, Edward. 2004. Longitudinal and panel data: Analysis and applications in the social sciences. New York: Cambridge University Press.

Fricker, Robert D., and Matthias Schonlau. 2002. Advantages and disadvantages of Internet research surveys: Evidence from the literature. *Field Methods* 14:347–67.

Gaber, Ivar. 2009. The slow death of the Westminster Lobby: Collateral damage from the MPs' expenses scandal. *British Politics* 4:478–97.

Galtung, Johan, and Mari Ruge. 1965. The structure of foreign news: The presentation of the Congo, Cuba, and Cyprus crises in four Norwegian newspapers. *Journal of International Peace Research* 1:64–91.

Gans, Herbert J. 1979. *Deciding what's news: A study of the CBS Evening News, NBC Nightly News, Newsweek, and Time.* New York: Vintage.

Gaziano, Cecile. 1997. Forecasting 2000: Widening the gap. *Journalism and Mass Communication Quarterly* 74:237–64.

Görke, Alexander, and Armin Scholl. 2006. Niklas Luhmann's theory of social systems and journalism research. *Journalism studies* 7:645–56.

Grabe, Maria E., Shuhua Zhou, and Brooke Barnett. 2001. Explicating sensationalism in television news: Content and the bells and whistles of form. *Journal of Broadcasting and Electronic Media* 45:635–55.

Grabe, Maria E., Shuhua Zhou, Annie Lang, and Paul D. Bolls. 2000. Packaging television news: The effects of tabloid on information processing and evaluative responses. *Journal of Broadcasting and Electronic Media* 44:581–98.

Graber, Doris A. 1990. Seeing is remembering: How visuals contribute to learning from television news. *Journal of Communication* 40:134–55.

Graber, Doris A. 2001. Processing politics: Learning from television in the Internet age. Chicago: Chicago University Press.

Graber, Doris A. 2003. The media and democracy: Beyond myths and stereotypes. *Annual Review of Political Science* 6:139–60.

Gunter, Barrie. 1987. Poor reception: Misunderstanding and forgetting broadcast news. Hillsdale, NJ: Lawrence Erlbaum.

Gunther, Richard, José R. Montero, and José W. Wert. 2000. The media and politics in Spain: From dictatorship to democracy. In *Democracy and the media: A comparative perspective*, eds. Richard Gunther and Anthony Mughan. Cambridge: Cambridge University Press.

Gunther, Richard, and Anthony Mughan, eds. 2000. *Democracy and the media: A comparative perspective.* Cambridge: Cambridge University Press.

Gurevitch, Michael, and Jay G. Blumler. 1990. Political communication systems and democratic values. In *Democracy and the mass media*, ed. Judith Lichtenberg. Cambridge: Cambridge University Press.

Gurevitch, Michael, and Jay G. Blumler. 2004. State of the art of comparative political communication research: Poised for maturity? In *Comparing political communication: Theories, cases, and challenges*, eds. Frank Esser and Barbara Pfetsch, 325–43. Cambridge: Cambridge University Press.

Hallin, Daniel. 1996. Commercialism and professionalism in the American news media. In *Mass media and society*, eds. James Curran and Michael Gurevitch, 243–6. London: Edward Arnold.

Hallin, Daniel. 2009. Not the end of journalism history. *Journalism* 10:332–4.

Hallin, Daniel, and Paolo Mancini. 2004a. Americanization, globalization, and secularization: Understanding the convergence of media systems and political communication. In *Comparing political communication: Theories, cases, and challenges*, eds. Frank Esser and Barbara Pfetsch, 25–44. Cambridge: Cambridge University Press.

Hallin, Daniel, and Paolo Mancini. 2004b. *Comparing media systems. Three models of media and politics*. Cambridge: Cambridge University Press.

Hallin, Daniel, and Stylianos Papathanassopoulos. 2002. Political clientalism and the media: Southern Europe and Latin America in comparative perspective. *Media, Culture and Society* 24:175–95.

Hallin, Daniel, and Paolo Mancini. 2012. Comparing media systems: A response to critics. In *Handbook of comparative communication research*, eds. F. Esser, Frank, and T. Hanitzsch, 207–20. New York: Routledge.

Hanitzsch, Thomas. 2009. Comparative journalism studies. In *The handbook of journalism studies*, eds. Karin Wahl-Jorgensen and Thomas Hanitzsch, 413–27. London: Routledge.

Hanitzsch, Thomas. 2011. Populist disseminators, detached watchdogs, critical change agents, and opportunist facilitators: Professional milieus, the journalistic field and autonomy in 18 countries. *International Communication Gazette* 73:477–94.

Hanitzsch, Thomas, Maria Anikina, Rosa Berganza, Incilay Cangoz, Mihai Coman, Basyouni Hamada, Folker Hanusch, et al. 2010. Modeling perceived influences on journalism: Evidence from a cross-national survey of journalists. *Journalism and Mass Communication Quarterly* 87:7–24.

Hanitzsch, Thomas, Folker Hanusch, Claudia Mellado Ruiz, Maria Anikina, Rosa Berganza, Incilay Cangoz, Mihai Coman, et al. 2010. Mapping journalism cultures across nations: A comparative study of 18 countries. *Journalism Studies* 12:273–93.

Harkness, Janet A. 2012. Comparative survey research. In *Handbook of comparative communication research*, eds. F. Esser, Frank, and T. Hanitzsch, 445–58. New York: Routledge.

Henningham, John. 1995. Political journalists' political and professional values. *Australian Journal of Political Science* 30:321–34.

Henningham, John, and Anthony Delano. 1998. British journalists. In *The global journalist: News people around the world*, 143–60. Cresskill, NJ: Hampton Press.

Hess, Stephen. 1981. *The Washington reporters.* Washington, DC: Brookings Institution.

Hess, Stephen. 1992. All the president's reporters: A new survey of the White House press corps. *Presidential Studies Quarterly* 22:311–21.

Hoffstetter, Richard C. 1976. Bias in the news: A study of network coverage of the 1972 presidential campaign. Columbus: Ohio State University Press.

Holz-Bacha, Christina. 2004. Germany: How the private life of politicians got into the media. *Parliamentary Affairs* 57:41–52.

Hopmann, David N., Claes H. de Vreese, and Erik Albæk. 2011. Incumbency bonus in election coverage explained: The logics of political power and the media market. *Journal of Communication* 61, 2, 264–282.

Iyengar, Shanto. 1991. *Is anyone responsible: How television frames political issues.* Chicago, IL: University of Chicago Press.

Iyengar, Shanto, James Curran, Anker Brink Lund, Inka Salovaara-Moring, Kyu S. Hahn, and Sharon Coen. 2010. Cross-national versus individual-level differences in political information: A media systems perspective. *Journal of Elections, Public Opinion, and Parties* 20:291–309.

Iyengar, Shanto, and Kyu S. Hahn. 2009. Red media, blue media: Evidence of ideological selectivity in media use. *Journal of Communication* 59:19–39.

Jackman, Robert W. 1985. Cross-national statistical research and the study of comparative politics. *American Journal of Political Science* 29:161–82.

Jacobs, Randy D. 1995. Exploring the determinants of cable television subscriber satisfaction. *Journal of Broadcasting and Electronic Media* 39:262–74.

Jensen, Anders T., Toril Aalberg, and Kees Aarts. 2012. Informed citizens, media use, and public knowledge of parties' policy positions. In *How media inform democracy. A comparative approach,* eds. Toril Aalberg and James Curran, 138–58. London: Routledge.

Jerit, Jennifer, Jason Barabas, and Toby Bolsen. 2006. Citizens, knowledge, and the information environment. *American Journal of Political Science* 50:266–82.

Johnstone, John W.C., Edward J. Slawski, and William W. Bowman. 1976. *The news people: A sociological portrait of American journalists and their work.* Urbana: University of Illinois Press.

Josephi, Beate. 2005. Journalism in the global age: Between normative and empirical. *Gazette* 67:575–90.

Kaase, Max. 1994. Is there personalization in politics? Candidates and voting behavior in Germany. *International Political Science Review* 15:211–30.

Kavanagh, Trevor. 2011. Downsizing? Not on the politics beat. *British Journalism Review* 22:55–9.

Kelly, Mary, Gianpietro Mazzoleni, and Denis McQuail. 2004. *The media in Europe: The Euromedia handbook*. 3rd ed. London: Sage.

Kepplinger, Hans Mathias. 2000. The declining image of the German political elite. *International Journal of Press/Politics* 5:71–80.

Kerbel, Matthew, Sumaiya Apee, and Marc Ross. 2000. "PBS Ain't So Different: Public Broadcasting, Election Frames, and Democratic Empowerment." *Harvard Journal of Press/Politics* 5:8–32.

Klaus, Elisabeth. 2009. Media systems, equal rights and the freedom of the press: Gender as a case in point. In *Press freedom and pluralism in Europe: Concepts and conditions*, eds. Andrea Czepek, Melanie Hellwig, and Eva Novak, 101–14. Bristol: Intellect.

Kleinnijenhuis, Jan. 1991. Newspaper complexity and the knowledge gap. *European Journal of Communication* 6:499–522.

Kleinnijenhuis, Jan, Anita M. van Hoof, and Dirk Oegema. 2006. Negative news and the sleeper effect of distrust. *International Journal of Press/Politics* 11:86–104.

Köcher, Renate. 1986. Bloodhound or missionaries: Role definition of German and British journalists. *European Journal of Communication* 1:43–64.

Kohn, Melvin L. 1989. Cross-national research as an analytical strategy. In *Cross-national research in sociology*, ed. Melvin L. Kohn, 77–102. London: Sage.

Kwak, Nojin. 1999. Revisiting the knowledge gap hypothesis: Education, motivation, and media use. *Communication Research* 26:385–413.

Larsson, Larsåke. 2002. Journalists and politicians: A relationship requiring manoeuvring space. *Journalism Studies* 3:21–33.

Latimer, Margaret K. 1984. Policy issues and personal images in political advertising in state election. *Journalism Quarterly* 61:776–84, 852.

Lazarsfeld, Paul F., Bernard Berelson, and Hazel Gaudet. 1944. *The people's choice: How the voter makes up his mind in a presidential campaign*. 3rd ed. New York: Columbia University Press.

Lecheler, Sophie K., and Claes H. de Vreese. 2011. Getting real: The duration of framing effects. *Journal of Communication* 36:400–25.

Lecheler, Sophie K., and Claes de Vreese. 2013. Forthcoming. What a difference a day makes? The effects of repetitive and competitive news framing over time. *Communication Research*, 40, 2, 147–175.

Liu, Yung-Ii, and Willaim P. Eveland Jr. 2005. Education, need for cognition, and campaign interest as moderators of news effects on political knowledge: An analysis of the knowledge gap. *Journalism and Mass Communication Quarterly* 82:910–29.

Livingstone, Sonia. 2003. On the challenges of cross-national comparative media research. *European Journal of Communication* 18:477–500.

Löffelholz, Martin, and David Weaver, eds. 2008. *Global journalism research: Theories, methods, findings, future.* Oxford: Blackwell Publishing.

Luskin, Robert C. 1990. Explaining political sophistication. *Political Behavior* 12:331–61.

Luskin, Robert C., and John G.Bullock. 2005. "'Don't know' means 'don't know.'" Paper presented at the annual meeting of the Midwest Political Science Association, Chicago.

Mancini, Paolo. 1993. Between trust and suspicion: How political journalists solve the dilemma. *European Journal of Communication* 8:33–51.

Mancini, Paolo. 2000. Political complexity and alternative models of journalism. In *De-Westernizing media studies*, eds. James Curran and Myung-Jin Park, 265–78. London: Routledge.

Marcus, Gregory E., and Michael B. MacKuen. 1993. Anxiety, enthusiasm, and the vote: The emotional underpinnings of learning and involvement during presidential campaigns. *American Political Science Review* 87:672–85.

Markus, Gregory. 1979. *Analyzing Panel Data.* Beverly Hills: Sage.

Mazzoleni, Gianpietro, and Winfried Schulz. 1999. Mediatization of politics: A challenge for democracy? *Political Communication* 16:247–61.

McChesney, Robert W. 1999. Rich media, poor democracy: Communication politics in dubious times. Urbana: University of Illinois Press.

McCombs, Maxwell E., and Amy Reynolds. 2009. How the news shapes our civil agenda. In *Media effects: Advances in theory and research*, 3rd ed., eds. Jennings Bryant and Mary Beth Oliver, 1–16. London: Routledge.

McCombs, Maxwell E., and Donald L. Shaw. 1972. The agenda-setting function of the mass media. *Public Opinion Quarterly* 69: 813–24.

McGraw, Kathleen M., and Neil Pinney. 1990. The effects of general and domain-specific expertise on political memory and judgment. *Social Cognition* 8:9–30.

McLachlan, Shelley, and Peter Golding. 2000. Tabloidization in the British press: A quantitative investigation into changes in British newspapers, 1952–1997. In *Tabloid tales: Global debates over media standards*, eds. Colin Sparks and John Tulloch, 76–90. Lanham, MD: Rowman and Littlefield.

McLeod, Jack M., Zhongshi Guo, Katie Daily, Catherine A. Steele, Huiping Huang, Edward Horowitz, and Huailin Chen. 1996. The impact of traditional and nontraditional media forms in the 1992 presidential election. *Journalism and Mass Communication Quarterly* 73:401–16.

McLeod, Douglas M., Gerald M. Kosicki, and Jack M. McLeod. 2002. Resurveying the boundaries of political communication effects. In *Media effects: Advances in theory and research*, eds. Jenning Bryant and Dolf Zilmann. Mahwah, NJ: Lawrence Erlbaum.

McLeod, Jack M., and Daniel G. McDonald. 1985. Beyond simple exposure: Media orientations and their impact on political processes. *Communication Research* 12:3–33.

McLeod, Douglas M., and Elizabeth M. Perse. 1994. Direct and indirect effects of socioeconomic status on public affairs knowledge. *Journalism Quarterly* 71:433–42.

McNair, Brian. 2000a. Journalism and democracy: A millennium audit. *Journalism Studies* 1:197–211.

McNair, Brian. 2000b. *News and journalism in the UK.*, 2nd ed. London: Routledge.

McNair, Brian. 2004. PR must die: Spin, anti-spin, and political public relations in the UK, 1997–2004. *Journalism Studies* 5:325–338.

McNair, Brian. 2009. Journalism and democracy. In *The handbook of journalism studies*, eds. Karin Wahl-Jorgensen and Thomas Hanitzsch, 237–49. London: Routledge.

McQuail, Denis. 2005. *McQuail's mass communication theory.*, 5th ed. London: Sage.

Merritt, David. 1995. Public journalism and public life. Why telling the news is not enough. Hillsdale, NJ: Lawrence Erlbaum.

Miller, Arthur H., Edie N. Goldenberg, and Lutz Erbring. 1979. Typeset politics: Impact of newspapers on public confidence. *American Political Science Review* 73:67–84.

Min, Young. 2004. News coverage of negative political campaigns: An experiment of negative campaign effects on turnout and candidate preference. *Harvard International Journal of Press/Politics* 9:95–111.

Mishler, William, and Richard Rose. 2001. What are the origins of political trust? Testing institutional and cultural theories in postcommunist societies. *Comparative Political Studies* 34:30–62.

Moloney, Kevin, and Rob Colmer. 2001. Does political PR enhance or trivialise democracy? The UK general election 2001 as contest between presentation and substance. *Journal of Marketing Management* 17:957–68.

Molotch, Harvey, and Marilyn Lester. 1974. News as purposive behavior: On the strategic use of routine events, accidents, and scandals. *American Sociological Review* 39:101–12.

Munck, Geraldo L. 2007. The past and present of comparative politics. In *Passion, craft, and method in comparative politics*, eds. Geraldo L.

Munck and Richard Snyder, 32–59. Baltimore, MD: Johns Hopkins University Press.

Mundorf, Norbert, Dan Drew, Dolf Zillmann, and James Weaver. 1990. Effects of disturbing news on recall of subsequently presented news. *Communication Research* 17:601–15.

Myers, R. Kelly. 1994. Interpersonal and mass media communication: Political learning in New Hampshire's first-in-the-nation presidential primary. *Sociological Spectrum* 14:143–65.

Negrine, Ralph, Christina Holtz-Bacha, Paolo Mancini, and Stylianos Papathanassopoulos. 2007. *The professionalization of political communication.* Bristol: Intellect.

Nelson, Thomas E., Rosalee Clawson, and Zoe M. Oxley. 1997. Media framing of a civil liberties conflict and its effect on tolerance. *American Political Science Review* 91:567–83.

Neuman, W. Russell. 1986. The paradox of mass politics: Knowledge and opinion in the American electorate. New York: McGraw-Hill.

Neuman, W. Russell, Marion R. Just, and Ann N. Crigler. 1992. *Common knowledge: News and the construction of political meaning.* Chicago: The University of Chicago Press.

Neveu, Erik. 2002. Four generations of political journalism. In *Political journalism: New challenges, new practices*, eds. Raymond Kuhn and Erik Neveu, 24–44. London: Routledge.

Newton, Kenneth. 1999. Mass media effects: Mobilization or media malaise? *British Journal of Political Science* 29:577–99.

Nimmo, Dan D. 1964. Newsgathering in Washington. A study in political communication. New York: Atherton.

Norris, Pippa. 2000. *A virtuous circle. Political communications in postindustrial societies.* Cambridge: Cambridge University Press.

Norris, Pippa. 2009. Comparative political communications: Common frameworks or Babelian confusion? *Government and Opposition* 44:321–40.

Oliver, Richard L. 1981. Measurement and evaluation of satisfaction processes in retail settings. *Journal of Retailing* 57:25–48.

Palmgreen, Philip. 1979. Mass media use and political knowledge. *Journalism Monographs* 61 (May).

Palmgreen, Philip, and J. D. Rayburn II. 1985. A comparison of gratification models of media satisfaction. *Communication Monographs* 52:335–48.

Papacharissi, Zizi, and Alan M. Rubin. 2000. Predictors of Internet use. *Journal of Broadcasting and Electronic Media* 44:175–96.

Papathanassopoulos, Stylianos. 2001. Media commercialization and journalism in Greece. *European Journal of Communication* 16:505–21.

Papatheodorou, Fotini, and David Machin. 2003. The umbilical cord that was never cut: The post-dictatorial intimacy between the political elite and the mass media in Greece and Spain. *European Journal of Communication* 18:31–53.

Patterson, Thomas E. 1980. The mass media election: How Americans choose their president. New York: Praeger.

Patterson, Thomas E. 1993. *Out of order*. New York: Alfred A. Knopf.

Patterson, Thomas E. 1998. Political roles of the journalist. In *The politics of news: The news of politics*, eds. Doris Graber, Denis McQuail, and Pippa Norris, 17–32. Washington, DC: CQ Press.

Patterson, Thomas E. 2000a. "Doing well and doing good." Research working paper, Kennedy School, Harvard University. (On file with authors.)

Patterson, Thomas E. 2000b. *How soft news and critical journalism are shrinking the news audience and weakening democracy*. Cambridge, MA: Shorenstein Center for Press, Politics, and Public Policy, Kennedy School of Government, Harvard University.

Patterson, Thomas E. 2005. Of polls, mountains. U.S. journalists, and their use of election surveys. *Public opinion quarterly* 69:716–24.

Patterson, Thomas E. 2008. Political Roles of the Journalist. In *The Politics of News, the News of Politics*, eds. Doris A. Graber, Denis McQuail, and Pippa Norris, 23 39. 2nd Edition. Washington, DC: CQ Press.

Patterson, Thomas E., and Wolfgang Donsbach. 1996. News decisions: Journalists as partisan actors. *Political Communication* 13:455–68.

Patwardhan, Padmini, Jin Yang, and Hermant Patwardhan. 2008. Understanding media satisfaction: Development and validation of an affect-based scale. Paper presented at the annual meeting of the Association for Education in Journalism and Mass Communication, Chicago.

Perse, Elizabeth, and Douglas A. Ferguson. 1993. The impact of the newer television technologies on television satisfaction. *Journalism Quarterly* 70:843–53.

Peter, Jochen. 2003. Why European TV news matters. A cross-nationally comparative analysis of TV news about the European Union and its effect. Doctoral dissertation, University of Amsterdam.

Peter, Jochen. 2004. Our long return to the concept of powerful mass media. *International Journal of Public Opinion Research* 16:144–68.

Peter, Jochen, and Edmund Lauf. 2002. Reliability in cross-national content analysis. *Journalism and Mass Communication Quarterly* 79:815–32.

Pfetsch, Barbara. 1996. Convergence through privatization? Changing media environments and televised politics in Germany. *European Journal of Communication* 11:427–51.

Pfetsch, Barbara. 2001. Political communication culture in the United States and Germany. *International Journal of Press/Politics* 6:46–67.

Pfetsch, Barbara. 2004. From political culture to political communication culture: A theoretical approach to comparative analysis. In *Comparing political communication: Theories, cases, and challenges*, eds. Frank Esser and Barbara Pfetsch, 344–66. Cambridge: Cambridge University Press.

Pfetsch, Barbara, and Eva Mayerhöffer. 2011. Vordergründige Nähe Kommunikations-kultur von Politik- und Medieneliten in Deutschland [Superficial closeness: On the communication culture of political and media elite in Germany]. *Medien & Kommunikationswissenschaft* 1:40–59.

Pinkleton, Bruce E., and Erica W. Austin. 2002. Exploring relationships among media use, frequency, perceived media importance, and media satisfaction in political disaffection and efficacy. *Mass Communication and Society* 5:141–63.

Plaisance, Patrick L., and Elizabeth A. Skewes. 2003. Personal and professional dimensions of news work: Exploring the link between journalists' values and roles. *Journalism and Mass Communication Quarterly* 80:833–48.

Porto, Mauro P. 2007. Frame diversity and citizen competence: Towards a critical approach to news quality. *Critical Studies in Media Communication* 24:303–21.

Preacher, Kristopher J., and Andrew F. Hayes. 2004. SPSS and SAS procedures for estimating indirect effects in simple mediation models. *Behavior Research Methods, Instruments, and Computers* 36:717–31.

Preacher, Kristopher J., and Andrew F. Hayes. 2008. Asymptotic and resampling strategies for assessing and comparing indirect effects in multiple mediator models. *Behavior Research Methods* 40:879–91.

Przeworski, Adam, and Henry Teune. 1970. *The logic of comparative social inquiry*. New York: Wiley.

Price, Vincent. 1989. Social identification and public opinion effects of communicating group conflict. *Public Opinion Quarterly* 53:197–224.

Price, Vincent, and Edward J. Czilli. 1996. Modeling patterns of news recognition and recall. *Journal of Communication* 46:55–78.

Price, Vince, David Tewksbury, and E. Powers. 1997. Switching trains of thoughts: The impact of news frames on readers' cognitive responses. *Communication Research* 24:481–506.

Price, Vince, and John Zaller. 1993. Who gets the news? Alternative measures of news reception and their implications for research. *Public Opinion Quarterly* 57:133–64.

Prior, Markus. 2003a. "News vs. entertainment: How increasing media choice widens gaps in political knowledge and turnout." Working paper, Princeton University. (On file with authors.)

Prior, Markus. 2003b. Any good news in soft news? The impact of soft news preferences on political knowledge. *Political Communication* 20:149–71.

Prior, Markus. 2007. Post-broadcast democracy: How media choice increases inequality in political involvement and polarizes elections. Cambridge: Cambridge University Press.

Prior, Markus. 2010. You've either got it or you don't? The stability of political interest over the life cycle. *Journal of Politics* 72:747–66.

Pritchard, David, Paul R. Brewer, and Florian Sauvageau. 2005. Changes in Canadian journalists' views about the social and political roles of the news media: A panel study, 1996–2003. *Canadian Journal of Political Science* 38:287–306.

Putman, Robert D. 2000. Bowling alone: The collapse and revival of American community. New York: Simon & Schuster.

Quandt, Thorsten. 2012. What's left of trust in a network society? An evolutionary model and critical discussion of trust and societal communication. *European Journal of Communication* 27 (3): 7–21.

Ragin, Charles. 1994. Introduction to qualitative comparative analysis. In *The comparative political economy of the welfare state*, eds. Thomas Yanoski and Alexander M. Hicks, 299–45. Cambridge: Cambridge University Press.

Ragin, Charles. 2000. *Fuzzy-set social science*. Chicago: University of Chicago Press.

Reese, Stephen D. 2001. Understanding the global journalist: A hierarchy-of-influences approach. *Journalism Studies* 2:173–87.

Rhee, June W. 1997. Strategy and issue frames in election campaign coverage: A social cognitive account of framing effects. *Journal of Communication* 47:26–48.

Riffe, Daniel, Stephen Lacy, and Frederick G. Fico. 2005. *Analyzing media messages: Using quantitative content analysis in research*. 2nd ed. London: Lawrence Erlbaum.

Rimmer, Tony, and David Weaver. 1985. Different questions, different answers? Media use and media credibility. *Journalism Quarterly* 64:28–36.

Robinson, John P., and Dennis K. Davis. 1990. Television news and the informed public: An information processing approach. *Journal of Communication* 40:106–19.

Robinson, John P., and Mark R. Levy. 1986. *The main source: Learning from television news*. Beverly Hills, CA: Sage.

Robinson, John P., and Mark R. Levy. 1996. News media use and the informed public: A 1990s update. *Journal of Communication* 46:129–35.

Robinson, Piers. 1999. The CNN effect: Can the news media drive foreign policy? *Review of International Studies* 25:301–9.

Roland, Asle. 2009. A clash of media systems? British Mecom's takeover of Norwegian Orkla media. *International Communiation Gazette* 7:263–81.

Roncarolo, Franca. 2009. News coverage of elections in the long transition of Italian democracy. In *The handbook of election news coverage around the world*, eds. Jesper Strömbäck and Lynda Kaid, 308–23. London: Routledge.

Rosen, Jay. 2005. Bloggers vs. journalists is over. (Accessed February 3, 2012, at http://archive.pressthink.org/2005/01/21/berk_essy.html.)

Rosenstiel, Tom. 1993. Strange bedfellows. How television and the presidential candidates changed American politics. New York: Hyperion.

Rössler, Patrick. 2012. Comparative content analysis. In *Handbook of comparative communication research*, eds. F. Esser, Frank, and T. Hanitzsch, 459–68. New York: Routledge.

Sampedro, Víctor, and Francisco Seonane Pérez. 2008. The 2008 Spanish general elections: "Antagonistic bipolarization" geared by presidential debates, partisanship, and media interest. *International Journal of Press/Politics* 13:336–44.

Scheufele, Dietmar A. 1999. Framing as a theory of media effects. *Journal of Communication* 49:103–22.

Scheufele, Dietmar A. 2002. Examining differential gains from mass media and their implications for participatory behavior. *Communication Research* 29:46–65.

Schlesinger, Philip. 1990. Rethinking the sociology of journalism: Source strategies and the limits of media-centrism. In *Public communication: The new imperatives. Future directions for media research*, ed. Marjorie Ferguson, 61–83. London: Sage.

Scholl, Armin, and Siegfried Weischenberg. 1998. *Journalismus in der Gesellschaft. Theorie, Methodologie und Empirie* [Journalism in society: Theory, methodology, and empirical results]. Opladen, Wiesbaden: Westdeutscher Verlag.

Schönbach, Klaus, and Edmund Lauf. 2002. The "trap" effect of television and its competitors. *Communication Research* 29:564–83.

Schönbach, Klaus, and Edmund Lauf. 2004. Another look at the "trap" effect of television – and beyond. *International Journal of Public Opinion Research* 16:169–82.

Schönbach, Klaus, Dieter Stürzebecher, and Beate Schneider. 1994. Oberlehrer und Missionare? Das Selbstverständnis deutscher

Journalisten [Head teachers and missionaries? German journalists' self-understanding]. Sonderheft [Special issue], *Kölner Zeitschrift für Soziologie und Sozialpsychologie* 34:139–61.

Schuck, Andreas, and Claes H. de Vreese. 2006. Between risk and opportunity. News framing and its effects on public support for EU enlargement. *European Journal of Communication* 21:5–32.

Schuck, Andreas, and Claes H. de Vreese. 2008. The Dutch no to the EU constitution: Assessing the role of EU skepticism and the campaign. *Journal of Elections, Public Opinion and Parties* 18:101–28.

Schuck, Andreas, Georgios Xezonakis, Matthijs Elenbaas, Susan A. Banducci, and Claes H. de Vreese. 2011. Party contestation and Europe on the news agenda: The 2009 European parliamentary elections. *Electoral Studies* 30:41–52.

Schuck, Andreas, Rens Vliegenthart, Hajo Boomgaarden, Matthijs Elenbaas, Rachid Azrout, Joost van Spanje, and Claes H. de Vreese. 2013. Explaining campaign news coverage: How medium, time, and context explain variation in the media framing of the 2009 European parliamentary elections. *Journal of Political Marketing*, 12, 1, 8–28.

Schudson, Michael. 1978. Discovering the news: A social history of American newspapers. New York: Basic.

Schudson, Michael. 1998. *The good citizen: A history of American civic life*. New York: Free Press.

Schudson, Michael. 2003. *The sociology of news*. New York: W.W. Norton.

Schudson, Michael, and Chris Anderson. 2009. Objectivity, professionalism, and truth-seeking in journalism. In *The handbook of journalism studies*, eds. Karin Wahl-Jorgensen and Thomas Hanitzsch, 88–101. New York: Routledge.

Schulz, Winfried. 1998. Media change and the political effects of television: Americanization of the political culture? *Communications* 23:527–43.

Schulz, Winfried, and Reimar Zeh. 2005. The changing election coverage of German television: A content analysis 1990–2002. *Communications* 30:385–407.

Semetko, Holli A., and Maria Canel. 1997. Agenda-sender versus agenda-setter: Television in Spain's 1996 election campaign. *Political Communication* 14:459–79.

Semetko, Holli A., and Patti M. Valkenburg. 2000. Framing European politics: A content analysis of press and television news. *Journal of Communication* 50:93–109.

Seymoure-Ure, Colin. 1974. *The political impact of mass media*. London: Constable/Sage.

Shoemaker, Pamela J., Stephen D. Reese. 1996. *Mediating the message: Theories of influences on mass media content.*, 2nd ed. White Plains, NY: Longman.

Sigal, Leon V. 1986. Sources make the news. In *Reading the news*, eds. R. K. Manoff and M. Schudson. New York: Pantheon.

Singer, Jane. 2011. Journalism in a network. In *Managing media work*, ed. Mark Deuze, 103–9. London: Sage.

Skovsgaard, M., Albæk, E., Bro, P. and de Vreese, C. H. 2013. A Reality Check: How Journalists' Role Perceptions Impact Their Implementation of the Objectivity Norm. *Journalism – Theory Practice and Criticism.* 14, 1, s. 22–42.

Skovsgaard, Morten, Erik Albæk, Claes de Vreese, and Peter Bro. 2012. Danish journalist. In *The global journalist*, eds. D. Weaver and L. Willnat, 155–70. London: Routledge.

Slater, Michael D. 2004. Operationalizing and analyzing exposure: The foundation of media effects research. *Journalism and Mass Communication Quarterly* 81:168–83.

Sotirovic, Mira, and Jack M. McLeod. 2004. Knowledge as understanding: The information processing approach to political learning. In *Handbook of political communication research*, ed. Lynda L. Kaid. Hillsdale, NJ: Lawrence Erlbaum.

Sparks, Colin. 2000. Introduction: Panic over tabloid news. In *Tabloid tales: Global debates over media standards*, eds. Colin Sparks and John Tulloch, 1–40. Lanham, MD: Rowman and Littlefield.

Sparrow, Bartholomew H. 1999. *Uncertain guardians: The news media as a political institution.* Baltimore, MD: John Hopkins University Press.

Starck, Kenneth, and John Soloski. 1977. Effect of reporter predisposition in covering controversial stories. *Journalism Quarterly* 54: 120–5.

Steger, Wayne P. 1999. Comparing news and editorial coverage of the 1996 presidential nominating campaign. *Presidential Studies Quarterly* 29:40–64.

Strömbäck, Jesper. 2005. In search of a standard: Four models of democracy and their implications for journalism. *Journalism Studies* 6:331–45.

Strömbäck, Jesper. 2008. Four phases of mediatization: An analysis of the mediatization of politics. *The International Journal of Press/Politics* 13:228–46.

Strömbäck, Jesper, and Daniela V. Dimitrova. 2006. Political and media systems matter: A comparison of election news coverage in Sweden and the United States. *International Journal of Press/Politics* 11:131–47.

Strömbäck, Jesper, and Lynda L. Kaid, eds. 2008. *The handbook of election news coverage around the world.* New York: Routledge.

Strömbäck, Jesper, and Óscar G. Luengo. 2008. Polarized pluralist and democratic corporatist models: A comparison of election news coverage in Spain and Sweden. *International Communication Gazette* 70:547–62.

Strömbäck, Jesper, and Adam Shehata. 2007. Structural biases in British and Swedish election news coverage. *Journalism Studies* 8:798–812.

Strömbäck, Jesper, and Peter van Aelst. 2010. Exploring some antecedents of the media's framing of election news: A comparison of Swedish and Belgium election news. *International Journal of Press/Politics* 15:41–59.

Swanson, David L. 1992. The political-media complex. *Communication Monographs* 59:397–400.

Tewksbury, David, Jennifer Jones, Matthew W. Peske, Ashlea Raymond, and William Vig. 2000. The interaction of news and advocate frames: Manipulating audience perceptions of a local public policy issue. *Journalism and Mass Communication Quarterly* 77:804–29.

Thomson, Elizabeth, Peter R.R. White, and Philip Kitly. 2008. Objectivity and hard news reporting across cultures: Comparing the news report in English, French, Japanese, and Indonesian journalism. *Journalism Studies* 9:212–28.

Tichenor, Philip, George Donohue, and Clarice N. Olien. 1970. Mass media flow and differential growth in knowledge. *Journalism Quarterly* 54:254–61.

Traquina, Nelson. 1995. Portuguese television: The politics of savage deregulation. *Media, Culture and Society* 17:223–38.

Tresch, Anke. 2009. Politicians in the media: Determinants of legislators' presence and prominence in Swiss newspapers. *International Journal of Press/Politics* 14:67–90.

Tuchman, Gaye. 1978. Making news. New York: Free Press.

Tumber, Howard. 2004. Scandal and media in the United Kingdom: From Major to Blair. *American Behavioral Scientist* 47:1122–37.

Tunstall, Jeremy. 1970. The Westminster lobby correspondents: A sociological study of national political journalism. London: Routledge.

Tunstall, Jeremy. 2004. The United Kingdom. In *The media in Europe: The Euromedia handbook*, 3rd ed., eds. Mary Kelly, Gianpietro Mazzoleni, and Denis McQuail, 261–74. London: Sage.

Uribe, Rodrigo, and Barrie Gunter. 2004. Research note: The tabloidization of British tabloids. *European Journal of Communication* 19:387–402.

Valentino, Nicolas A., Thomas A. Buhr, and Matthew N. Beckmann. 2001. When the frame is the game: Revisiting the impact of "strategic" campaign coverage on citizens' information retention. *Journalism and Mass Communication Quarterly* 78:93–112.

Valkenburg, M. Patti, Holli A. Semetko, and Claes H. de Vreese. 1999. The effects of news frames on readers' thoughts and recall. *Communications Research* 26:550–69.

Van Aelst, Peter, and Toril Aalberg. 2009. Between love and hate. A comparative study on the informality of the relationship between politicians and political journalists in Belgium, Norway, and Sweden. Paper presented at the annual conference of the International Communication Association, Chicago.

Van Aelst, Peter, Kees Brants, Philip Van Praag, Claes H. de Vreese, Michiel Nuytemans, and Arjen van Dalen. 2008. The fourth estate as superpower? An empirical study of perceptions of media power in Belgium and the Netherlands. *Journalism Studies* 9:494–511.

Van Dalen, Arjen. 2012. Structural bias in cross-national perspective. How political systems and journalism cultures influence government dominance in the news. *International Journal of Press/Politics* 17:32–55.

Van Dalen, Arjen. 2012. The people behind the political headlines: A comparison of political journalists in Denmark, Germany, the United Kingdom, and Spain. *International Communication Gazette* 74(5) 464–483.

Van Dalen, Arjen, Erik Albæk, and Claes H. de Vreese. 2011. Suspicious minds: Explaining political cynicism among political journalists in Europe. *European Journal of Communication* 26:147–62.

Van Dalen, Arjen, and Morten Skovsgaard. 2011. Er en politisk skandale en politisk skandale? Danske medierede politiske skandaler I et komparativt perspektiv [Is a political scandal a political scandal? Danish mediated political scandals in comparative perspective]. *Tidskrift Politik* 17–26.

Van de Vijver, Fons, and Norbert K. Tanzer. 1997. Bias and equivalence in cross-cultural assessment: An overview. *European Journal of Applied Psychology* 47:263–79.

Van Dijk, Teun A. 1988. *News as discourse.* Hillsdale, NJ: Lawrence Erlbaum.

Van Herk, Hester, Ype H. Poortinga, and Theo M.M. Verhallen. 2004. Response styles in rating scales: Evidence of method bias in data from six EU countries. *Journal of Cross-Cultural Psychology* 35:346–60.

Van Santen, Rosa. 2009. Popularization and personalization in political television journalism: A conceptual exploration. Paper presented at the Annual Conference of Communication Science, Nijmegen.

Van Zoonen, Liesbet. 1998. A professional, unreliable, heroic marionette (M/F): Structure, agency, and subjectivity in contemporary journalisms. *European Journal of Cultural Studies* 1:123–43.

Van Zoonen, Liesbet, and Christina Holtz-Bacha. 2000. Personalization in Dutch and German politics: The case of talk show. *Javnost/The Public* 7:45–56.

Vettehen, Paul H., Koos Nuijten, and Johannes W. J. Beentjes. 2005. News in an age of competition: Sensationalism in Dutch television news 1995–2001. *Journal of Broadcasting and Electronic Media* 49:282–95.

Voltmer, Katrin, ed. 2006. Mass media and political communication in new democracies. London: Routledge.

Vos, Timothy P. 2002. Role enactment: The influence of journalists' role conceptions on news content. Paper presented at the 85th conference of the Association for Education in Journalism and Mass Communication, Miami.

Vos, Timothy P. 2009. Journalistic role conceptions: A bridge between the reporter and the press. Paper presented at the annual conference of the International Communication Association, Chicago.

Waisbord, Silvio. 2000. *Watchdog journalism in South America*. New York: Columbia.

Walgrave, Stefaan, and Peter van Aelst. 2006. The contingency of the mass media's political agenda setting power: Towards a preliminary theory. *Journal of Communication* 56:88–109.

Wang, Tai-Li, and Akiba Cohen. 2009. Factors affecting viewers' perceptions of sensationalism in television news: A survey study in Taiwan. *Issues and Studies* 45:125–57.

Weaver, David H, ed. 1998. *The global journalist: News people around the world*. Creskill, NJ: Hampton Press.

Weaver, David H. 2008. Methods of journalism research – survey. In *Global journalism research: Theories, methods, findings, future*, eds. Martin Löffelholz and David Weaver, 106–16.Oxford: Blackwell.

Weaver, David H., Randal A. Beam, Bonnie J. Brownlee, Paul S. Voakes, and G. Cleveland Wilhoit. 2007. *The American journalist in the 21st century: U.S. news people at the dawn of a new millennium*. London: Lawrence Erlbaum.

Weaver, David H., and Dan Drew. 2001. Voter learning and interest in the 2000 presidential election: Did the media matter? *Journalism and Mass Communication Quarterly* 78:787–98.

Weaver, David H., and Martin Löffelholz. 2008. Questioning national, cultural, and disciplinary boundaries: A call for global journalism research. In *Global journalism research: Theories, methods, findings, future*, eds. Martin Löffelholz and David H. Weaver, 3–12. London: Blackwell.

Weaver, David H., and G. Cleveland Wilhoit. 1986. *The American journalist: A portrait of U.S. news people and their work*. Bloomington: Indiana University Press.

Weaver David H., and Lars Willnat, eds. 2012. *The global journalist in the 21st century*. London: Routledge.

Weischenberg, Siegfried, Maja Malik, and Armin Scholl. 2006. *Die Souffleure der Mediengesellschaft: Report über die Journalisten in Deutschland* [The prompters of the media society: Report about journalists in Germany]. Konstanz: UVK.

Werner, Oswald, and Donald T. Campbell. 1970. Translating, working through interpreters, and the problem of decentering. In *A handbook of Method in Cultural Anthropology*, eds. Roul Naroll and Ronald Cohen, 398–420. New York: National History.

Williams, Bruce A., and Michael X. Delli Carpini. 2011. *After broadcast news: Media regimes, democracy, and the new information environment*. Cambridge: Cambridge University Press.

Wirth, Werner, and Steffen Kolb. 2004. Design and methods of comparative political communication research. In *Comparing political communication: Theories, cases, and challenges*, eds. Frank Esser and Barbara Pfetch, 87–111. Cambridge: Cambridge University Press.

Wirth, Werner, and Steffen Kolb. 2008. Comparative research. In *The international encyclopedia of communication*, ed. Wolfgang Donsbach. Oxford: Blackwell.

Wonneberger, Anke. 2011. Coping with diversity: Exposure to public-affairs TV in a changing viewing environment. PhD dissertation, University of Amsterdam.

Zaller, John R. 1992. *The nature and origins of public opinion*. Cambridge: Cambridge University Press.

Zaller, John R. 2003. A new standard of news quality: Burglar alarms for the monitorial citizen. *Political Communication* 20:109–30.

Zhang, Ping, and Gisela M. von Dran. 2000. Satisfiers and dissatisfiers: A two-factor model for website design and evaluation. *Journal of the American Society for Information Science* 51:1253–68.

Zhu, Jian-Hua, David H. Weaver, Ven-hwei Lo, Chongshan Chen, and Wei Wu. 1997. Individual, organizational, and societal influences on media role perceptions: A comparative study of journalists in China, Taiwan, and the United States. *Journalism & Mass Communication Quarterly* 74:84–96.

Index

241

Other Books in the Series (*continued from page iii*)